THE BIG 50
CHICAGO BEARS

The Men and Moments That Made
the Chicago Bears

Adam L. Jahns

TRIUMPH
BOOKS

Library of Congress Cataloging-in-Publication Data

Names: Jahns, Adam, author.
Title: The big 50 Chicago Bears : the men and moments that made the Chicago Bears / Adam Jahns.
Other titles: The big fifty Chicago Bears
Description: Chicago, Illinois : Triumph Books, [2020] | Includes bibliographical references. | Summary: "The Big 50: Chicago Bears is an amazing look at the fifty men and moments that have made the Bears the Bears. Longtime sportswriter Adam L. Jahns explores the living history of the team, counting down from number fifty to number one. This dynamic and comprehensive book brings to life the iconic franchise's remarkable story, including greats like Ditka, Payton, Urlacher, and more"— Provided by publisher.
Identifiers: LCCN 2020029892 (print) | LCCN 2020029893 (ebook) | ISBN 9781629377612 (paperback) | ISBN 9781641255356 (epub) | ISBN 9781641255363 (kindle edition) | ISBN 9781641255370 (adobe pdf)
Subjects: LCSH: Chicago Bears (Football team) | Football players—Illinois—Chicago. | Football team owners—United States—Biography.
Classification: LCC GV956.C5 J34 2020 (print) | LCC GV956.C5 (ebook) | DDC 796.332/640977311—dc23
LC record available at https://lccn.loc.gov/2020029892
LC ebook record available at https://lccn.loc.gov/2020029893

This book is available in quantity at special discounts for your group or organization. For further information, contact:

Triumph Books LLC
814 North Franklin Street
Chicago, Illinois 60610
(312) 337-0747
www.triumphbooks.com

Printed in U.S.A.
ISBN: 978-1-62937-761-2

Design by Andy Hansen

For my beautiful wife, Colleen.
It's always been you and for you.

[Contents]

[Foreword]

Being drafted by the Bears in 1998 as the last pick in the sixth round and ending up playing 245 games and 16 seasons—both of which are franchise records—is beyond a dream come true. After retiring in 2013, I still pinch myself that my Bears career really happened.

As a kid playing sports, I would always try to mimic my favorite athletes. Didn't we all? I was 10 years old when the world experienced the phenomenon that was the 1985 Chicago Bears. I learned all about the greats like Walter Payton, Mike Singletary, and Jim McMahon. Headbands became hip to wear. Playing offensive line looked cool after seeing the "Black 'n' Blues Brothers" poster. And that defense... wow! What a force of nature.

Recently, I was cleaning out my closet with my wife and came across some mementos I kept from childhood. One of them was a Dr. Seuss book called *My Book About Me*, from when I was 10 years old. It's the type of book where you write your favorite colors and foods, height and weight, favorite subject in school, etc. On one of the last pages was: "What do I want to be when I grow up?"

Well, I wrote "astronaut" and then erased that and wrote "football player." One of the main reasons I wrote that was because of the '85 Bears and the impact they had on sports and on me. Fast forward 12 years after that Super Bowl and I was fortunate to become part of the historic franchise. I never would have dreamed that when I was filling out my Dr. Seuss book as a kid.

My rookie year with the Bears was in 1998. I was just in awe that I was there. My head was spinning. I was trying to learn and keep up as best I could. It really wasn't until the next year, and years beyond, that I realized just how special it was to be a Chicago Bear. I learned about the history of the team and the legacy that George Halas left. Halas Hall, the facility where we practiced in Lake Forest, was decorated and continually updated with photos and memorabilia from this historic franchise.

There was a long hallway between the locker room and training room and the walls were lined with team photos from every year. I would find myself studying these photos and reading the rosters and seeing names like Red Grange, Bronko Nagurski, Link Lyman, George McAfee, Clyde "Bulldog" Turner, Gale Sayers, Doug Atkins, and more. The list goes on and on. Seeing that history displayed on those walls really showed how impressive this franchise is in the history of the NFL. I still can't believe my name and photo grace those hallways today.

I am fortunate to be in 16 of those team photos. And in the photos with me are a lot of great teammates. We always had a special locker room when I was with the Bears. Olin Kreutz and I were in the same draft class and spent 13 years playing together. He would always say, "Who would have thought a little ol' boy from Honolulu and a kid from Marietta, Georgia, would ever become friends?" That sums up our locker room. We all came from different places and backgrounds, yet we all became friends—not just teammates. I can't even begin to name all the teammates and staff members who have had an impact on me over my football career. But I would like to thank them for the memories and our continued friendships.

The Bears truly are a family organization. I felt a connection with the McCaskey family during my tenure with the team. In 2010, my brother-in-law, who was living with us at the time, passed away tragically during the off-season. The funeral service for him was at St. Patrick's Church in Lake Forest and who was one of the first people to arrive? Virginia McCaskey. That really sums up the kindness and integrity of this family. They care. I never played for any other organization, but I am happy that I got to spend my career with a family-run operation.

And what to say about the fans? There really is nothing like a Chicago Bear fan. Early in my career I remember James "Big Cat" Williams telling me, "Just wait until we win." As a team we struggled my first few years until 2001 and then we went 13–3. And, man, did

I feel what he was talking about. Bears fans certainly are intense! I learned that the fans can get on you real hard when you lose, but when you win they love you twice as much. That to me is what a fan base should be like: passionate.

This is why many of us former players have never left this city and continue to call it home. It's because of our experience with the Bears franchise, the fans, and the great city of Chicago.

Bear down.

—Patrick Mannelly

Chicago Bears career leader in games played (245) and a member of the team's official 100 Greatest Bears of All-Time list.

1

SWEETNESS

A day spent on the property of Walter Payton in South Barrington, Illinois, filled veteran sportswriter Rick Telander with disbelief. A Bears icon became more iconic, almost mythical.

Throughout Telander's interview, Payton shot a bow and arrow as they walked together throughout the grounds of his estate.

"He finally got bored and shot it as far as he could and shot it half a mile in the air," Telander said. "God knows where it landed. He says, 'Come on, ask questions, let's go.'"

Payton's arrows were gone. But there were plenty of saplings.

"We're walking through these trees and he stops and he starts pulling," said Telander, who wrote for *Sports Illustrated* before joining the *Chicago Sun-Times*. "There's this tree, a sapling, and this is the springtime, and he's just got it. And he started to rock it like this and everything, back and forth."

Payton kept at it, too. It wasn't in Payton to quit. At anything. Ever.

"He gets down like a young King Arthur and the sword in the stone, and he starts pulling this thing up, 'Arghhhhh,'" Telander said. "And then all of sudden, 'Psshhhhh!' This tree just explodes from the ground, roots and everything and dirt's flying and everything.

"He just drops that, walks on, and goes to another one. He's pulling trees out of the ground."

Telander, who became close to Payton covering his career, saw it as a challenge. He was in his thirties and in relatively good shape. He played football at Northwestern and had a cup of coffee in the NFL. Why not try it himself?

"It won't even budge, let alone pull out of the ground," Telander said. "It would have taken me all day if I ever could have done it. I just started laughing. Walter is going along, and then all of a sudden, there would be this twisting and twisting, and then this explosion of dirt and another tree is pulled out of the ground."

Telander's experience was another feat of strength from a career that was full of them. This one just happened to occur off the football field.

Payton is not only revered, but anointed in Bears history. No player embodies Bears football more than Payton. He is the Bears, and the Bears are him. He is *the* legend for a franchise that's full of them.

"We loved the way he played the game and he exemplified the spirit that we all wanted to play with," former Bears defensive lineman Dan Hampton said. "He never changed. He was always the heart and soul of the team."

* * *

Jarrett Payton's favorite run by his father came against the Minnesota Vikings on November 12, 1978. It's a 19-yard touchdown run on a sweep to the left.

"He runs through the line. He jumps over someone with that Bear-ified leap that he had in the air," said Jarrett Payton, a sports broadcaster in Chicago. "And then he hits somebody. Another guy hits him, stands him up, and he finds his way into the end zone."

But a son always sees more in his father.

"To me, that run embodies everything that he was all about," Jarrett Payton said. "His toughness. His never-die-easy attitude. And just his nose to smell the end zone and taking hits while he's doing it."

When Payton retired after the 1987 season, he was the NFL's rushing leader, surpassing another legend, Jim Brown, with 16,726 yards. Emmitt Smith passed Payton in 2002. But Payton remains the Bears' all-time leading rusher and is unlikely to be reached.

Payton's No. 34 was retired and, when the Bears practice indoors, it's in the massive Walter Payton Center, which was named after him in 2000. There is a short quote from Payton in the Bears' remodeled locker room. In the running backs room, the team has his most famous message on the wall.

"Never die easy. Why run out of bounds and die easy? Make that linebacker pay. It carries into all facets of your life. It's okay to lose, to die, but don't die without trying, without giving it your best."

On September 3, 2019, two days before the Bears opened their 100th season against the Packers, a trophy of Payton was unveiled outside Soldier Field, just steps away from one of George Halas, the team's founder and longtime coach.

"You never know where you're going to go in the NFL draft," Jarrett Payton said. "My dad lucked up and came to the charter franchise, was lucky enough to work hard and to achieve the ultimate goals for him. That was to win a Super Bowl, go to the Hall of Fame, and I never asked him, but I think the rushing record was a huge deal. At that position, you're getting handed the ball every single time. You're trying to get yards. Those three things, he got a chance to achieve those."

It was an amazing career, one that started with being the fourth overall pick in 1975 and concluded with 16 NFL records.

But even though Payton was a decorated high school player, major colleges—predominantly white ones—didn't pursue him. Instead, he followed his brother, Eddie, to Jackson State, a historically black university in Mississippi. The Paytons were from the small, segregated town of Columbia, Mississippi.

"He went to Jackson State and he didn't win the Heisman [Trophy], which you can't give to a guy who goes to Jackson State," said Telander, who first met Payton in 1975. "But that tells you everything you need to know about where he came from, about segregation and about the times....

"It all started for him in the Deep South—a segregated high school and then they came together. And that's when all the people in Mississippi and Louisiana—all the white people—started going to private schools and stuff. So it was integration in theory, but it wasn't really. But that's why a guy like him would go to a tiny school like Jackson State. So that informed everything about him."

Payton got his nickname, "Sweetness," at Jackson State, as he became a three-time Black College All-American and a coveted NFL prospect. He didn't win the Heisman Trophy but would become arguably the greatest player in NFL history. Three months after he was drafted by the Bears, his hometown of Columbia held "Walter Payton Day."

His nickname followed him to Chicago, where it came to mean so much more. People always bring it up to his son, Jarrett Payton.

"Sweetness is kind; it's gentle, respectful," said Jarrett Payton, who moved his father to tears when he presented him for the Hall of Fame in 1993. "But it also means toughness, hard work, never giving up, or, as my dad would say, 'Never die easy.' It's the mixture of both things. That's the definition for me. It's a combination of sweet and toughness. I think about it all the time."

Sweetness was the true star of the star-studded '85 Bears, too. It was how he ran on the field, but also how he lived off it. He was endearing.

"That whole team, we all wanted to be the man," Hampton said. "Ditka wanted to be the man. Buddy Ryan wanted to be the man."

But Payton was different. Hampton, the fourth overall pick in 1979 and a future Hall of Famer, knew it. Every player and coach will tell you that from that beloved team.

"Anybody that walked in that front door, you were going to be B-team to him," Hampton said. "He was the man. A lot of people would have engendered jealousy and back-biting, but not Walter."

* * *

In the second week of the 1983 season, Jay Hilgenberg messed up against the Buccaneers and in one of the first starts of his career at the Bears' center.

Hilgenberg, who went undrafted out of Iowa, remembered being excited but also tested by coach Mike Ditka, who wanted to see him against All-Pro nose tackle Dave Logan.

"The first play we ran off tackle to the right and I just got all loaded up," Hilgenberg said. "I was just going to bury Dave Logan. And so I came off the ball and I can just tell, 'Oh, I got him. I'm just going to crush him.' He gave up on the block and he tossed me and he threw me play side into the hole. I like, landed on my belly and I just popped up real quick and I look behind to see what was going on and all of a sudden I see Walter come through this huge hole. I'm trying to duck out of the way.

"You know how he always did that kind of leap with that one leg out. He was trying to jump over me and I was trying to get out of the way, and I caught his knee and he just did this kind of somersault and went down. I went, 'Man,'—literally in my head—'one of my first plays in the NFL and I tackled Walter Payton.' On the way back to the huddle, he looks at me and goes, 'Hey, next time just stay on the ground.'"

It's a story that Hilgenberg, who went on to become a seven-time Pro Bowl center for the Bears, can share with a hearty laugh.

It helps that Payton loved to laugh, too. Hilgenberg sat next to him in the Bears' locker room for six years. There wasn't a more feared practical joker than No. 34. Everyone had to look out for him.

"I got to know Walter well," Hilgenberg said. "He used to ride and give me some hard times, but he was great. Walter was a superstar. You could just look at the guy and know that he was special."

There were many victims of Payton's pranks. There's that famous photograph of him pulling down the pants of fullback Matt Suhey, a close friend. The McCaskey family, the owners of the team, were fair game, too.

"He said, 'All those McCaskeys look alike'—he said that at a banquet," said Patrick McCaskey, a board member who has held various roles with the team.

"When he answered the phone in my father's [Ed's] office, he said, 'This is Bernice. Mr. McCaskey can't come to the phone right now because I'm giving him a full-body massage.'"

Those who played with, worked with, or covered Payton remember different things about him.

For Doug Plank, the former Bears safety, it's meeting Payton for the first time and then seeing him play during a three-day rookie camp in Orlando after they were both drafted. Plank and Payton were part of the Bears' 1975 draft class. They also roomed with each other.

"I'll be honest you, I never heard of Walter Payton until I got to the Chicago Bears," said Plank, who played at Ohio State with Archie Griffin.

"But No. 1, when he came out to the field, I was impressed. This was before practice. We had a kicker who was kicking field goals. Walter went over and started kicking the ball and kicking it farther than the field goal kicker. He could punt. He was punting farther than the punter. He could throw the ball farther than the quarterback could even throw the ball."

The players didn't hit during that three-day camp, but they didn't need to to notice Payton.

"You can't hide power and speed and change of direction and attitude," Plank said. "I had never seen anybody like him.... I just knew great things were going to happen when I saw him in that three-day camp."

For guard Tom Thayer, who is from the Chicago area, it was feeling starstruck initially. But blocking for Payton became an honor. Over the course of a 13-year career, Payton touched the ball 4,330 times. Former general manager Jim Finks once called him a more complete player than O.J. Simpson.

"It was a thrill; it was exciting," Thayer said. "It was different than him being a teammate because I was so enamored with everything Walter was in terms of his greatness and what he was accomplishing on a team, that in his early years, didn't have a great deal of success."

For Hub Arkush, the former Bears radio analyst and longtime publisher of *Pro Football Weekly*, it's Payton's success on the field combined with his success off it as a businessman.

"He became a multimillionaire," Arkush said. "He was one of the smartest football players I ever met. He understood the media. He understood the game. He understood business. He was just one of those unique individuals that don't come around often.

"I think the one thing that people never understand or give him enough credit for is what a complete person he was. He wasn't just a football player. And you don't meet a lot of guys like that."

For Patrick McCaskey, it was how Payton would "goose" people with his sense of humor or how he would answer questions in the media.

"Every interview he gave was a gem," he said.

But it was also the man's handshake. There was none like it.

"He had a tremendous handshake," McCaskey said. "Very, very strong. He really gave you a grip."

For Hampton, it was playing in the band Chicago 6 with Payton, who was the drummer, or in Pro Bowls and golf tournaments.

"He was a movie star in a sense that he was the biggest name in the game of football and he was right there next to you," Hampton said.

And then it was seeing how that movie star treated the people he met.

"And never once, never, ever, that there was anything negative that you could attribute to him," Hampton said. "He was exemplary always and in all facets."

For Telander, it's getting a pinch in the leg after interviewing him in the locker room or later walking his property and seeing him pull trees or talk to his landscapers over the phone in Spanish.

"I used to love doing stuff with him," Telander said. "But he'd drive you crazy because he'd exhaust you. He could not just sit still and be questioned. You had to walk or do something with him."

It's also being flattered when Payton invited him to a private dinner with friends at his restaurant, the Round House in Aurora.

"I remember sitting next to him," Telander said. "We ordered and he didn't eat a thing, and he reached over and grabbed one of my French fries and ate like part of it.

"Obviously, nobody is going to beat whatever liver cancer or whatever the hell he had. He was so sick and no complaining, no nothing. It was almost like he just wanted to see some people before he died. It was really a touching moment. Nobody really knew what to say. I wish I could have filmed the whole thing, but he wouldn't have allowed it."

There was a soft side to that tough man, one who played in 186 consecutive games despite fractured ribs, a chronic turf toe, a nerve injury in his shoulder, and so much more.

"As strong and impregnable as he was as a football player and on the surface, he was that soft, that tender, that vulnerable and delicate underneath," Telander said. "That's why he was so upset about not scoring in the Super Bowl, which none of us thought about. Watching that game, it was like, 'What the hell? They're toying with these Patriots.' They're toying with them because they're so good."

* * *

Payton died on November 1, 1999, after his fight with a rare liver cancer. He was 45.

Six days later, the Bears beat the Packers 14–13 at Lambeau Field. Defensive end Bryan Robinson blocked a field goal by kicker Ryan Longwell as time expired for the victory.

It was a magical, almost mythical ending.

It became known as the Walter Payton Game.

"I think Walter Payton actually picked up a little bit and boosted me up in the air because I can't jump that high," Robinson said after the game. "Walter had a lot to do with it. I know he did."

Payton lives on. He's a legend. Stories about him are passed on by generations of fans. His jersey is still one of the most popular in Chicago. Players show up to training camp wearing them, too.

Seeing the No. 34s always will give Jarrett Payton chills.

"We didn't know how his memory was going to be remembered," Payton said. "We had no clue. Then the internet came along. YouTube came along and that right there was the saving grace.

"We could talk about it as long as we want to but for people to be able to go to the internet and look at old videos and the highlights. That right there, in my mind, was the saving grace to be able to help keep his memory alive."

And so is the Walter Payton Man of the Year Award. The annual honor, which recognizes a player "for outstanding community service activities off the field as well as excellence on the field," is awarded ahead of the Super Bowl during the NFL Honors.

It was previously the NFL Man of the Year Award, which Payton won in 1977. It was renamed for Payton in 1999, before Super Bowl 34.

"It's the biggest honor," Jarrett Payton said. "The guys that want to be remembered for being great, that want it. You know there's guys just in the NFL because they're there and then there's other guys who are the top of the top, they want to leave their legacy and they get a chance to.

"This reward has really elevated my dad on a national stage and it happens every single year in the biggest game on the planet."

Each team nominates a player. And the Payton family takes their part in the selection process seriously. It's his award, his lasting legacy on the game of football. It has created a new fraternity for players, one that includes former Bears cornerback Charles Tillman. It's the final award of NFL honors and the winning player is honored on the field before the Super Bowl begins.

"It's a testament to who my dad was as a football player but also as a person off the field," Jarrett Payton said.

There will never be another like him. He was the best player on the best NFL team ever, a living legend who went too soon.

"We all loved him," Hampton said. "We were all so proud to not only to have him as a teammate, but to have him call us a friend."

2

MAMA BEAR

The Bears' preseason game was over, and the real party in Canton, Ohio, was just getting going.

In a hotel, the career of linebacker Brian Urlacher was celebrated. Old teammates, old coaches, and old trainers were there among family and friends.

And then royalty showed up.

At about 11:45 PM, owner Virginia McCaskey, who was 95 at the time, arrived after the Bears played the Ravens in the 2018 Hall of Fame Game.

"She's amazing," Urlacher said. "She showed up with her family. Just an amazing woman. I have so much respect for her and that family."

She stayed to about 1:30 AM, too.

Truth be told, it wouldn't have been a real Bears party without her. She's adored and beloved.

Every former Bears player seemingly has a personal story about her. So do those who have covered the team for decades. In Urlacher's case, it was her attending his Hall of Fame party.

"Royalty," Urlacher said. "She is pro football royalty in my opinion. She's a sweet, sweet woman, and I truly believe she cares about every player on that team."

* * *

Virginia Halas was born on January 5, 1923. Warren G. Harding was still the president, and the Chicago Bears were only four years old. The NFL was only two and consisted of the Hammond Pros, Rock Island Independents, Canton Bulldogs, Milwaukee Badgers, and others.

In other words, McCaskey grew up while the NFL grew.

"She's seen most of it," said Patrick McCaskey, one of Virginia McCaskey's 11 children.

It included accompanying her father, George Halas, and the league's first star, Red Grange, on the barnstorming tour—or better known as The Red Grange Tour—when she was a toddler. She attended the 1932 Championship Game inside Chicago Stadium that still smelled like the circus and she watched the Bears pound Giants quarterback Y.A. Tittle in the 1963 Championship Game in Wrigley Field.

Then came the days of Walter Payton and Mike Ditka, followed by Lovie Smith and Brian Urlacher and now Matt Nagy and Khalil Mack.

"She's a beautiful, soft-spoken devout Catholic woman, who owns one of the oldest franchises in the National Football League," former cornerback Charles Tillman said.

"I had the great honor of introducing her or presenting her with an award that the NFL gave her at the owners meetings [in 2019]. I think it's pretty amazing what she's seen, but also what she had dedicated her life to. In her mind, her husband or her brother, they were just going to do the football thing. It wasn't her."

But it became hers.

On December 16, 1979, her brother George "Mugs" Halas Jr. died of a heart attack. He was 54. Not long after, on October 31, 1983, her father, George Halas Sr., passed away.

Team control was turned over to Virginia and her husband, Ed McCaskey, who served in the U.S. Army in World War II and later became a salesman and a singer. Ed McCaskey was a vice president/ treasurer for the Bears but was named chairman of the board in 1983. Their son, Michael, became team president that year, too.

There were great days immediately. Her father hired Mike Ditka in 1982. The Bears' roster was loaded, too. The McCaskeys had former general manager Jim Finks, who left for the Cubs after the 1983 draft, to thank for that.

The difficulties came later. Replacing Ditka proved problematic. Michael McCaskey fired him and replaced him with Dave Wannstedt.

And then came the botched hiring of Dave McGinnis, who previously coached linebackers under Ditka. McCaskey wanted to hire him after firing Wannstedt in 1998.

The Bears issued a press release and scheduled a news conference for McGinnis, but there was a problem. There was no deal in place. An angry McGinnis passed on the job. It was an embarrassing episode for the proud franchise, who eventually hired Dick Jauron.

"Probably one of the hardest decisions [Virginia McCaskey] had is that she had to fire her son and make him step down," Tillman said. "That's a tough thing to do when it's a family business. But she's been there. She's made the tough decisions."

For longtime observers, it was telling, if not impressive. A change needed to be made and Virginia McCaskey made it. It was more impressive to longtime observers than her decision to disband the Honey Bears, the team's cheerleaders, in 1986.

On February 10, 1999, Ted Phillips was named team president, replacing McCaskey. Phillips was previously the Bears' vice president of operations and director of finance.

"Irrespective of football, she is one of the four or five most impressive people I've met in my lifetime," said Hub Arkush, a former Bears radio broadcaster and longtime publisher of *Pro Football Weekly*.

It's the decision to remove her son, but also being the matriarch of a family business—one with varying agendas—that grew to be worth billions.

"She took it upon herself to be a steward of that history," Arkush said. "[It's] maintaining the family commitment to this organization and in many respects most of the players who have come through Halas Hall have become her children, step-children, whatever you want to call them. Obviously, some closer than others."

* * *

For Jeff Joniak, the Bears' radio play-by-play broadcaster since 2001, boarding the team plane after a loss and seeing Virginia McCaskey is the worst.

"Your eyes go right to Virginia, win or lose," Joniak said. "And when we lose, you could see it in here face. And when they win, it's a bright smile.

"But one of the hardest things to do is to look at her when they lose because you feel for her. They want to win badly. She wants to win badly."

On December 29, 2014, George McCaskey, the Bears' chairman since 2011, said his mother was "pissed off" as the team fired general manager Phil Emery and coach Marc Trestman following a disastrous 5–11 season.

"I can't think of a 91-year-old woman that that description would apply," George McCaskey said at a news conference that day, "but in this case, I can't think of a more accurate description."

Of course, Virginia McCaskey would never use such words, but it was an apt description that fit her competitiveness. It's an inherited trait.

"She's like her father," said Patrick McCaskey, a team board member and one of her 11 children. "She's tough and competitive."

Over the years, many came to see it, including Arkush, whose radio booth was right next to the McCaskey's at Soldier Field before it was remodeled.

"She sat through every game sometimes with a 5x9 pad or sometimes just a back of an envelope with a pencil and she took game notes," Arkush said. "She really knows football."

Over the years, many players and staff members have heard her speak, too. Stories about the '40s and '60s leave an impression, but so do the messages behind them.

"The rich history that the Bears have, it's hers," said former long snapper Patrick Mannelly, who played in the most games in team history.

"She's the living piece of it. So anytime you saw her, you could feel it. It was tangible. You can feel the history. When we were lucky enough to have her come speak to us, that's the quietest you'd ever hear a room. And it's not because she's older and spoke in a soft voice, we just revered her. She's the godmother of pro football."

Former players don't only feel remembered by her. They know they are. It's attending a Bears game at Soldier Field and being approached by a McCaskey family member who says, "Mom wants to see you."

"I know how much her father's legacy—and I know how much the team—means to her," said former receiver Tom Waddle, who became a radio host on ESPN 1000. "There's a lot of conversations about how owners treat their players regardless of sport. She's a genuine carer.

She cares about all of her employees, including those in the front office, though some of them are her children, and certainly everyone that has ever worn that jersey."

Former safety Gary Fencik, a member of the Bears' 1985 team, got to know McCaskey when they worked together in Bears Care, the charitable arm of the franchise.

"I'd go, 'Virginia, how many guys do remember that wore No. 41?'" Fencik said. "She'd rattle off three or four names."

It's also her knowledge of position changes over the years and her ability to vividly recall her first game at Wrigley Field.

"To me, it's extraordinary," Fencik said. "She is one of the historians for the Chicago Bears, but also the NFL."

* * *

On March 4, 2009, Jarrett Payton needed the help of Virginia McCaskey. It was his wedding day and the reception—on March 4—was at Soldier Field.

"They were telling us that we couldn't turn the lights on in the stadium for our reception," Payton said.

That was unacceptable for McCaskey. After all, this was the son of Walter, one of her favorite players of all time.

"She said, 'No, no,'" Payton said. "She had them turn the lights on."

It allowed for better pictures with friends and family. And in this case, McCaskey is family. She was close with Walter Payton and she's in the wedding pictures that Jarrett Payton sees at his own home.

"I walk by her every day," Jarrett Payton said. "I'm like, 'That's Mama Bear'.... Virginia, she's just everything to our family. She's a big part of helping keep my dad's legacy alive."

Much of Virginia McCaskey's legacy will live on in anonymity. She's a devout Catholic woman who has maintained a humble home in Des Plaines. She's the reason the Bears have a chapel in their updated facility.

McCaskey is very charitable, but the full of reach of her donations will never be made public. Before the Bears' centennial celebrations, interviews with her were rare. But the team history is her history, too. She shared the best of it.

"She's sharp. She's witty. She's calm. She's intense," Joniak said. "And she just loves this franchise. She loves what her father put together. It means everything to her and her family."

The stories that former players share about Virginia McCaskey tend to be personal, too. They're drawn to her. They enjoy seeing her arrive at training camp on a golf cart. The small talk with her is big talk to them.

"She wants to engage in conversations with you," Tillman said. "She's not just an owner. She's not just a face of the franchise. She's a kind, sweet woman who wants to know about you. She knows my family."

Former guard Tom Thayer, who became a radio analyst, shared with her the book *Broken Mary* and then received a handwritten letter from her. George Halas was known for his letters, too.

"Her penmanship is as beautiful as an artist's painting," said Thayer, who is from the Chicago area. "I saved the letter and I'll always save it because it meant so much to me that she took the time out after reading the book to pen a letter and just the beautiful flow of her penmanship, where we should all strive to be able to write like that. Her, to be able to do it, means a lot to me. She comes off as beautiful in her penmanship as she as a person."

Those letters are cherished by those who receive them. Longtime Bears writer Dan Pompei received an autographed copy of the Bears' centennial book that he co-wrote with Don Pierson, who, like Pompei, is in the Hall of Fame as a Dick McCann Memorial Award winner.

"There is nobody like her in the NFL," Pompei said. "You're talking about someone who was on the Red Grange tour and has seen more NFL history than anyone alive or anyone who has ever existed. She's very different in that regard. She is someone who is universally respected and people who know her really think highly of her. She's been very kind to me professionally and personally."

* * *

The snow was falling on January 21, 2007, at Soldier Field, and for every player there, it made the night that much better.

Urlacher hoisted the George Halas Trophy over his head after the Bears defeated the Saints in the NFC Championship Game. A few steps away from him was Virginia McCaskey—a wide, glowing smile on her face.

It's a moment in Bears history that will live on forever, one captured in photographs and one etched into the players' minds.

"That means so much to you, just looking at her," former center Olin Kreutz said. "You're almost winning it for her."

Throughout that season, former coach Lovie Smith emphasized that point. He often talked about McCaskey and her family, the team's history and the city of Chicago.

"When you're there and when you're playing hard, you have her in mind," Kreutz said. "Gosh, we want to win a Super Bowl."

It's the ultimate sign of how endearing she is. Her history—the team's history—became the players' history. They felt like they were a part of something bigger, something grand.

"It's the amount of respect you have for her when you're in that building," Kreutz said. "She's just a central figure of that building."

It's generational feeling, too. She's seen it all. She's lived the NFL.

"She means something to every football fan in the world," Thayer said. "Because to have the actual eye-on account of the growth, the development, the dedication to the entirety of the NFL, seeing it from where it started to what it's become, we'll never have that person in our lives again."

3

BRIAN URLACHER

When it comes to the Bears and linebacker Brian Urlacher, Patrick Mannelly remembers the cleats. A ton of them.

"He would wear a lot of cleats during the week," the Bears' longtime long snapper said.

Urlacher could do that. He had a Nike contract.

But instead of having the Bears dispose of them, Urlacher would do something different.

Mannelly, who played in more games for the Bears than anyone, assisted charities over his long career. He'd ask teammates for autographs, especially Urlacher, the face of the team.

"I bugged Brian way too much but he never batted an eye," Mannelly said. "He'd be like, 'Nah, listen just take a shoe. I'll sign both of them. Maybe they can sell both of them.' That's the one thing that I remember vividly off the field."

But that's who Urlacher was.

He didn't win a Super Bowl, but he was the face of a team that was the Bears' best since the days of Mike Ditka. A first ballot Hall of Famer in 2018, Urlacher revolutionized the inside linebacker position with his blend of size, speed, and smarts. He was a rare breed. It's a description that applies to him off the field, too.

Urlacher wasn't only the best player on the Bears over his 13-year career; he was the best teammate. That's how his teammates remember him.

"The most humble superstar I ever met," Mannelly said. "He was the glue to our locker room because nobody, whether you were drafted as a first-round pick or a high-priced free agent to come in, could be bigger than him. He always kept it just that way.

"He knew everybody's name in the building, from the undrafted rookie free agent to somebody who worked upstairs and that we never saw. That's the first part that I would mention most about him—and then obviously just an unbelievable player."

For a generation of fans, Urlacher is the Bears.

"Brian was a star; he was the face of the team," former cornerback Charles Tillman said. "But he always made you feel like you were the star. He wasn't about that limelight. He wasn't about taking credit for anything... He's just a kind, quiet soul who is beloved by his teammates and the whole damn state of Illinois."

Determined to be Great

Working the Bears' sideline meant watching the stars, which meant always being aware of what Urlacher was doing. So over 14 years as the team's radio sideline reporter, Zach Zaidman learned just how smart Urlacher was as a football player as he interacted with coach Lovie Smith and linebackers coach Bob Babich.

"After the first defensive series in nearly every game, he'd come back to the sideline and Bob Babich and Lovie would go to him, and he'd basically say, 'Here's what's working, here's what isn't. This is what we have to change,'" Zaidman said. "He was a brilliant player, a great player, a great teammate."

It didn't always look that way after the Bears selected Urlacher with the ninth overall pick in 2000. His start under former coach Dick Jauron and defensive coordinator Greg Blache had its inauspicious moments.

Urlacher was a hybrid safety/linebacker at New Mexico. Learning how to play linebacker in the NFL would require time and effort and highs and lows. His first NFL position coach, Dale Lindsey, was a backbreaker, too.

"I remember covering his first camp," ESPN 1000 radio host Marc Silverman said. "He had a lot to learn."

There was that time that he got pancaked by tight end Alonzo Mayes.

"Everybody is sort of looking at each other, 'Oh Boy,'" Silverman said.

With Barry Minter at middle linebacker, Urlacher started at "Sam" linebacker and played close to or on the line of scrimmage. It was an adjustment after playing in space in college.

"Being up there right away wasn't for him," former center Olin Kreutz said.

But the skepticism never lasted long. There was too much talent, too much effort. Minter suffered an injury, which moved Urlacher to the middle. Kreutz felt the difference immediately.

"I was a decent center and I could get out and cut off linebackers." Kreutz said. "Lach took off running that day at middle linebacker. I came back to the huddle, and I'm like 'That guy's fast.' I remembered that about him. The first thing you remember about him is how big he was, but it's how fast he was. He was just fast."

A star was born. Urlacher made 125 tackles and eight sacks for a 5–11 team as a rookie. He was hope in hard-hitting form. He was named Defensive Rookie of the Year.

"Boy, there were frustrating times for him, where he really didn't want to do it, but he did it anyway," Bears radio play-by-play broadcaster Jeff Joniak said. "It was all about what he wasn't able to do, not what he was able to do.

"I bring that up because he wasn't just anointed as a Hall of Famer. He had to work at it. In many respects, he was a self-made player. I always have a great respect for the guys that were self-made, lunch-bucket guys. That guy worked at it, man."

In his second season, Urlacher had Ted Washington and Keith Traylor, two 300-pound brutes, in front of him to eat blocks. It helped him earn his first All-Pro honors.

But in 2004, everything changed. Jauron and Blache were fired. Gone were the days of his big-bodied protectors. In Smith's version of the Tampa Two defense, he was asked to do so much more, especially against the pass. He was asked to drop and cover the deep middle. It wouldn't be easy, but he had the gifts and willingness.

"And he still had 200 tackles," said John "Moon" Mullin, a longtime Bears writer for the *Daily Herald, Chicago Tribune*, and NBC Sports Chicago. "He wasn't scheme dependent. I'm still shaking my head. I never saw a player like that. Athletic freak doesn't even say it."

As a result, the Bears redefined the position that the franchise essentially created with Bill George in the 1950s and 1960s.

"People say Lovie played the Cover 2, well, I called it Cover Urlacher," Kreutz said.

It was his ability to line up directly over the center, then drop straight into coverage. Most linebackers couldn't do that, let alone ones that were officially listed at 6'4" and 258 pounds.

"No one else in the league could do this," Kreutz remembered telling Smith. "You could make an argument that that wasn't the system for him. It just shows how great he is, that he made the Hall of Fame anyway."

A Superstar with a Smile

Urlacher didn't have Butkus' bloody knuckles or snarl. And he didn't have the wide eyes and verbose, gospel-like ways of Singletary. Urlacher was something completely different. He simply smiled. A lot.

"I've never seen somebody enjoy playing football as much as he did," Mannelly said. "He would hit people and truly smile. It's not snot coming out of his nose and spitting in their face. He will just kind of smile and laugh at them."

With Lance Briggs at his side, the smiles only multiplied. Everyone saw it, and everyone loved it.

"I think people truly enjoyed competing against [Urlacher]," Mannelly said. "Because the other thing that I loved about Brian, and Lance as well, they would go up and smack somebody and they'd get up laughing. Like hammer somebody. They'd be laughing instead of that snarl and nastiness. They truly enjoyed like just beating the hell out of everybody."

Urlacher's story wouldn't be complete without Briggs, one of his best friends on the team. They were a dynamic tandem on the field. But it's also everything they did off it.

From finding unflattering pictures of each other and other linebackers and sharing them during training camp to ping-pong matches and dodge ball in the locker room to their beloved "box game"—where empty equipment boxes were slammed over the heads of unsuspecting teammates—Urlacher's Bears always had fun.

"He is just a fun-loving guy, a small-town kid that made good on his talent and his abilities," Briggs said. "For us, we laughed virtually every day. We played pranks on each other. We always pushed each other, but if one of us tripped and fell, the other guy would make it overdramatic. We were always waiting for that one little slip up so that we can laugh dramatically at the other guy to kind of tick him off."

Smith allowed it because of how good they remained on the field. Smith's Bears were fun-loving and feared defensively. It started with Urlacher.

"You just kind of enjoyed the locker room," former Bears kicker Robbie Gould said. "He was a guy that led the charge and the games of whiffle ball and dodge ball that made it fun for the guys. Because it's a grind. The seasons are a grind, and I think he's the guy who ultimately everyone looked up to and followed his lead."

It didn't occur in the same vein as Singletary or Butkus or George. But it worked. The Bears did as Brian did.

"When I say leader, I don't give everybody that name," superstar returner Devin Hester said. "Brian was a leader on and off the field. He was a leader in the locker room. He was a leader to the practice-squad guy. He was a guy that treated everybody equal.

"That's when I start giving out names to leaders, when a guy [doesn't] look at another person because of the situation and the status that they have. He was the guy that treated the starting quarterback just like a walk-on guy, the scout team. He was that type of leader where everybody felt comfortable around him."

To Mullin, whose coverage of the Bears spanned decades, Urlacher became a "put down my pen" player to watch and cover. It turned out that he was watching the career of a first-ballot Hall of Famer—a dynamic and rare player who made 41½ sacks and 22 interceptions and was voted to eight Pro Bowls.

"You know the guys that I'd compare him to? Barry Sanders and Brett Favre," Mullin said. "[It's] just seeing Brian do stuff that somebody who is 260 pounds shouldn't be able to do that. So Lovie told me, 'Brian let us do things that no other player could of.' It all sounds cliche-ish until you see him. He's one of those rare guys that he always looked like was having fun."

The Leader of the Midway

On October 1, 2000, Urlacher introduced himself to the Packers and quarterback Brett Favre at Lambeau Field. It officially came on third-and-10 from the Bears' 38 early in the second quarter.

"Favre is rolling right and goes to pat the ball and he looks back and the next thing you know he is just on his back," Mannelly said. "You saw Favre kind of look at him, like "Ah, [expletive], there is a new guy in town I've got to deal with.'"

The Bears defeated their rivals 27–24 that day. It was Urlacher's rookie season and his first game in Green Bay. The teams' long-standing rivalry would intensify. A new superstar had entered the fray.

"Brian just impressed the hell out of Brett Favre and now he knows that he has to worry about him," Mannelly remembered thinking at the time.

Mannelly wasn't wrong. Explained through multiple interviews since, Favre and Aaron Rodgers came to appreciate not only Urlacher's physical prowess, but the chess match with him.

"By far the most special and smartest player I've ever played the game of football with," Gould said. "I remember sitting on the sideline with him in the preseason in game and he would just know based on formation and shifts what the offense—whether it was our offense or their offense—what they were going to do. He was always a step ahead and one of the smartest guys on the field."

It made him more formidable, but also transcendent. When longtime Bears writer Dan Pompei presented Urlacher to Hall of Fame voters, that was part of his point.

"He would have been a great player I think in any scheme," Pompei said. "He was a really special guy and also a guy like Singletary, like Butkus, like George, who was a great team leader and led in a different way probably than any of those guys, but had the respect of every person in the locker room. It was well-deserved."

The fans will remember Urlacher's highlights and him hoisting the Halas Trophy in the snow after winning the NFC Championship Game against the Saints.

But his teammates will remember the teammate. His lasting impact on the Bears always will be felt there.

"Nothing was as important to him as the team and just playing ball," Kreutz said. "Those kind of guys, they can't fake it, right? You're either like that or you're not and Urlacher was like that through his whole career.

"As long as our offenses were bad, you never heard a word from him about our offense. Most times, you're going to hear something, right? You might not hear it in the media, but you'll see this frustration in the building. But not with Lach. It was never like that.

"It was always just about what I can do to help the team win. He practiced the hardest. He always enjoyed his days in the building. But the thing about Lach, you can tell when it's fake, with him, it never was. He just wanted to be one of the guys."

4

DA COACH

It was second-and-36 with less than five minutes left to play, and the Bears trailed the Steelers in Pittsburgh by three points.

If the Bears were going to hold off the rival Packers in the standings, they needed something special to happen, something unworldly.

What the Bears got was a short pass from quarterback Bill Wade to tight end Mike Ditka in the flat.

In the huddle moments before, Ditka said he was too tired to run a longer route. But with the ball in his hands, the Bears would still get something heroic.

"Everybody on the team hit him at least once," former Bears offensive tackle Bob Wetoska said.

Ditka couldn't be stopped. He turned a short catch into a 63-yard thunderous run in an important game from the Bears' championship 1963 season.

"He bowled them over," former Bears defensive end Ed O'Bradovich said. "The first two or three guys that he hit, he ran over them. And he wouldn't go down. He wouldn't damn go down."

When the Steelers finally stopped him, it was too late. Ditka was dragged down on the 15-yard line. In exhaustion, Ditka laid on his back for a few moments, his chest gasping for extra air. It was his seventh catch of the day. He gained 146 yards.

"That's what really got us into the championship," Wetoska said.

Three plays later, Roger LeClerc made a field goal for a 17–17 tie on November 24, 1963. The Bears were able to maintain their half-game edge over the rival Packers, who won the previous two NFL championships, in the standings.

Nearly a full month later, the Bears defeated the New York Giants 14–10 on December 29 to win the championship at Wrigley Field.

"That's one of the greatest runs in Bears history and certainly in the NFL," O'Bradovich said.

Over time, Ditka's on-field heroics have seemingly been forgotten. He's an endless endorser of products, a restaurant owner, a supporting cast member in movies, an inspiration for *Saturday Night Live* skits or Halloween costumes, and a frequent interviewee in Chicago for anything and everything.

But he's an NFL icon first—a championship player from the best Bears team in decades who later became a championship coach for arguably the best team ever. The Bears simply aren't the Bears without Mike Ditka.

"He gave 100 percent in practice; he gave 100 percent in games," Wetoska said. "And he was not afraid if he felt that you weren't putting out to the best of your ability, that he'd let you know right to your face. I respected him, and he was the absolute greatest."

Da Player

In the opinion of Hub Arkush, the longtime publisher of *Pro Football Weekly* and a former Bears radio broadcaster, it's Mike Ditka and then John Mackey.

"What [Ditka] doesn't get credit for is that he pretty much created the tight end position," Arkush said. "John Mackey came after him. It was him and Mackey, and he was probably the first tight end who became a significant offensive position."

It all started in 1961. Owner George Halas selected Ditka out of the University of Pittsburgh with the fifth overall pick. It was the result of the advice from assistant George Allen.

Mackey, who has a college award for tight ends named after him, didn't arrive in the NFL until 1963 as the 19th overall pick by the Colts.

"They were inventing the position," Arkush said. "They brought these guys in who could block and be tough, but as a pass catcher and a run-after-the-catch guy, nobody had really seen anything like [Ditka]."

As a rookie, Ditka made 56 catches for 1,076 yards and 12 touchdowns—and did so after making only 11 catches in his final collegiate season.

It was unheard of production as the end position became what's now the tight end in the NFL. Halas and offensive assistant Luke

Johnsos were changing the game—and doing it with Ditka, a fiery mad man on and off the field.

"I think Ditka is probably the best all-around football player I'd ever seen," Wetoska said. "He was so tough and he had so much ability that he could have played on the offensive line, he could have been running back. He could had been on defense. He was just an animal."

The best team he was a part of came in 1963. The Bears' defense was loaded with Bill George, Doug Atkins, Joe Fortunato, Richie Petitbon, and Rosey Taylor. Ditka was the face of the offense, who had Wade at quarterback and Willie Galimore and Rick Casares at running back.

"One of the toughest guys I've ever seen," Arkush said. "When you think of that era and that style, you've got Mike Ditka.... Any player that you can think of when they pop in your mind and there's blood on them somewhere, that's who he was."

As a player, Ditka wasn't afraid to get on his teammates or his coaches. Much like Halas, Ditka enjoyed a good fight. But that's how things ended, too.

After six seasons with the Bears—which included five consecutive Pro Bowl honors—Halas traded Ditka to the Eagles in 1967. It came after Ditka's now-legendary quote about Halas throwing nickels around like manhole covers—a clear mocking of the Bears owner's frugality and stinginess.

But Ditka and the Bears would always have that 1963 season, and that 63-yard run against the Steelers. It came two days after President John F. Kennedy was assassinated in Dallas and the same day that Lee Harvey Oswald was shot and killed.

Vice president Lyndon B. Johnson wanted the NFL to play its games to help the nation heal. In his home state, Ditka delivered just that; he made his own history by changing the Bears'.

"That's what a true champion is as a player," O'Bradovich said. "He understood the game. He understood the situation that we were in. We were playing in Pittsburgh after the president of the United States gets assassinated and we got to go out and play football. But we knew what it was. We knew what he had as a team."

The Bears knew what they had in Ditka.

"The will to win,' O'Bradovich said. "The will to win has to burn, just so deep in you that every day is precious."

Da Coach

Admittedly, players weren't sure what they were getting when Halas stunned the NFL world and hired Ditka to be the team's head coach in 1982.

"I think initially because he had never been an offensive or defensive coordinator and he was a former Bear, there were positives and negatives on that," said former safety Gary Fencik, who had already been with the Bears for six seasons at the time.

"If you talk to some of the players around the league, they were like, 'Oh, Mike Ditka. Come on. Hot head. Special teams coach.'"

The players' impressions of Ditka changed with his first message.

"He was the first head coach who really articulated what the goals of the organization were. It wasn't just to get to the Super Bowl but it was to win," Fencik said. "Well, you may say, of course. Everybody knows that's the goal. But in an organization, if you're not orally articulating the goals of the organization, it's kind of hard to see what your measuring stick is.

"He gave that speech, and he said, 'But when we get there, half of you won't be there.' And if you look at the turnover from the time that he gave that speech, which I did, till the time we got to the Super Bowl, it was about a two-thirds turnover in players that heard that initial comment. He did hold players accountable. He was very impatient."

That fire—that will to win—still burned in Ditka. Halas knew it, too. After his playing career ended, Ditka became the special teams coach for the Cowboys and Tom Landry.

But his heart belonged to the Bears. Sixteen years after their separation, Ditka wrote Halas a letter, stating his dream to coach his team. How could Halas say no? Ditka turned out be a loaded personality who was just right for Halas' loaded teams of the 1980s.

Some players, including center Jay Hilgenberg and Hall of Fame defensive tackle Dan Hampton, don't think Ditka gets enough credit for the Bears' Super Bowl–winning 1985 team. To them, Ditka's impact stretched beyond making things work with defensive coordinator Buddy Ryan, a holdover from the previous staff.

"Ditka's leadership and talent evaluation was just fantastic, and I don't think he ever gets enough credit for that," Hampton said. "It's almost like people treat him like a hood ornament to our team. They were so great, blah, blah, blah. Anybody could have coached them. Yeah, maybe. Maybe.

"But he was able to get us not only to the Super Bowl and win it, but how they rank the teams now, we were like No. 1 team in football for a long time there. And it would have never happened without Mike Ditka."

In some ways, he was the second coming of Halas. He was intense and stubborn. He sparred with his players, particularly his quarterbacks, Jim McMahon and Jim Harbaugh.

Sportswriter Rick Telander described him as a "loose nut" who became part of what the Bears were as a franchise in the 1980s, which included the passing of Halas and the departure of general manager Jim Finks.

"I was out of touch with reality for about 20 years," Ditka joked during a panel at the Bears 100 celebration in 2019.

But Ditka still fit what the 1985 Bears were. It took a level of crazy to coach a crazy good team, especially in that decade.

"They could go to places and get absolutely hammered and get into fights," Telander said. "They could do crazy stuff all together, which they did. And then they had these unique personalities. And then all of it, I want to say was tolerated because it was Ditka. He tolerated it."

But only if the players worked and won. Earning his praise—"Hey, good job"—became significant because he rarely did it.

"He knew what it took to be dedicated to be great," former guard Tom Thayer said. "It wasn't something he said all the time. He had expectations of work ethic, work effort, the physical style of play that he expected of you."

He expected his players to be like him—a blue-collar, give-it-your-all tough guy. Ditka was a Hall of Fame player who won 106 games as the Bears' coach, which trails only Halas.

"Ditka had three rules for us: show up on time, pay attention, and play like hell," Hilgenberg said. "After that, he said I don't care what you guys do. That was an open door for us. We had fun. We enjoyed what we did.

"If you weren't prepared, ready for your day and if you had any type of mental errors during the day, your life was miserable. But if you showed up on time, paid attention, played like hell, it was a great experience. He's great. There's no way the Chicago Bears don't win the Super Bowl without Mike Ditka as the head coach."

5

PAPA BEAR

In the back of a business park in Lake Forest, Illinois, about a mile north of Illinois Route 60, is the home of the Chicago Bears.

It has its own street address—1920 Football Drive—and some of it can be seen by passing drivers on Interstate 294.

A winding private road takes you past the massive Walter Payton Center, a garden dedicated to Ed McCaskey, and to a two-story gray building that bears the words "Halas Hall." The yellow goal posts from two practice fields can be seen behind it.

In front of the entrance, an 8-foot-8-inch statue of owner, founder, and coach George Halas stands tall, walking and pointing.

Inside the building, which was expanded and upgraded from 2017 to 2019, there is a 13,000-square-foot strength and conditioning room, an indoor practice turf with a full-wall projection system, a hydrotherapy room, a modern cafeteria, and so much more. Millions and millions were spent on it. There are two new practice fields behind the Walter Payton Center, too.

What would Halas—whose name is on the building and who once lived in a modest apartment in Chicago when the Bears were based in the city—think of the Bears' modern facility?

"He'd be very honored," said Patrick McCaskey, a Bears board member and one of Halas' 11 grandchildren from his daughter, Virginia McCaskey. "He'd be very humble about it and grateful."

Of course, it wouldn't exist without him. What left is there to say about Halas? The NFL wouldn't be what it is today—a multi-billion dollar behemoth—without him. He was and always will be the league's foremost pioneer.

"He was dedicated to the Bears and to the league and his family," McCaskey said. "He was the son of immigrants from what is now Czechoslovakia. He believed in hard work and he had fun doing it."

CHICAGO BEARS

* * *

"Nobody who ever gave his best regretted it."—Halas

Born in 1895, Halas' story is long and amazing. Encapsulating it has its difficulties. He had the life and experiences that only come through a man who served in two World Wars and lived through the Great Depression. It's really the stuff of legends

Halas was the eighth child born to his parents, Frank and Barbara, but only four survived past infancy. The son of a tailor, Halas' life had its rough, personality-molding moments, especially growing up on the West Side of Chicago and attending Crane Tech High School.

At 20 years old, he worked for Western Electric and was supposed to be on the SS *Eastland*, which was set to cross Lake Michigan on July 24, 1915, for a company picnic. But Halas missed it. The *Eastland* overturned, killing 844 people.

Halas was an exceptional athlete. After Crane Tech, he attended the University of Illinois, where he lettered in football (under legendary coach Bob Zuppke), basketball, and track while earning a degree in civil engineering.

Halas also was intensely patriotic. Toward the end of World War I, he joined the Navy and was an ensign stationed in the Great Lakes Naval Station in North Chicago, Illinois. He played for their football team and in the 1919 Rose Bowl against the Mare Island (California) Marines. He was named the game's most valuable player, too.

It's often said that Halas' first love was baseball and the Cubs. He even played for the New York Yankees. One of his favorite tall tales to tell was saying that he was replaced by Babe Ruth, but Ruth arrived one season after him.

In 1920, Halas was hired by A.E Staley of the Staley Manufacturing Company in Decatur, Illinois. He would not only learn the cornstarch business, but Staley wanted him to start, coach, and play for the football team that became the Decatur Staleys.

At 47 years old—and with the Bears under his ownership—Halas re-enlisted in the Navy to serve during World War II. He left the team in the middle of the 1942 season and went to the Pacific. The Bears were undefeated at the time.

"He was a lieutenant commander in the Navy in World War II," said Hub Arkush, the publisher of *Pro Football Weekly* and former Bears radio broadcaster. "At that point, in his mid-forties, he left the team for whatever it was, two or three years."

You can do that when you're George Halas.

The Decatur Staleys had already turned into the Chicago Bears and then the Monsters of the Midway by then. Five championships already were won by his team. A league that once needed Halas' "Red Grange Tour" was growing, but it wasn't easy.

Halas was present for the meeting on September 17, 1920, in Canton, Ohio, when the league was founded. Two years later, upon Halas' suggestion, the American Professional Football Organization was re-named the National Football League.

"George Halas, to the league, was George Washington," Arkush said. "He was Abraham Lincoln. It's that real…. I don't think you can overstate his importance to the National Football League."

The growth of the NFL was paramount to Halas. He successfully pushed for expansion into Minneapolis and Dallas and he promoted revenue sharing as television sparked new growth. Halas understood the importance of the draft and maintaining competitive balance. He loaned money to the Giants and even to the rival Packers, knowing that the Bears and the league couldn't exist without them.

All of it is a source of pride for the family.

"For about the first 40 years of the league and the Bears, it was a struggle," Patrick McCaskey said. "And then when the television money came in, equally distributed among each of the NFL teams, regardless of the size of the market, then there was some stability. Prior to that, my grandfather had to borrow money to prepare for the next season, which he paid back once the gate receipts came in.

"It was always a worthwhile struggle. It was always a struggle to make ends meet. My grandfather was once asked what was his greatest thrill in sports and he said just to be part of the growth of the National Football League. It's tremendous."

* * *

"Nothing is work unless you'd rather be doing something else."—Halas

Attending Proviso East High in the western suburbs of Chicago and playing at the University of Illinois, defensive end Ed O'Bradovich knew all about Halas when the Bears drafted him in the seventh round of the 1962 draft.

"He's the guy that basically started this league," said O'Bradovich, who played 10 seasons with the Bears, including five under Halas.

"And I know all the different things. He gave other teams money decades ago to stay in this league. It was his belief. He basically started it. And for that, I give him all the respect in the world. If there wasn't a George Halas, you may not have seen what's going on here today."

But playing for the legend still had it difficulties. O'Bradovich, who later became a successful businessman and radio broadcaster, said that he had a "love and hate thing" with Halas. He wasn't alone, of course.

Mike Ditka had his famous spat with Halas, where he said the Bears owner threw nickels around like manhole covers. Halas, who also enjoyed a good barb and argument, agreed. Halas traded Ditka, the future Hall of Fame tight end, to the Eagles, but he still brought him back to be the Bears' coach.

"I was hired by Mr. Halas twice," Ditka told reporters during the Bears 100 celebration in 2019, "and it was the greatest time of my life."

Ditka was part of the last championship team that Halas coached in 1963—a special, loaded group, particularly on defense with linebacker Bill George and defensive end Doug Atkins.

Halas always had innovative assistant coaches in George Allen, Luke Johnsos and Clark Shaughnessy at his side, too. Through them, came the T formation and evolutions of the middle linebacker with George and tight end with Ditka. It was on Halas to keep things civil amongst them all. But he also was a motivator.

"As a coach, of course, he was a legend," said former offensive tackle Bob Wetoska, a starting offensive tackle for that 1963 team and a Bear for 10 seasons. "He ran the practices. He set the tone for everything. But I think he was more of a real motivator than what you would call somebody as a coach.... When the guys were lousy, he'd build them up. When they were too high, he'd set them down. He really knew how to motivate people."

Sometimes Halas did that with his frugality. Other times it was a sternness from the streets of Chicago. Or it was a combination of everything. Halas simply knew how to get his players going—good, bad, and sometimes, ugly.

"Guys had their disagreements with him and they'd fight with him, and he'd fight right back," Wetoska said. "He was a tough guy to argue with. He loved discipline. He really liked to get into the finer points. He established weights for guys. How much weight they could carry. And he gave you a three-pound surplus before he would fine you. And every week, he'd have weigh-ins on Thursday.

"Wednesday nights all the steam baths in town were filled with Bears players trying to lose weight for the weigh in. But that's what he did, all the time. It was aggravating. But it was just something else to stir the pot. But that's what he loved to do. He loved to stir pot and motivate guys that way from a lot of different angles, either get them angry or build them up or whatever. It was quite something to be able to play for a legend like that."

Players often would talk about Halas' stubborn ways, especially when it came to their money and his.

"He was penurious," Wetoska said. "Everybody used to bitch about that. You weren't making enough money and you were losing money. And then when the season is over, in those days, they'd withhold 25 percent of your salary, and at the end of the year, you'd go in and settle up with the Old Man and go over the season, and he'd take out what you owed in fines from that 25 percent."

In time, players would learn that Halas was charitable. He was always willing to help players if they needed it. His stubbornness had its limits. There were reconciliations with jilted players, the most notable being Ditka and Dick Butkus. But Halas had his ways.

"He always kept the pot stirred, Halas," Wetoska said. "That's the way he was. He never let you get comfortable."

* * *

"Many people flounder about in life because they do not have a purpose, an objective toward which to work."—Halas

On September 24, 2019, Bears chairman George McCaskey appeared in a video with linebacker Danny Trevathan, tight end Trey Burton, defensive lineman Akiem Hicks, and quarterbacks Mitch Trubisky and Chase Daniel.

This was the Bears' social justice committee, and the team was about to wear a throwback jersey from 1936, which was a year from an era in NFL history where African American players were essentially banned from playing in the NFL.

Halas, who is McCaskey's grandfather, had a role in it. A murky part of Halas story was detailed in 2019 by fan/team historian Jack Silverstein in a story for the website, Windy City Gridiron.

"This Sunday against the Vikings our players will wear the 1936 classic jersey," McCaskey said in the team-produced video.

"That was from a time when unfortunately African Americans were not included on the Bears or other NFL rosters. Integration of the NFL and the Bears was too long in coming. But we're proud that this year's Bears will be the first African Americans to wear these jerseys."

Through the first 14 seasons of the league, African Americans played in the league. And then for 12 years, there weren't any. It's a shameful, almost forgotten period of time in league history. It was a ban led by Washington owner George Preston Marshall but Halas' Bears were a part of it. The team acknowledged as much in its centennial scrapbook.

"I think that any successful people or any famous people or people with a lot of public action, there's going to be pieces of their story that gets sanded away the longer you move away from their lives, especially if it's something uncomfortable to begin with that they're able to push people away from that truth at the outset," Silverstein said in a 2019 interview. "This is just to me another piece of his story. I don't think it has to be more or less than that. I think for some people it will totally change the way that they view George Halas. For other people, they don't care."

In time, Halas' Bears broke down barriers.

The Bears were the first team to draft a black player in running back George Taliaferro in the 13th round of the 1949 draft, but Taliaferro decided to play for the Los Angeles Dons of the All-America Football Conference.

In 1952, the Bears integrated by drafting running back Eddie Macon. In 1953, Halas signed quarterback Willie Thrower, the first black player to play in the Big Ten. It was his only season with the team. The Bears later made Gale Sayers and Brian Piccolo what's believed to be the first interracial roommates in the NFL during a time of racial turmoil in the United States.

"[The ban] adds nuance, another layer to his story," Silverstein said. "It deepens people's understanding of who he was and what he did, his life in totality."

In a way, that's what makes the video with McCaskey and the players more notable. It's another piece of Halas' legacy. In the video, Hicks and Burton said in statements that they were proud to be the first African Americans to wear the jerseys.

"Wearing this jersey is a sign, a symbol for the people who came before us that weren't allowed to wear this jersey," Hicks said.

In those jerseys, the Bears won, too—defeating the Vikings 16–6 in a dominant defensive performance. It was the type of victory that Halas surely would have enjoyed.

"From a mythology standpoint and from an iconography standpoint and from a storytelling narrative—from that perspective—the Chicago Bears are the NFL," Silverstein said. "From a very tangible perspective, you're talking about the charter franchise."

And it belonged to a man named George Halas.

6

DEVIN HESTER

When it comes to star returner Devin Hester, former Bears fullback Jason McKie remembers a dispute that he had with his position coach, Tim Spencer.

McKie was the only fullback on the Bears roster, and the coaching staff was contemplating taking him off kickoff return.

"I remember telling him, I said, 'No,'" McKie recalled. "'Take me off offense before you take me off kickoff return.' That's how much guys wanted to be on that kickoff return team blocking for him."

Something special might happen. McKie and many others wanted to be a part of it. There was no one like Hester in the NFL.

And there might not never be again.

"I always wanted to be labeled as one of the most feared guys in the NFL with the ball in his hand," Hester said. "That's pretty much how I want to stamp my name—as one of the most feared guys that ever touched the football."

It was that way from the beginning, too. The Bears wouldn't be what they were in 2006—the NFC champions—without him. If the Bears were going to rely on defense under coach Lovie Smith and run the ball on offense, they needed to excel on special teams.

With Hester, the Bears didn't only dominate their competition on special teams; they burnt it. Hester, whom the Bears selected in the second round with the 57th overall pick that year, returned 47 punts for 600 yards and three touchdowns and 20 kickoffs for 528 yards and two more scores as a rookie. He didn't merely flip the field; he ran all over it. The Bears had one of the most exciting and most dangerous players ever.

"Special teams used to be a time where you'd go back to the fridge, get some beer, go to the bathroom. You take a break, right? You couldn't," former Bears sideline reporter Zach Zaidman said. "Any moment was the moment. He made special teams a part of the offense because there was a while there the Bears' offense was special teams— their ability to do unique things. He was unstoppable. He was this force of nature. He was an incredible player. Just the moves."

Hester's teammates will debate their favorite return, but to him, the conversations start with two touchdowns from his rookie season: his 83-yard punt return against the Cardinals in the "the Bears are who we thought they were" game and his game-opening 92-yard kickoff return in Super Bowl XLI against the Colts.

The former was surprising because it came in the fourth quarter of a one-score game and it turned into the game-winning play for the Bears in a 24–23 victory, which famously set off Cardinals coach Dennis Green.

The latter was shocking because the Colts' kick and punt coverage units were considerable weaknesses. Coach Tony Dungy referred to Hester as a "nuclear weapon" as he and his staff debated kicking or punting to him at all.

"I thought, no way in hell that they're going to kick to him," long snapper Patrick Mannelly said. "I just said, 'There's no way.' Then when you saw it go up in the air, you're like, 'Oh boy,' because they didn't have the greatest special teams unit.

"We kind of knew that maybe that was one of the advantages that we had. Yes, they had Adam Vinatieri, a very good kicker, but other than that, they weren't one of the best teams that we played all year."

All of it made Hester an instant fan favorite. He was too dynamic on the field and too soft-spoken and team-oriented off it not to be. He had a vibe to him. Fans loved it when Hester danced to "Crank That" by Soulja Boy before his returns at Soldier Field. With the same song reverberating, the loudest cheers received by any player at the Bears 100 celebration belonged to Hester, too.

"They say that Gale Sayers did similar things," Zaidman said. "But nobody was able to impact the game as long in that area as Devin Hester."

One of the best parts of Hester's story is that a native Chicagoan found him and believed in him. Mark Sadowski grew up in the Bridgeport neighborhood and went to St. Rita of Cascia High School. He was the Bears' Southeast area scout when Hester was coming out of Miami. Teams were uncertain of which position would best fit Hester in the NFL, but Sadowski was 100 percent certain that he was a special playmaker. He strongly went to bat for Hester in pre-draft meetings with Smith and general manager Jerry Angelo. Some staff members had their doubts.

"He fought for me, man," Hester said. "I tip my hat to the guy because he was the guy, at the end of the day, who really convinced Jerry Angelo and those guys in that draft room, that 'Hey, you won't regret drafting this kid.' It's him standing on the table and saying, 'Hey, don't pass up on this guy. You're going to regret it.' He is one of the main reasons why I am a Chicago Bear."

One of the most unfortunate parts of Hester's story is that he didn't break the NFL record for return touchdowns in a Bears uniform. He almost had it, too. On November 24, 2013, in St. Louis, he broke free for a 62-yard score on a punt in the fourth quarter, but it was brought back because of a holding penalty on safety Craig Steltz.

It was Hester's last season with the team, which still was being overhauled by general manager Phil Emery after firing Smith following the 2012 season. Hester scored his 20th return touchdown, breaking a mark set by Hall of Fame cornerback Deion Sanders, as a member of the Falcons on September 18, 2014. That time his 62-yard punt return counted.

"He was truly transformational as a return man," said Bears radio play-by-play broadcaster Jeff Joniak, who famously called him "ridiculous" during a return against the Rams and also gave him the nickname "Windy City Flyer."

"It was an honor to call all those. You couldn't wait until he got back there. You were especially dialed in and revved up about it. You look at the sideline and all the players got up off the bench and they were watching, too. You just never knew what you were going to get for his entire career."

Hester should be a Hall of Famer because he changed how people did their jobs. Opponents had to game plan for him, where kicking away from him out of fear still resulted in favorable field position for the Bears.

Hester's pairing with special teams coordinator Dave Toub worked, too. Hester changed what the Bears did on special teams, but Toub excelled in coaching them. Players no longer wanted to rest on such plays. They wanted to be a part of them.

"Dave Toub played a huge role in helping Devin, scouting and helping the other 10 guys [with] the blocking schemes," former cornerback Charles Tillman said. "I've been on teams and some years, 'Oh, damn, we got special teams.' But when Devin is on the field, 'Oh, no, we got special teams! We're going to block for Devin.' Guys wanted to be on the field."

It's why McKie fought with his position coach to stay on the field. Everyone wants to play with special players.

"Greatest special teams player ever," McKie said. "He always told me, 'I can envision it before I even get the ball. Before the ball is kicked, I can envision how the return is going to be, where I am going to go.'"

If Hester's teammates couldn't play with him, they did everything they could to watch him.

"The other funny story about Devin Hester is that you would hear [linebackers coach] Bob Babich on [fourth] downs screaming at the defense to get their asses over to the bench so they could go through adjustments but they wouldn't because they wanted to watch Devin return kicks," Mannelly said. "You could see them on special teams tape. They're jogging off and they would turn around."

Hester, who also caught 255 passes for 3,311 yards and 16 touchdowns in his 11-year career, was truly unique. Everyone wanted to see him.

Teammates wanted to be on the field with him or watch him, while opponents feared him. It was must-watch television. He truly changed how fans tuned in at home and handled their time in stadiums.

"It was like watching the greatest hitter in baseball take an at bat," said ESPN 1000 radio host Marc Silverman, a former Bears reporter. "You couldn't turn the TV off or get a beer. You knew after the return is when you may want to go to the bathroom because you could not miss Devin Hester doing what he did."

7

DICK BUTKUS

Dick Butkus was drafted in the heat of the NFL/AFL war—and he was a coveted star.

The year was 1965.

Quarterback Joe Namath had turned down the NFL's Cardinals for the AFL's Jets.

What would Butkus do? His hometown Bears drafted him and running back Gale Sayers in the first round that year. The AFL's Broncos also had Butkus' rights.

"There was some general panic around the NFL as they were losing some of the best talent," said Hub Arkush, the publisher of *Pro Football Weekly* and a former radio broadcaster for Bears. "The biggest concern going in was are they going to be able to get these guys? Because [George] Halas already had the reputation of not being willing to pay for anybody."

But the Broncos, despite their recruitment of Butkus, never really had a chance. Butkus had Chicago in his blood. He went to Vocational High School on the South Side and then the University of Illinois.

"He was a Chicago kid," Arkush said. "There was general excitement for no other reason because everybody here knew who Dick Butkus was. I don't think the rest of the league realized what he was."

But, oh, would they learn—in a hard, painful way, too. Not that there weren't warnings. Scouts certainly knew what was coming. He was widely considered the best linebacker in college. *Sports Illustrated* writer Dan Jenkins wrote what was to come in the NFL with his cover story on Butkus' All-American career at Illinois.

"If every college football team had a linebacker like Dick Butkus of Illinois, all fullbacks would soon be three feet tall and sing soprano," Jenkins wrote in October 1964. "Dick Butkus is a special kind of brute whose particular talent is mashing runners into curious shapes."

Over Butkus' nine years in the NFL, there was violence. Lots of it. But it was the type that was endearing, especially in Chicago. Deacon Jones, a Hall of Fame defensive end, once called him "a stone maniac... a well-conditioned animal." Those were compliments. Butkus' brand of mean, in-your-face violence was special, if not, unmatchable. And it belonged to his hometown team.

"Nobody had ever seen anybody play the game as physically as he did," Arkush said. "Butkus became like a cultural icon because of his style."

Replacing a Legend

When Butkus joined the Bears in 1965, the team still belonged to Bill George, who revolutionized the middle linebacker position. George was an eight-time All-Pro selection and a world champion. Two years earlier, the Bears defeated the Giants 14–10 for the NFL championship.

But even George knew what Butkus' arrival meant for him and the team. Butkus was too good, too dominant, too darn physical, and too damn nasty.

"Bill George often said, once Butkus came on the field, he knew his tenure with the Bears was over," said Bears offensive tackle Bob Wetoska, who played with both players. "And it was. He just kind of took over that position right from the start."

The 1965 season was George's last with the Bears. The torch was passed. Butkus was an All-Pro as a rookie, making five interceptions and recovering seven fumbles.

"The big difference between the two of them was Dick was a more physical player," said defensive end Ed O'Bradovich, who also played with both players.

"Smart and physical. Bill George, it's hard to say. Does one really have a gigantic leap over the other one? No. They pretty much had all it takes for a middle linebacker. Calling the signals. Studying the game. I think one thing Dick learned from Bill George—when Dick was drafted and came here and saw Bill George—was Bill George's ability to understand defenses. It came back to that knowledge."

And punishment. It was different when it was delivered by Butkus.

"When Bill George tackled them, they would go down," O'Bradovich said. "But with Dick, he'd hit 'em and he wanted to try to break them in two before they hit the ground. He wanted them to know who the hell tackled him."

To do that, Butkus would often lord over his opponent on the ground.

"For a little extra a thousand and one count," O'Bradovich said. "I asked him one time. 'What the hell are you doing?' He says, 'I want them to look at me and know how the hell they got to that ground.' I said, 'Okay, that's good enough for me.'"

That was Butkus. It's what he always did, from running over catchers in Little League and getting booed by mothers, to leaving a football practice in high school to beat up four boys who were harassing his girlfriend and future wife, Helen, to using the jackets of opposing players in the NFL to wipe his cleats or even spitting on them before the game. He was feared but always respected.

"The stories you hear about him biting guys in the huddle and poking people in the eyes, yeah, that was happening," Arkush said.

Seemingly forgotten amidst all the bone-jarring hits and stories of intimidation is how talented and skilled Butkus actually was as a player. He backed everything up with violence but also his athleticism. He wouldn't have made 22 interceptions or recovered 27 fumbles in his career without it.

"The thing that people don't realize about Dick is that he was an unbelievable athlete," Arkush said. "He was like the first middle linebacker to cover passes. He would be able to drop and run with tight ends on everything."

But it's not as though Butkus had a problem with his rough-and-tough image. He fostered it. He became a legend despite only playing on two winning teams in his nine-year career. The internet kept his legend alive, too. Stories from fathers to sons can now be seen and then shared again.

In the NFL Films' series "Best Ever: Professionals" in 1981, narrator John Facenda encapsulated what Butkus' career was and always will be as videos of him snarling and intercepting a pass against the Oilers—and then showing it off—ran.

"Butkus stretched his passion for competition to its ultimate limits," Facenda said. "He played his own game, set his own standards. It was as if the football field was Butkus' private playground and he could do anything he wanted."

The Softer Side

In the 1990s, the Bears' radio broadcast team had a tradition for games in Green Bay.

It started with Butkus. The Hall of Famer–turned analyst would fly into O'Hare International Airport. Butkus had appeared in several movies at this point and lived in Malibu, California, but was a white-knuckle flyer. Some planes—the ones that would connect you to Green Bay—weren't for him.

So Arkush would drive. He'd pick up play-by-play man Wayne Larrivee first and then Butkus at O'Hare.

"So we're driving to Green Bay and we decide we're going to stop at the Brat Stop," Arkush said. "It's a two o'clock on a Saturday afternoon and the place is fairly empty."

But those there in the Kenosha, Wisconsin, restaurant still noticed Butkus.

"They'd come to the table and Dick is gracious about it," Arkush said.

It later turned into a conversation about why Butkus never came out to dinner with them on the road. That was another tradition.

"'You really want to know why,'" Arkush recalled Butkus saying. "'I'd love to have dinner with you guys, but I get in some of these places, people won't people leave alone. And then they think I'm a jerk because I just want to have dinner with my friends.'

"Wayne and I are like, 'Wow, it can't be that bad.'"

But then Butkus proved it to them when they arrived at the Bears' team hotel in Appleton. Instead of Butkus going through his usual back door, he entered with everyone else through the front.

"It was like locusts descending," Arkush said. "We got 15 feet in the door and either you signed for everybody or you're a jerk. So finally, I cut it off. I grabbed him and started pulling him away and everybody is yelling at me, which was fine. We got him away. We get to the desk, we get to the elevator, and he goes, 'See.' And it was true."

It's not that Butkus wanted to avoid fans. He just wanted to avoid extra attention. He had a private side. Some folks would say he even had a quiet side. He preferred not to be pressed for interviews or to take pictures. He was that way in college, too.

But once you're a star of Butkus' caliber, you're always a star.

After his career, Butkus appeared in more than a dozen movies and had recurring roles in television shows. He was in commercials for Miller Lite, Prestone (a brand of antifreeze), and more. Butkus had two stints on the Bears' radio broadcast, starting with the beloved 1985 team, and was briefly a television analyst.

A year after that trip to Green Bay, Arkush remembers being with Butkus in Dallas' airport, when Butkus was stopped by a security agent. It was around Christmas and the place was empty.

"There is this little old lady during the security check and in those days you just went right up," Arkush said. "We put our stuff down and this lady is looking at him. He's looking at her. He's looking at me.

"And she finally says, 'I know you. I know who you are.' Dick looks up and he kind of smiles and he goes, 'That's nice. Who do you think I am?' She goes, 'You're that guy in that movie *Hamburger*.' She had no idea. So he's hugging her, and I'm trying to explain to her who he is.

"And he's saying, 'Is there anybody in your family who is a football fan and would probably like some autographs?' She goes, 'Oh, no, we're just big movie buffs.' She didn't even want his autograph. It was kind of like my favorite Butkus moment."

'The Ultimate Bear'

In 1979, George Halas' autobiography, *Halas by Halas*, was released. There were autograph signings and Butkus attended one.

"To Dick Butkus," Halas wrote. "The greatest player in the history of the Bears. You had that old ziperoo."

It was a reconciliation. After his career, Butkus sued the Bears and their doctor. His body was ravaged. The court battle lasted for two years before a settlement was reached.

As a result, Halas turned on Butkus. But he could only do so for so long. Similar to the story of Mike Ditka, Halas could never fully say goodbye to such a player. Butkus meant too much to Halas, too much to his team, too much to Chicago.

In the Bears' centennial scrapbook, team owner Virginia McCaskey, the daughter of Halas, described Butkus as "the ultimate Bear."

"Being from Chicago, I played my high school, college, and pro football all in the state of Illinois," Butkus told reporters during the Bears 100 celebration in 2019. "My parents, my family, brothers, all got to see me play.

"It's very humbling, I tell you. I guess it is kind of unusual because I don't see too many people doing that. People come from all over and everything. I'm just very proud. I'm very proud of this city, to come from this city, to kind of exemplify the trademark of people in Chicago that work hard."

8

1985

On January 27, 1986, the Bears and their fans partied in the cold—bitter, painful, frostbite-inducing cold. With the wind chill, the temperature in Chicago was minus-30.

But no one cared. They were too ecstatic, too euphoric.

A day earlier, the Bears absolutely destroyed the New England Patriots 46–10 in Super Bowl XX in New Orleans. And now the team would be paraded around a frigid city that still burned to see them up close.

"Bears Bring it Home," read the front page of the *Chicago Tribune*.

The Bears' chartered flight was an hour late getting into O'Hare International Airport. From there, the team was loaded into buses, traveled down the Kennedy Expressway, and into the city, where they eventually gathered at Daley Plaza with mayor Harold Washington.

A million people packed the streets, many of them covered in blankets. There was paper confetti everywhere.

But certain stars, including running back Walter Payton and quarterback Jim McMahon, were missing. The Bears' best players were off to Hawaii for the Pro Bowl.

"I wasn't in Chicago for the parade," center Jay Hilgenberg said. "I missed that because they took us out to the Pro Bowl the next day, which was kind of a bummer. But I was always thinking, 'Okay, I'll go to the next one.'

"I remember when I came back from Hawaii. A few weeks later, I went up to Halas Hall and I remember Jerry Vainisi saying something, 'Oh, there is never going to be a year like that one.'

"I just remember going, 'What? What are you talking about? This thing is just starting. Let's don't start thinking negative on the train right now.'"

But Vainisi, who was promoted to general manager after Jim Finks left for the Cubs in 1983, was right, even though he probably didn't mean to be. Of course, the Bears thought more championships were coming. Their roster was the best in the NFL, but that's also part of the specialness of the 1985 team. It was the only one to win it all.

"We were the greatest of all time, on and off the field," Hilgenberg said. "We really got the nation's attention more so than a lot of NFL teams previously."

It's not only what that team did to their competition on the field, but who they were off it. It's why there are 40 pages dedicated to them in the Bears' centennial scrapbook.

Built by Finks and scouts Bill Tobin and Bill Parmer, and coached by Mike Ditka, the 1985 Bears were unique for their success, but also because of their array of personalities. The team had nicknames that Chicago will never forget, from "Da Coach" to "Sweetness" to "the Punky QB" to "Mongo" to "Samurai" to "the Fridge" to "the Hit Man" to "L.A. Mike" to "Butthead." There will never be a group like it—ever—not with the changes in media coverage and attention paid to the NFL and rise of social media. You'll never see another "Super Bowl Shuffle"— before the game is actually won. The 1985 Bears were a phenomenon.

"Rising to the top and then falling is a very almost mythical way of looking at things, where that's kind of like a Greek tragedy," said longtime sportswriter Rick Telander, who chronicled much of the team on and off the field for *Sports Illustrated*. "You rise to the top and you don't stay there. If you do stay there, then you're this noble hero that rises often to heaven or something like that when it's all over. These guys fell to earth."

* * *

Despite having covered the NFL for more than 30 years, Dan Pompei still thinks of his first. How he could not? In retrospect, there was nothing like it.

Pompei, who entered the Pro Football Hall of Fame as the 2013 Dick McCann Award winner, started his career by covering the Bears in 1985.

"It was unlike anything I've experienced since," said Pompei, a Hall of Fame voter. "I think part of it was that the team was so dominant. It was probably the best team that I've ever seen in terms of the ability to dominant an opponent when they were on their game, both from the standpoint of physical superiority and having a cutting-scheme on defense. They were just hitting on all cylinders as a team. It was a lot of people, ideas, strategies peaking at one time. It all came together in that year."

It started with the Bears' devastating 46 defense, which was run by coordinator Buddy Ryan. Owner George Halas opted to keep Ryan on staff after receiving a letter from players asking him to do so, knowing that head coach Neill Armstrong likely was going to be fired after the 1981 season. Halas was touched by the letter, which was signed by more than 20 players. When he hired Mike Ditka as coach, Ryan stayed on Ditka's staff.

"Mike comes in and inherits Buddy Ryan, and I think a lot of people forget that dynamic," said Bears safety Gary Fencik, who wrote the letter. "Buddy Ryan was hired by George Halas before George hired Ditka, so it led to a really dynamic tension for a couple of years."

But that was the Bears in those years.

Ditka, a Hall of Fame tight end from the Bears' 1963 championship team, was different from Armstrong in terms of personality. He still lived and acted like some of his players: fiery, short-tempered, impulsive and extremely competitive. He was perfect for that team, even if meant clashing with McMahon and Ryan at times.

"A coach like him is just a rare thing," Telander said. "The personality, the outspokenness, sometimes the lunacy, the uncontrollable nature that he had. Now you get so many of these guys that are just like automatons. They don't have much say. If they do, they're very careful about what they say."

Ditka, though, allowed Ryan to do his thing. Ryan relentlessly attacked his opponents with his 46 defense, which was designed years earlier, but was perfected with Dan Hampton, Richard Dent, Mike Singletary, Otis Wilson, Wilber Marshall, Steve McMichael, Fencik, and others in it.

"When you look at the numbers of the '85 defense, the 64 sacks, the 34 interceptions, six rushing touchdowns they've limited their opponent to, all the other numbers that go along with it, what are the numbers that are accomplishable in today's game?" said former guard Tom Thayer, a member of that team who is now the team's radio analyst.

"I don't know if you're going to have the opportunity to get 64 sacks anymore in the NFL. Is it reasonable or feasible to think that you can get 34 interceptions as a team?"

It might be possible with how much teams throw in today's NFL. But the rules changed, too. Defense can't be as physically imposing as the Bears were in the 1980s. Today's rules are designed to protect quarterbacks. The '85 Bears destroyed quarterbacks.

"The dominance that they showed in some games was like you prepared to watch an annihilation and you got it," Telander said. "When they played right, they were so much better than anybody else in the league that it was ridiculous. The defense had done something where you probably can't do it again. You leaped ahead of the league by like two years.

"They had like a two-, maybe three-year window where nobody knew what they were doing.... The fact that they knew that you would not be able to run most of your plays—your passing plays—because you would not have the time to set it up, that was different and you started to recognize that as the season went on."

It's all part of '85 team's lasting bravado. The city that loved Dick Butkus adored them too—and still does.

"They also came along kind of in a magical time," said longtime Bears writer John "Moon" Mullin, who worked for the *Daily Herald*, the *Chicago Tribune*, and NBC Sports Chicago. "It was *The Bonfire of the Vanities*. It was the mid-80s. It was junk bonds. America was kind of going crazy. It was like the Roaring '20s and here's the perfect team for it.

"What made them so unique is that they were the bullies that everybody loved. They'd kick your ass and then go have a beer with you. Or you want to have a beer with all of them."

Many did and still do.

"We were the team that had the most fun that won," McMahon told reporters during the Bears 100 celebration. "We did. We had a great time. We had a great time together."

It's the stories and jokes that '85 Bears would tell. For the most part, they didn't hide who they were. Nowadays, with social media, they likely would.

"This was just beginning of the era of when people were really starting to pay attention to sports in a way that they never did before, that went beyond just what happened on the field," Pompei said. "The Bears had all these incredible personalities. It started with the head coach, Mike Ditka, who was unafraid of being himself and open and honest and just really different from the typical NFL head coach. And the team took his lead and they all went out and were completely themselves. I know [Bears coach] Matt Nagy says 'Be you,' and it's on his call sheet and everything, but they really were 'Be You.' These guys are not 'Be you'— nowhere near the same way."

* * *

For Jarrett Payton, the '85 Bears are family. The guys from that team, he said, are like his uncles. They call him and check on him. With former fullback Matt Suhey, it's even more.

"Matt Suhey handles my family's estate," Payton said. "My dad left him in charge. Matt's my dad's best friend. They were super close. Now I deal with Matt on a regular basis. We do lot of stuff together when it comes to anything image and likeness with my dad."

Everyone loved Walter Payton. Stories about the 1985 Bears aren't complete without him. He was Superman on a team of superstars. He ran for 1,551 yards and nine touchdowns that season behind a powerful offensive line centered by Hilgenberg. The Bears were second in the NFL in scoring that season, too.

"It was almost how much were we going to win by and not really thinking about losing," said Thayer, a starter for that mauling offensive line.

One of the bittersweet parts of that memorable season was Payton not scoring in the Super Bowl. His touchdown went to rookie defensive lineman William "Refrigerator" Perry. But a lasting legacy of that season is the connection they all share. It lives on through Walter's son, Jarrett. On the anniversary of his father's passing, he still hears from the '85 Bears, including McMahon.

"They see a lot of my dad in me," Payton said. "So they kind of feel not that I'm him, but we say the same things and we're pretty similar with how we deal with people. It's cool just to see them interact with me. And now I get to do it with them."

There will never be a group like them. Ryan left to coach the Eagles in 1986 and Payton retired after the 1987 season. McMahon, to the dismay of many teammates, could never stay healthy. But for one year that were an imperfect blend of characters who were nearly perfect on the field'; they went 15–1 in the regular season, losing only the Dolphins and quarterback Dan Marino. There are other legendary teams in NFL history, but nothing like the '85 Bears.

It was having five Hall of Fame players—Payton, Hampton, Dent, Singletary, and offensive tackle Jimbo Covert—led by a Hall of Fame coach and former player in Ditka but also having Hall of Fame characters. They're the best team of all time—and they know it.

"It's like every year somebody is voted into the Rock 'n' Roll Hall of fame, but you're already in there and get to show up and party with them," McMichael said during the Bears 100 celebration. "It's what the Gladiator meant in the movie. When Russell Crowe said, 'Your name echoes through eternity.'"

9

1963

Locked into a conversation with Dan Hampton and Richard Dent—two members of the 1985 Bears—Ed O'Bradovich had to defend himself, his team.

Never one to shy away from a conflict, O'Bradovich wouldn't allow anyone to disparage what the Bears had in 1963, not even two Hall of Famers. Otis Wilson, another member of the '85 Bears, might have been there, too.

"They're talking, 'Oh you guys were all small then,'" O'Bradovich said, his voice rising. "I looked them and said, 'What the hell? Smaller? I said you guys are the smaller team. Not us.' I said, 'Dan, let me tell you and Richard, did you guys have a defensive end that's 6'8" and weighed 280 on your team? No.'"

That would be Doug Atkins.

"'Did you have a strong-side safety that was 6'3" and weighed 217? No.'"

That would be Richie Petitbon.

"'Did you have a linebacker in Bill George who was 6'2½" and weighed 235? Did you have a middle linebacker like that? No.' So that was the end of that conversation."

Before the '85 Bears wreaked havoc in the NFL and enthralled Chicago, there was the 1963 Bears. They were the franchise's standard to beat. In that era, they were just as dominant, too. They should never be forgotten.

The Bears lost only one game that season and defeated the Giants 14-10 in the NFL Championship Game before 46,000 fans at Wrigley Field. It was the final title won by the Bears with founder/owner George Halas as their coach.

Since there wasn't a Lombardi Trophy, mayor Richard J. Daley presented the Bears with the John Fitzgerald Kennedy Memorial Trophy, which honored the president who was assassinated that year.

From George to Atkins to Petitbon to linebacker Joe Fortunato to tight end Mike Ditka to receiver Johnny Morris to running back Rick Casares, the '63 Bears had their legends, too.

"You were a Bear, you were a king," Casares told the *Chicago Tribune* in 2013.

An Emotional Season

The radio was on and players were silent on the bus as the Bears headed to their game against the Steelers in Pittsburgh on November 24, 1963. Two days earlier, President John F. Kennedy was assassinated.

And now, a broadcast covered the transport of Lee Harvard Oswald as if it were play-by-play of a sporting event.

"We're getting closer to the stadium and getting ready to get off the bus," said offensive tackle Bob Wetoska, a starter on that team, "and this guy is narrating this transfer from this facility to another facility and then all of a sudden you hear bang, bang, bang, and he said, 'My God, he's been shot! He's been shot!' Of course, Halas jumped out of his seat, 'Goddammit, you shouldn't be listening to this...'"

Halas broke that radio.

It was an emotional, transformational time for the United States. Vice president Lyndon B. Johnson and NFL commissioner Pete Rozzlle wanted the games played to help facilitate the healing process.

The Bears had the Steelers—"The Steelers are always tough," Wetoska said—and a run at a championship to continue. The Packers were only a half game back in the standings. They had the NFL West division to win.

"We get off the bus, getting ready for the game," Wetoska said. "Everything is somber. Go out to the field, there is no music, there's no noise, there's no public address system. There's no nothing. There are all these people sitting in the stands in this somber situation."

But it still was a homecoming game for tight end Mike Ditka. The Aliquippa, Pennsylvania, native and former star at the University of Pittsburgh had friends and family in the stands. And he delivered one of the most memorable plays in Bears history.

On second-and-36, Ditka turned a short pass from quarterback Bill Wade into a powerful, almost awe-inspiring 63-yard romp. He broke tackle after tackle after tackle after tackle. He was finally brought down on the Steelers' 15. Three plays later, Roger LeClerc made a field goal for a 17–17 tie. The Packers didn't catch the Bears in standings.

"The difference was that tie in Pittsburgh when Ditka had that unbelievable run," said Hub Arkush, the longtime publisher of *Pro Football Weekly* and a former radio broadcaster for the Bears. "You've probably seen film of the Walter Payton run against the Kansas City Chiefs. The Ditka catch-and-run against the Steelers was better. It was unbelievable. Walter's run was great. But Ditka just literally beat people up on the way."

A Rivalrous Cause

Patrick McCaskey, a current board member of the Bears, will always remember what his grandfather said about the 1963 season before it began.

The Packers, as winners of the 1961 and 1962 championships, played the college All-Stars in an exhibition game. It was an annual tradition. And this time, they lost.

"After the game, my grandfather said, this is very encouraging," said McCaskey, one of Halas' 11 grandchildren from his daughter, Virginia. "And of course, the Bears won the championship that year and were able to beat the Packers twice."

Every season is about beating the Packers, but it was particularly true in 1963. The Packers, under coach Vince Lombardi, had become the best team in the league.

"It wasn't just the Bears-Packers rivalry," Arkush said. "It was Halas and Lombardi and it was just bigger than life. And Halas was much bigger than Lombardi. Lombardi had only been there since '59, so four years. But the Bears had had, in some respects, their first stretch of hard times after dominating the league in the early era."

Halas embraced it. He was in the middle of his fourth stint as the Bears' coach. Beating the Packers had become everything.

"When we met in the opening training camp, [Halas] had a meeting for the whole team," Wetoska said. "He said he was dedicating this training camp to beating the Green Bay Packers. And he said that every session of practice, when we were down in Rensselaer, Indiana, which is just out in the middle nowhere and two-and-a-half to three hours from Chicago. He said we were going to devote 15 minutes of every practice to playing against the Packers, either offense or defense or some portion of the game.

"So that's what we did. We went up there for the first game against them and, of course, we ended up beating them, and that kind of started us on the right track."

Of course, there was more to it. Halas had an innovative coaching staff with George Allen, Luke Johnsos, and Clark Shaughnessy.

Johnsos turned Ditka into a Hall of Fame tight end. Shaughnessy mentored George, who became the first modern linebacker. Allen's contributions were all-encompassing, from drafting to practice routines to advanced defensive game planning.

"The team that we had in '63, you couldn't believe the intensity on every moment," O'Bradovich said. "George Allen changed the way we practiced. We would have interception drills, fumble drills, every day. Every day, be alert, be alert, no mistakes. Instead of running around and doing all kinds of things, he got right down to the business of the game."

O'Bradovich would know. His pass rush frustrated Giants quarterback Y.A. Tittle in the title game, but he also intercepted a screen pass and powered his way 10 yards to the Giants' 15. Five plays later, quarterback Bill Wade scored on a quarterback sneak for the final margin.

It was another dominant performance by the '63 defense, one that Ditka described as better than the Bears' acclaimed '85 unit during a panel at the team's centennial celebration in 2019. The '63 defense allowed only 10 points per game.

"They were great football players," Ditka said. "They didn't get the acclaim they would get today."

But the '63 team still deserves it.

10

JAY

Tom Waddle and Marc Silverman were live on the air hosting their popular *Waddle & Silvy* show on ESPN 1000 in Chicago when Bears quarterback Jay Cutler called. And they couldn't believe it. It was too random.

In the past, the radio show would get a call from Jim Christman, the Bears' media relations director who worked directly with Cutler.

"Hey, Jay wants to go on with the guys," Silverman said Christman would say.

But that didn't happen this time. He called in by himself.

"'Hey, it's Jay Cutler. I want to go on with the guys,'" recalled Silverman, who covered the Bears for ESPN before being paired with Waddle.

"And you know you never want to get burned by a fake caller. So we're quizzing Jay if it's really him on the other line."

It was. The wheels were in motion. Something bigger—better—was coming.

On June 7, 2012, ESPN 1000 announced that there would be "The Jay Cutler Show" with Waddle and Silverman.

It wouldn't merely be a segment similar to what Eli Manning and Tom Brady did in their respective markets. It would be a full hour with him live in studio or on locations. It was ground-breaking, especially in Chicago.

The show's connection with Cutler started when they met him for the first time during training camp one year in Bourbonnais, Illinois. But Cutler, who was from Santa Claus, Indiana, also grew up a fan of Waddle, a hard-nosed, blue-collar receiver for the Bears who had his best seasons in the early '90s.

"I know Jay's not the most-liked in the history of the Chicago Bears," Waddle said. "But when you get through the veneer or you get inside or you get to know him, there's really redeeming and good qualities with him. I found him to be fiercely loyal. I found him to be funny as shit. He had a great personality. He's smart. I think that we gave him a platform where people could kind of see him in a different light."

It didn't end in the most positive fashion. Then again, that's how things tended to always work out for Cutler.

But for three seasons, *Waddle & Silvy* provided an inside look at arguably the most polarizing figure in the history of Chicago sports. Cutler no longer was the moody quarterback who scoffed at the media and threw too many interceptions, but a relatable dude with a witty, smart-aleck sense of humor.

"It was more about him than it was us," Waddle said. "We gave him a platform where I think he was comfortable. I think he knew we would be honest and we'd be fair. We would be critical when it was necessary, but we'd be fair and we'd give him a forum to not just talk about the game but express his personality."

* * *

On April, 3, 2009, Bears radio play-by-play broadcaster Jeff Joniak was on vacation in Boca Raton, Florida. He played softball with his daughter, but his phone kept ringing.

"I'll worry about it later," Joniak remembered thinking at the time.

But his phone kept going. It wouldn't stop. What the heck was going on?

"I finally look at my phone and it's my boss," Joniak said. "'Where are you? They got Jay Cutler.' And I was just floored.... My first impulse was that we got our quarterback."

Finally.

Bears fans were overwhelmed with joy, including the one that Joniak ran into at the airport leaving his Florida vacation. Joniak remembered that the fan was wearing Bears sneakers. They had Jay Cutler written on them.

"He started bawling," Joniak said. "He's like, 'Oh, my God, we got our quarterback.' He was emotional. He was just some fan who recognized me in the airport. It almost gives me goosebumps because that's how thirsty he was to have a quarterback.

"The traits. The arm. I remember going to one of his first practices. You can hear it sometimes from all quarterbacks. I heard it consistently. That ball whistled when he threw it—*whistled*. You could hear it coming. That's how hard he threw the football on a tight spiral. Just gifted."

The Bears acquired Cutler from the Denver Broncos, who drafted him in the first round in 2006, for two first-round picks, a third-round pick, and quarterback Kyle Orton. The Bears also received a fifth-round pick in return.

It was a blockbuster move in every facet. The Bears didn't do such things. But on this day, former general manager Jerry Angelo did. He took a homerun swing at fixing a longstanding problem position for the NFL's founding franchise.

"We were all excited," long snapper Patrick Mannelly said. "I was jacked. I can still remember the first OTA practices. He threw a deep out and I'm standing there with [special teams coordinator Dave] Toub, and we both looked at each other and we go, 'Holy Shit.' We haven't seen that in years. Perfect line drive ball right over the corner. Just boom. You're like, 'That's an NFL arm.' Yeah, there were some throws that you saw in practice that were unreal."

* * *

On January 23, 2011, something seismic happened on the lakefront of Chicago. The Bears were playing the Packers in the NFC Championship Game, but Cutler was on the sideline. He was in a long coat and had a winter hat on. His face lacked expression.

It soon turned into a social-media experiment gone wrong. It was announced that Cutler was questionable to return because of a knee injury. But Twitter still questioned why. On that day, Cutler became one of the first athletes to feel the wrath of social media.

Everyone and anyone had a voice, a message—wrong or not—to share, including NFL players Darnell Dockett and Maurice Jones-Drew. They absolutely ripped Cutler for not playing without knowing the full extent of his knee injury.

"All I'm saying is that he can finish the game on a hurt knee.... I played the whole season on one," Jones-Drew said.

It was later revealed that Cutler had a Grade 2 MCL sprain, an injury that can take weeks to recover from. His teammates knew that. Cutler struggled to move.

But the damage was done. The Bears lost to the Packers 21–14—and the Packers would go on to win the Super Bowl. A perception of Cutler was cemented. A story about him walking up some stairs while out to dinner later fueled the anger, the frustration.

"That was a big moment," said Rick Telander, a longtime sportswriter who covered the game as a columnist for the *Chicago Sun-Times*. "The debate about that, a guy with a stone face—seemingly completely oblivious to what his team was doing or any kind of teamwork and not seeming to be hurt—is suddenly not playing. While the game is going, he's being savaged by people. The interconnectivity of the world is what has changed."

For the Bears and Cutler, the NFL would never be the same again. His narrative changed. It was a seminal moment.

"The team was okay, but something really happened in that NFC Championship Game where Cutler hurt his knee and was playing terribly," said John Mullin, a Bears reporter for the *Daily Herald*, *Chicago Tribune,* and NBC Sports. "Some air went out of the balloon. Something was revealed to Chicagoans, Bears fans, and maybe Bears players, and everybody that just took the joy out of stuff, that made things just seem very negative."

A season later, the Bears arguably had a better team. They were 6–3 going into Week 11 against the Chargers. In the fourth quarter, on second-and-8 from San Diego's 30, Cutler was intercepted by cornerback Antoine Cason after receiver Johnny Knox slipped on his slant route. In an effort to prevent a pick-six, Cutler chased after Cason and reached at him with his right hand before falling awkwardly.

Cason didn't score, but Cutler suffered a fractured right thumb on his tackle attempt in a 31–20 victory for the Bears. Therein lies the tragedy of Cutler's story. The Bears were formidable with him, then went 1–5 without him and missed the playoffs. Everyone thought the Bears had another playoff run in them, then Cutler got hurt.

"We always hung to the thought that Jay was going to be that great quarterback that we had been lusting for for years," Waddle said. "Shit, it just never came to be."

* * *

On December 17, 2014, Bears coach Marc Trestman held a meeting with Cutler and backup Jimmy Clausen. The Bears were 5–9 and an off-the-rails trainwreck.

A season that started with playoff hopes spiraled quickly into conflict. Receiver Brandon Marshall was a divisive problem, one who yelled at his kicker after a loss, quarreled with an assistant coach at practice, and then questioned Cutler on the radio.

But Trestman had issues on his own staff. Earlier in December, an explosive report by the *Chicago Tribune* revealed that offensive coordinator Aaron Kromer was the source behind an NFL Network report that was critical of Cutler.

The report included the description of "buyer's remorse" in regards to Cutler's seven-year, $126.7 million contract that included $54 million guaranteed. It was the largest deal in organization history.

Kromer denied making the "buyer's remorse" comment, but he still made a tearful apology to Cutler and players afterward. Nonetheless, he remained on Trestman's coaching staff.

"I just want to say I made a very poor decision of talking about things outside the building and I admit that," Kromer said then. "I can't take that back. But I recognize that I made a mistake."

Cutler, though, wasn't out of the Bears' internal crosshairs. It was Trestman's turn. In that meeting, Trestman told him that he would be benched in favor of Clauson for their next game in Week 16 against the Lions.

For Trestman, it was a desperate attempt to save his job. A day later, Cutler was asked if he played his last game for the Bears.

"I think that's a fair question," Cutler said. "I don't know if I can answer it for you, though. At this point in my career, it's out of my hands. Whatever happens, management—Trestman, Phil [Emery], those guys—will make that decision, and we'll talk about that when that happens, I guess."

It was the end of the plan to build around Cutler. Emery executed it with the best intentions. He finally did what many argued that Jerry Angelo and Lovie Smith should had done years ago. Cutler was surrounded by high-end pass catchers in Marshall, Alshon Jeffery, and Martellus Bennett. Better yet, Emery paired him with offensive-minded head coach in Trestman.

It didn't work. Instead, the Bears got a two-year stretch in 2013 and 2014 that the organization would like to wipe from the books. On top of Cutler's own struggles and widespread discord, the Bears' defense had the two statistically worse seasons in franchise history.

Interesting enough, the *Waddle & Silvy* show had a part in it. Cutler and Marshall had a falling out in Denver, but conversations with both of them on ESPN's airwaves seemed to change things, at least in Silverman's opinion. The Bears acquired Marshall from the Dolphins on March 13, 2012.

"I don't want to say, make it happen, but sort of making it a realistic possibility," Silverman. "We had him on. We would talk to Jay about it. It sort of smoothed over their once-icy relationship."

It got frosty again in 2014. *Waddle & Silvy* experienced that, too, as Cutler and Marshall split time on air.

"One week it would be Brandon, and the next week it would be Jay," Silverman said. "And in the commercial breaks, Brandon would take off the headset and MF—literally MF—Jay. 'Could you believe Jay did this? Ask me about that. Can you believe this?'

"And the next week, we'd have Jay on. And then in the commercial breaks—this is all in-person—he would take off his headset, and he would be MF-ing Brandon. Waddle and I, we really couldn't use it because they were telling this all this in confidence. We would then say on the shows that they weren't on, that 'Things aren't good.'"

* * *

On March 7, 2017, a representative for Cutler released a statement through the *Chicago Sun-Times* and the NFL Network. It was time for the maligned quarterback to say thank you and his goodbye.

An eight-season run that started with overwhelming optimism was over. Ryan Pace, who was the third general manager that Cutler played for in Chicago, released him. The prohibitive portions of Cutler's lucrative contract had run out. It was finally time for the franchise to move on and find their next quarterback.

"I would like to first thank the city of Chicago and its passionate fans for a memorable eight years," Cutler said in his statement. "I grew up in Indiana rooting for the Bears as a kid, so it was an honor to wear the Bears uniform and play quarterback at Soldier Field for my favorite childhood team."

Cutler's run with the Bears will be remembered for its excitement and disappointment. He was never as bad a teammate as some said he was, but he also never became the great, franchise-changing quarterback that everyone hoped he'd be, either.

There are reasons for that. He had too many offensive coordinators and too few weapons. He couldn't stay healthy, but his teammates still considered him tough as hell. He might have looked and acted as if he didn't care, but his teammates saw a passionate competitor in games and practices. Some teammates didn't like him, while others seemed to adore him.

In a way, his numbers reflect everything he was and wasn't, too. Cutler set franchise records for passing attempts, completions, passing yards, passing touchdowns, and passer rating, but he still finished with a 51–51 record—a mark recognized by owner Virginia McCaskey in the Bears' centennial scrapbook—as a starting quarterback.

For some of Cutler's former teammates, he should be remembered for exactly what his record says. He's a .500 quarterback. He was good, but never quite good enough to turn the Bears into a consistent winner.

"Jay should be remembered as a guy we traded for, gave up a lot for, and probably wasn't the quarterback they thought he was, but a very good quarterback," former center Olin Kreutz said.

"I think too much is made out of what kind of guy he was, what kind of teammate he was. Look, if you're a good player, no one really cares what kind of guy you are, what kind of teammate you are. His career, in no way was it a failure. But the problem people had with Jay was that people expected him to be elite and that's really where the frustration comes from."

Cutler also had a damned-if-you do, damned-if-don't quality about him. When he bumped and yelled at maligned left tackle J'Marcus Webb against the Packers in Week 2 of the 2012 season, it was perceived as a negative. He was trying to win but he still couldn't win in the public arena.

"He expects you to be great; he expects himself to be great; he wants everybody else around him to be great," Mannelly said. "That's just his passion. I think that kind of went with J'Marcus Webb. J'Marcus wasn't good with confrontation. I don't think he liked criticism. And that's what started it. And Jay was trying to challenge him and it came across like more than it was."

* * *

On July 8, 2018, the country got to see a new side of Cutler. The show *Very Cavallari* debuted that night. It starred his wife, Kristin Cavallari, a reality TV star whom Cutler married when he was with the Bears.

Cutler spent the 2017 season with Dolphins and coach Adam Gase. In their one season together for the Bears, Cutler had a career-best 92.3 passer rating. But even that success was tough to replicate for Gase, who needed a quarterback after Ryan Tannehill was injured.

But it didn't matter. Cutler was now a reality star of his own. The witty, dry sense of humor that his teammates often referenced was now on television. Not that Waddle and Silverman were surprised.

"'The Jay Cutler Show' is some of the most fun that we've had because whether it was on the air or off the air before the show or during breaking, you got an insight into who Jay was and the personality," Waddle said. "We all knew the guy that kind of stole the show the last years on *Very Cavallari*. We knew that guy. None of us were surprised that he went on that show and basically was the star of the show. None of us were."

Therein lies the tragedy of Cutler's story again, too. The Bears needed that guy earlier in his career. He joined a team that was led by Kreutz and linebacker Brian Urlacher, but he was still the quarterback. He needed to be more than he was. Fair or not, it comes with the position.

"Like you see now in that TV show, he can be entertaining," Mannelly said. "He's witty as hell and he would open up a little bit for you guys and let you in. That's what he should have done more with his teammates when he was there."

In some ways, his transformation from a moody, pudgy quarterback to a married father with stylish hair became complete. His teammates saw that transformation late in his career.

"It's just how it goes," kicker Robbie Gould said. "I think your perspective on life, what matters, kind of the importance of things around you, change when you have kids. I think it's about setting a good example and I think he was one of those guys when he had a family and got married and had his kids around, it kind of put things into perspective for everybody."

It's just another part of Cutler's story. In some ways, it'll always feel incomplete.

"The one thing that I think was the biggest misconception was that Jay didn't care because he had whatever look on his face," Waddle said. "I can tell you with 100 percent certainty that Jay cared. Jay wanted to win. Jay may not have always communicated things in a 'normal' way, but I would always attest to his desire to succeed and win. And he was tough as shit, too."

11

THE TRADE FOR MITCH TRUBISKY

When the Bears traded up from the third pick to the second in the 2017 draft, ESPN's cameras turned to Adam Schefter for answers. If anyone knew what the Bears were up to—whom they were targeting with this blockbuster move—Schefter, the league's preeminent insider, would know.

"The Bears come up to No. 2. The player they've been eyeing all along has been Solomon Thomas from Stanford," Schefter said on the broadcast.

Then came the bombshell.

NFL commissioner Roger Goodell announced that the Bears selected quarterback Mitch Trubisky from North Carolina. As far as moments go in Bears history, this one on April 27, 2017, was one of the biggest. There simply isn't another draft selection like it. For better or worse, taking Trubisky was a transformational move by general manager Ryan Pace, who had been looking for his quarterback for years.

Forgive Schefter. No one, outside a select few at Halas Hall, saw the selection of Trubisky coming. The Bears parted ways with Jay Cutler after eight seasons in March, but also signed Mike Glennon to a three-year, $45 million contract, which included a guarantee of $18.5 million, in free agency.

"I didn't see that coming at all," Trubisky said after his selection. "I was surprised."

In the end, Glennon turned out to be only cover for the team's adoration of Trubisky. Their entire scouting effort was discreet. It included Pace sitting in the stands with fans for North Carolina's final matchup that year against Stanford in the Sun Bowl. There was a private workout followed by a private dinner at Bin 54, a sumptuous steakhouse in Chapel Hill, North Carolina, where Trubisky made reservations for him and the Bears under the name of "James McMahon."

The draft was in Philadelphia, but the shock of it reverberated throughout Chicagoland. It became a lightning-rod moment in Chicago sports history, the kind where you remember where you were and what you were doing.

Adam Hoge, a reporter/host for WGN Radio, was live on the air at that time as part of his station's draft show.

"About an hour before the draft, I got this weird gut feeling that Pace was going to draft a quarterback," Hoge said. "I remember telling fellow WGN Radio host Justin Kaufmann that if he did it, it would probably be Trubisky. But that didn't stop me from literally yelling 'Oh!' into my microphone when Roger Goodell announced the pick."

Bears radio play-by-play broadcaster Jeff Joniak was hosting a draft show in an Irish bar in Oak Lawn, a south suburb, that night.

"The reaction was raw from everybody in the bar," Joniak said. "First of all, there was not a familiarity with the name. There was some shock. So during the commercial break, people kept coming up, 'What do you know about this guy?' He didn't have a lot starts in college. People did their research. It continued the whole night. That's all anyone wanted to talk about at that little draft party is Mitch Trubisky."

Tom Waddle and Marc Silverman, from the popular *Waddle & Silvy* show on ESPN 1000, watched the draft that night at the Clayton, a ritzy cigar bar in Chicago. Their producers were there, too.

"I'm thinking, 'They traded up for Solomon Thomas! What the...' and then they announce for Mitch Trubisky," Silverman said. "I jumped. I physically jumped up from the couch we were sitting on."

In some ways, the shock of the pick never wore off; it followed Trubisky into the early years of his career. No one likes to be surprised, especially reporters and Bears fans who have been desperate to root for a franchise quarterback.

The trade mattered, too. Did the Bears really have to move up one spot to select him? That would follow Trubisky into the early years of his career, too. He was booed when he was introduced at a Bulls game at the United Center.

"It was still shocking that it actually happened," Hoge said. "Processing the trade part of it in the moment was difficult because you don't know the specifics of who else might have been trading up to get Trubisky. In the Twitter world we live in, Pace was getting criticized almost instantly.

"My instinct was to defend the idea that if you truly covet a specific quarterback, a few mid-round picks are absolutely worth the price of making sure you don't lose that quarterback. I still believe that. People were—and still are—too obsessed with the draft picks that were traded."

On draft night, the calls that Pace took turned into his own call for action. If the Bears were getting calls about the third overall pick from teams trying to move up to select a quarterback—and rebuffing them—then logically the 49ers were getting calls for the second pick. Nothing changes a draft like the flurried pursuit of quarterbacks by teams that don't have one.

The Bears, of course, were one of them—and Pace wasn't going to allow them to miss on their guy. He was too close.

"If we want to be great, you just can't sit on your hands," Pace said after Trubisky's selection. "There are times when you've got to be aggressive. And when you have conviction on a guy, you can't sit on your hands. I just don't want to be average around here. I want to be great and these are the moves you have to make."

It was a move that was criticized for its cost—the 49ers took Thomas, too—but also praised for its gumption and bravado. Chicago finally had a GM with guts—all-in, make-no-excuses guts.

"Did the 49ers fleece the Bears? Listen, if that's your guy, I don't care what you give up to go get him," Waddle said. "I'm cool with it. I don't know who is kicking the tires. I don't know what was true and what was false. But I do know if you believe in this guy at the most important position in sports, I don't have a problem with what Ryan did. That was my starting point."

Patience was preached from the moment of the pick. Trubisky's selection was more about the Bears' projection than about instant production. He didn't have the same experiences that Patrick Mahomes had at Texas Tech or anything that resembled the résumé that Deshaun Watson built at Clemson.

Trubisky, though, always would be held to a high standard—one that he didn't create for himself. Fair or not, he would always be compared to Mahomes and Watson. The Chiefs traded up for Mahomes at No. 10, and the Texans did the same for Watson at No. 12. They had motivation; Trubisky had pressure.

It was a trade and selection that would change the Pace era for the Bears. John Fox was fired and replaced by Matt Nagy after Trubisky's rookie season. The Bears went all-in on their quarterback. The debate about him, Pace, and the Bears didn't only begin, but started to rage on.

"I hope everybody's excited about it," Pace said after the draft. "The most important position in all of sports is quarterback. And I don't think you're ever a great team until you address the position and you address it right. I think everybody should respect that."

12

PEANUT

Bears receiver/returner Devin Hester didn't like practicing against Charles Tillman. Neither did fullback Jason McKie. No one who caught passes or carried the ball did.

Tillman, the Bears' 6'2" cornerback, would attack you with punches.

"It's sad to say but I had to go against this guy every day in practice," Hester said. "For me, I got the worst of it. Whenever you get a pass and you're running the ball, you're not even worried about running."

Instead, you looked out for No. 33.

"All you're really doing is trying to secure the ball," Hester said. "All the moves and slick moves and trying to score a touchdown go out the window because you see Peanut coming."

Tillman went for the ball. Every single time. If you lost it, you paid. Literally.

"We hated—hated!—Peanut in practice because we knew if we could catch a pass and run downfield, he'd come up and punch the ball out," McKie said. "And we got fined for that. So if you caught one in practice, it was like $50 bucks."

If you had the ball, you had to be aware of every him at every moment. He was coming for you.

"You would be walking back to the huddle after a play and Peanut would come and punch the ball out," McKie said. "That's how much he practiced his craft."

A factor in the game and a statistic that was once reserved for the best pass rushers had extended to the secondary—and no one was better at it than Charles "Peanut" Tillman. He became feared over the course of forcing 44 fumbles, the most ever by defensive back, in his career.

"He revolutionized the game," McKie said.

An Underrated Star

On second-and-goal from the Bears' 10 in the final minutes of a one-score game, the Vikings did what everyone knew they'd do at Soldier Field. It was time for Daunte Culpepper to throw a jumpball to wide receiver Randy Moss.

The problem is that the Bears drafted an answer for Moss in the second round before that season. It was time for Tillman, who played at Louisiana-Lafayette, to show just how good of a player he could be in the NFL.

"You saw me turn into a man in front of your own eyes," Tillman would later say.

Not only did Tillman, who is 6'2", get the better of Moss on that play, he ripped the ball from the superstar's grasp for an interception. It sealed the Bears' 13–10 win at Soldier Field on December 14, 2003. The Bears had a star of their own.

"That started it right there," Bears radio play-by-play broadcaster Jeff Joniak said. "Purely there to take on receivers like that with size and speed. Randy Moss, Adrian Peterson, those guys, they didn't have a lot of fun at Soldier Field those games."

Tillman had a career that deserves more adulation than it got as it played out. He didn't go to his first Pro Bowl until his ninth season and wasn't named an All-Pro until his 10th. But in its totality, the numbers that Tillman produced over 12 seasons with the Bears tell you he's one of the best players ever to play for the team.

"I thought that Peanut was always one of the best corners in the game for a very long time," said linebacker Lance Briggs, who was drafted in the same year.

Tillman's 42 forced fumbles are the most in team history. He's also third in interceptions with 36, trailing Gary Fencik (38) and Richie Petitbon (37). Tillman also recovered 11 fumbles.

As the *Chicago Tribune* highlighted in their series of the 100 greatest Bears players in 2019, "the sum of those three stats, 89, is far more than any other Bear, with Fencik's 63 the next most." It's elite production.

"He may be one of the most underrated players that have come through in the last 20 years in NFL history—seriously," Joniak said.

Tillman was not only the perfect cornerback for Lovie Smith's Tampa Two defense, but a vital cog in Smith's takeaway machine. Those who played with Tillman said that he took Smith's calls for takeaways to heart. As a result, he tortured his teammates as he perfectly his "Peanut Punch" in practice.

The evolution of it can be traced back to Louisiana-Lafayette. Tillman said he would change his angle of pursuit on tackles, knowing that he was fast enough to catch ball carriers.

"Instead of taking a great pursuit angle, I'd take a pretty good pursuit angle and then at last the second, I would just get behind the tailback so he wouldn't see me coming," Tillman said in 2019.

And then whack.

"I would let him get in front of me, then I would just run behind him and then punch the ball out," Tillman said. "I did that numerous times in college."

But Tillman said he perfected it in the league, once he adjusted to the speed of everyone. In his 10th season, Tillman forced a season-high 10 fumbles. One of the highlights from that season, which turned out to be Smith's last, was the four fumbles that Tillman caused in 51–20 rout of the Titans in Nashville, Tennessee in Week 9. Traveling Bears fans drank Nashville's famous Broadway Street out of beer that day.

"That was insane," long snapper Patrick Mannelly said of Tillman's performance. "That was like a joke. Numerous times you would hear guys yell at other offensive players, 'We told you all week. You've got to hold onto the ball.' You would hear coaches yell and players yell at them. I definitely heard that in the Titans game."

A Lasting Legacy

On first-and-goal from the Bears' 3, defensive back Sherrick McManis rode his blocker on a quick receiver screen by the Raiders and right into receiver Trevor Davis. Instead of going for the tackle, McManis balled up his fist and swung at the ball.

"Davis is close," Fox play-by-play broadcaster Dick Stockton said "Fumble recovered by the Bears. Davis lost it. Unbelievable at the 1-yard line."

The replays showed that McManis—in the middle of the commotion of the play— knocked the ball free from Davis.

"Look at that punch," analyst Mark Schlereth said. "That's Peanut Tillman-esque right there."

Yes, it was, and it came on October 6, 2019, with the Bears in London. Tillman retired three years before that. McManis, of course, was a former teammate of Tillman's. He's been out of the league for a while, but his Peanut Punch is still mentioned on NFL and even college broadcasts. His move is now taught by coaches at all levels.

"It's changed the NFL," Briggs said. "You can see the effect that it's had. I think he has definitely changed the NFL, but has everyone bought in the way that Peanut bought in? No, I don't think so. Not on that level yet. When you see somebody that's literally punching every time that somebody else gets the ball, then you see the real Peanut Punch pupil that's on the rise."

Bears defensive coordinator Rod Marinelli had highlight-reel films of running backs and then two cars would crash.

"Balls would fly out of the cars and stuff," center Olin Kreutz said. "That's what Tillman was like. It was almost like he was Marinelli's highlight film. Here's a guy that changed the whole NFL by punching balls out."

Tillman was feared because of it. His teammates remember that, too.

"It's amazing going into a game and seeing receivers act differently when they have to play against us," said Hall of Fame linebacker Brian Urlacher, who played with Tillman. "Because when they catch the ball, all they care about is taking care of the football. They don't care about getting yards. If Peanut's around, that ball is going to be protected with two hands and he still made them fumble. That's what's amazing to me because you know all week long they practiced it and they worked on it. They're worried about Peanut knocking that ball out, and not just receivers, anyone on the field with him."

Off that field, Tillman was special as well. In 2013, he was named the Walter Payton Man of the Year for his charitable work through his

Cornerstone Foundation. He gave a touching, tear-filled speech upon receiving it. Part of that was his upbringing.

"He's a military kid who moved around a lot," said Briggs, one of his closest friends on the team. "He's a man that understands the world different than others."

There was always a very human side to Tillman. He loved football and his family. His teammates remember that about him, too. Tillman always found motivation in being from a small college. But in 2008, his life changed when his daughter, Tiana, was diagnosed with a heart condition and required a transplant as an infant.

"You talk about another guy who has been great in the community," kicker Robbie Gould said. "The things that he's done and how he handled his situation with his daughter, how he was in the locker room managing working out while taking care of his family and being responsible, I think those are things that as a younger player growing up, you can appreciate now that you have kids. You can appreciate what he went through. It's definitely one of those situations where, I think you look at it, he probably deserved a lot more respect than he got when he played."

A conversation with Tillman eventually will turn into praise for his former teammates. He will go on and on listing them for minutes.

How great was his own career? He'd rather leave that for everyone else to decide. But the recognition is deservedly pouring in now. He's no longer playing in the NFL, but you still hear about the Peanut Punch nearly every week.

"It took a while [to get recognition]," Tillman said. "I don't know why it took a while, maybe because I wasn't a loud, boisterous, trash-talking corner. I was just kind of quiet and did my own thing. And year after year we would create takeaways, and my stats, I felt like they were pretty consistent. No one really noticed until the end of my career. And then when you look at everything, 'Oh wow, he was doing this entire career.'"

13

THE BUDDY RYAN LETTER

Gary Fencik was cleaning out his garage in 2018, preparing it for new flooring and updated cabinetry, when he came across a letter that he should have never forgotten.

"To have it personally signed by George Halas, that's pretty cool," the longtime Bears safety said. "It was December 22, 1981."

It was Halas' thank you to Fencik being the man who authored the letter that asked the Bears owner to consider keeping defensive coordinator Buddy Ryan and his staff despite looming staff changes.

"I covered my butt and had all the players sign it by the way," Fencik recalled with a laugh. "This was a team effort all the way."

Either way, it turned out to be the most important letter written in franchise history. Halas, of course, fired coach Neill Armstrong and replaced him with Mike Ditka, but Ryan and his staff were retained. Halas loved that letter from his players, which was written on December 9, 1981. Halas said as much in his personal letter back to Fencik.

"I was kind of in shock," Fencik said "He goes, 'Gary thanks a lot for sending me the reasons why you want to retain Buddy Ryan. This is a magnificent letter. It is a beautifully written letter. It is the highest tribute a coach could receive.'

"Then he goes, 'I could tell you without fear of contradiction that this is the first time in the 61-year history of the Chicago Bears that such a letter was written about a Bear coach. I think I can also say that this is the first time any owner in the NFL has received such a letter.'"

The players had good reasons to write it, especially since they sensed what coming after another disappointing season for the franchise. It was Armstrong's fourth year in charge. When the letter was written, the Bears were 4–10 and eventually finished 6–10.

Defensively, the numbers didn't show dominance. But there was improvement. It was a young unit, too. Some of the signatures on that letter included future starters and stalwarts of the Bears' 1985 team:

Fencik, Dan Hampton, Mike Singletary, Otis Wilson, Leslie Frazier, and Steve McMichael

"The arrow was pointing up; don't monkey with this," Hampton said. "We wanted to make sure that not only was there a stable plan going forward. But we had started to get to the point where we were pretty damn salty and we could see and project where this defense was going."

To do it right, a meeting was called. It included Fencik and Hampton, but also veterans Doug Plank and Alan Page. Plank and Page's tenure would end soon, but they signed the letter, too. Every defensive player, young and old, sensed what was being built.

Ryan joined the Bears in 1978 after being the defensive line coach for the Vikings' feared Purple People Eaters for two years. By 1979, he had designed a cutthroat attack—the 46 defense, which was named for Plank. The Bears were going to attack opposing offenses, specifically quarterbacks, with ruthless aggression and a cutting-edge scheme.

"We just simply had a little team meeting right there on defense and said, listen, the year is not going very well and there is going to be some changes at the end of the year without a doubt," Plank said. "Buddy has done a great job in improving the defense, statistically. You couldn't necessarily look at it like in the wins and losses because that wasn't a reflection of the job that he was doing."

Fencik, who was an All-Pro in 1981, can accurately recall much of the letter word-for-word by memory. The final two sentences of it turned out to be an accurate prediction.

"We feel that if there is to be a change in the coaching staff Buddy Ryan and his staff should be retained in order to avoid a setback for our defense. We feel that we are a good defensive team and that with their help we can be a great defensive team in the near future."

It happened after the strike season of 1982. In 1983, the Bears were 8–8 and the defense was ranked fifth. In 1984, the Bears improved to 10–6 and the defense was third. And then in 1985, the Bears won the Super Bowl. Their defense wasn't only first in the league, but arguably the best ever in the history of the NFL.

A five-paragraph letter that was typed up by Fencik and signed by 22 players made sure that future happened. Halas seemed to sense it, too. He visited the defense at practice after receiving it and told the players how much that letter meant to him. Halas also told them that Ryan and his staff would return.

"Halas came in and he basically had tears in his eyes and said, 'When I started this league, I was hoping that it would be played by men that cared, that cared deeply about the Bears and the future of the Bears. You guys exemplify that,'" Hampton said. "He was wonderfully gracious and complementary, instead of being resentful, and saying, shut the hell up. I know what's best the team. No. It was just the opposite. He trusted us, and boom, look what happened."

For Fencik, the Bears' franchise leader in interceptions, finding Halas' personal letter to him was like finding a lost treasure.

"I thought the letter was kind of cool because I forgot about it," Fencik said. "History certainly bore out the fact that it was a good idea to save Buddy's job."

14

JIM FINKS' 1983 DRAFT

Tom Thayer knew that he was a part of a special draft class in 1983 before he officially became a part of it in on the field for the Bears.

"Back then we went to three different combines," Thayer recalled. "We had a combine in Tampa. We had a combine in Detroit. We had a combine in Seattle. So you have a chance to see and know some of these guys throughout the time."

So he was familiar with Pittsburgh offensive tackle Jimbo Covert, whom he played with in the Hulu Bowl. Thayer had already played with safety Dave Duerson, the Bears' third-round selection that year, at Notre Dame.

"That whole crew of guys that you had a chance to know and learn a little bit about before the draft ever took place," Thayer said, "you kind of understood, going, 'Wow, this is a talented group of people.'"

Thayer just didn't join what the Bears drafted that year until 1985 after a brief run in the upstart USFL, starting with the Chicago Blitz and coach George Allen, who was an innovative and invaluable assistant and personnel boss for George Halas years earlier.

"In the '83 draft, I announced that we had drafted Tom Thayer," said Patrick McCaskey, a grandson of George Halas, a Bears historian, and a member of the team's board of directors.

"[Radio broadcaster] Brad Palmer pipes up and says, 'The Chicago Blitz just announced that he signed with them.' Jim Finks' reaction was, 'We eventually think he'll be in the Bears' stable.' And he was."

Finks often was right over his tenure with the Bears, which started in 1974 and ended after the 1983 draft. He was hired to modernize the Bears, becoming the first boss that wasn't a Halas. To the dismay of his father, George "Mugs" Halas Jr. gave Finks power and a lengthy title: executive vice president, general manager, and chief operating officer.

"If that needs further explanation, he was brought here to run the show," Mugs once said.

Finks' 1983 draft is considered the best in Bears history. It provided the Bears with the final pieces for their Super Bowl-winning team in 1985. Seven starters were drafted: Covert, receiver Willie Gault, cornerback Mike Richardson, safety Duerson, guard Thayer, defensive end Richard Dent, and defensive-tackle-turned-guard Mark Bortz.

"Jim Finks was the type of a guy that could filter through all that talent within that draft class and figure out who best fits the Bears at that point and where they were needed the most," Thayer said. "And then have the forethinking of looking at a guy like Mark Bortz and going, 'Okay, this guy's an All–Big Ten defensive lineman and probably could have played in the NFL as a defensive lineman, however, we're going to take this guy, flip him to the other side of the ball, and we're going to make an offensive lineman out of him, and he's going to become a Pro Bowler."

Finks previously built the Vikings into an annual contender before joining the Bears. He brought an influx of ideas and changed the Bears' scouting. In the opinion of McCaskey, Finks' eye for talent and affinity for lineman is rooted in Finks' own playing career.

"He was in the habit of drafting linemen high," McCaskey said. "He knew that they were very important partly because he was a quarterback for the Steelers when they didn't have good offensive lines. He remembered."

The Bears made the playoffs in 1977 and 1979. But the Bears' best years would come after he left for the Cubs following the 1983 draft. He drafted future Hall of Famers in running back Walter Payton in 1975, defensive tackle Dan Hampton in 1979, linebacker Mike Singletary in 1981, and Covert and Dent in 1983. Finks wasn't there when the Bears won the Super Bowl, but he was undoubtedly the architect of that team, signing 20 of the starters who played in it, including quarterback Jim McMahon.

"He was the model for a sports executive," McCaskey said. "He didn't overreact. He was very thorough in his evaluations and everything. He joined the Bears in 1974 and he got us going towards the playoffs and then championship in the 1985 season. He was tough and fair. He had a sense of humor. He was dedicated and he was funny.

"He built the Vikings, he built the Bears, and he built the Saints. He was a strong candidate to succeed Pete Rozelle as commissioner of the league. He was very highly regarded throughout the league. He was president of the Cubs when they made the playoffs in 1984."

Finks also is the reason why the Bears are based in Lake Forest, Illinois. He moved them there from downtown offices to Lake Forest College, where a new facility was built. Training camp also was moved there from St. Joseph College in Rensselaer, Indiana.

Friction was part of Finks' story, too. Similar to Halas, Finks was a hard bargainer with players. But in 1982, it was Halas who upset Finks. After Mugs died in 1979, Halas re-assumed an active role. Halas hired Ditka in 1982, firing Neill Armstrong, who was hired by Finks.

In the Bears centennial scrapbook, owner Virginia McCaskey said she had questions about her father's decision to hire Ditka, especially in light of Finks' authority. But that's the way it was with Halas. It's said that he always had issues with his team being out of family control.

As it turned out, the 1985 Bears needed Ditka as much as the Bears needed Finks to fix them.

"Jim Finks' contribution was unmatched, something I'll always be grateful for," McCaskey said in the centennial book. "I don't think there is anyone else who could have done what he did."

The Bears eventually recognized that, too. Finks died in 1994 at 66 years old. In 1995, Ed McCaskey, as the chairman of the Bears, presented him for the Pro Football Hall of Fame.

"Jim Finks," Thayer said, "is the guy that kind of put all the pieces in place."

15

"THE BEARS ARE WHO WE THOUGHT THEY WERE"

Devin Hester took the field against the Cardinals with three minutes, 17 seconds left in the game, and told himself that he was a player made for such moments. He just didn't believe that the Cardinals would give him the opportunity—not in a one-score game—to show it.

But the world apparently needed to learn just how great Hester was as a returner and also another viral soundbite to share for years.

"I just told myself, 'Big-time players make big-time plays in big-time games,'" Hester said. "I just kept saying that to myself. If you get the opportunity, you best make the best of it."

Clinging to a six-point lead, the Cardinals punted to Hester. The rest, as they say, is history. The Bears then became who we thought they were.

"The moment the ball was kicked, I was like, 'I can't believe this is your opportunity right here to make it. Let's make the play,'" Hester recalled. "I did what I could. There were great blocks and it was a great play call by [special teams coordinator] Dave Toub. My teammates rallied around and we were able to get it into the end zone."

It was an 83-yard punt return that gave the Bears a 24–23 lead with less than three minutes to go. It turned into the final margin after Cardinals kicker Neil Rackers missed a field goal on *Monday Night Football*. Hester's touchdown was one of many astounding highlights made by the Bears in Week 6 of the Bears' memorable 2006 season, which ended in Super Bowl XLI against the Colts.

"You're looking for the signature play of the game," said longtime Bears writer John "Moon" Mullin, who covered that game at University of Phoenix Stadium. "But there was one after another. Oh, that's the biggest play. Oh wait, there's another one.... That was nuts."

Then-Arizona coach Dennis Green went nuts, delivering one of the most viral postgame speeches of all time. He erupted after being asked a question about Bears quarterback Rex Grossman, who threw four interceptions but was still a winner.

"The Bears were what we thought they were," Green shouted. "What we thought they were. We played them in preseason. Who the hell takes the third game in the preseason like it's bullshit? We played them the third game, everybody played three quarters. The Bears are who we thought they were. That's why we took the damn field.

"If you want to crown them, then crown their ass. But they are who we thought they were. And we let them off the hook."

Of course, the Bears remember Green's rant. Who doesn't? It's been spliced into advertisements since. Some of them saw it in the locker room after the game. It was on the televisions.

"We were just laughing, because you could imagine the frustration," center Olin Kreutz said with a smile. "There is no way that they should have lost that game."

But the players remember even more from that game than the rant. It's also known as the "Brian Urlacher Game." The Hall of Fame linebacker made a career-best 25 tackles and ripped a fumble from running back Edgerrin James that cornerback Charles Tillman returned 40 yards for a touchdown with five minutes left in the game.

"He put the team on his back and willed it to win," longtime long snapper Patrick Mannelly said. "I'm like, 'What is going on? How are we doing this?' And that first half was brutal, where you're going to stink it up some days and we did against the Dolphins [in Week 9] and ended up losing and that was our first loss of the season.

"But to have that feeling of, 'Alright, we're having an off day but we can still win because our defense can now become our offense'— and Brian was the leader of all that. That just showcased how great he is."

The Bears fell behind 20–0 after the first half. The first time they found the end zone was with two seconds left in the third quarter. On second-and-10 from the Cardinals' 15, defensive end Mark Anderson had a strip sack of quarterback Matt Leinart. Safety Mike Brown picked up the loose ball and ran into the end zone for a three-yard score.

It was a vintage Mike Brown play. He threw the ball into the stands in celebration. But on the Bears' next defensive series, Brown suffered a Lisfranc fracture in his right foot and was lost for the rest of the season.

"If that 2006 defense stays healthy, if you turn the film on of the first five or six games, that speed, you don't even see that now," center Olin Kreutz said. "They were playing at an amazing pace at that time."

At halftime, Brown was at Kreutz's side when Kreutz delivered a memorable, impassioned speech. Every player asked about their rally against Cardinals brought up on Kreutz's speech. It was another impactful moment delivered by a team leader.

"You had Olin Kreutz in locker room at halftime saying, 'Hey, we're going to win this game—no matter what,'" fullback Jason McKie said.

And that was regardless how bad the Bears' offense was playing with Grossman.

"We couldn't even get a first down," McKie said. "It was almost like Arizona had our playbook."

But the Bears believed Kreutz. It was a sign of their bond that season.

"He's like, 'We will win this game,'" Tillman said. "For whatever reason, we did. We had a great locker room. We all bought into what Olin was saying. Olin being the leader that he is, we all believed it.

"We split up on offense and defense. We made our adjustments. [Defensive coordinator] Ron Rivera challenged us about getting the ball back, 'It's not over. We just got to get crazy takeaways.' The one thing that coach Smith always talks about is take the ball away. It's not a turnover. But take it away. Let's go take the ball from them."

The Bears took footballs away and more from the Cardinals that night. It was a magical performance, one that buoyed the Bears' confidence for their Super Bowl run.

"It was like, 'What are we watching here?'" Mullin said. "It was like a video game almost. Another turnover? It was like watching the Globetrotters against the Washington Generals and Denny Green [was] coaching the Washington Generals. *The Bears are who we thought they were.* No, they were a lot better than you thought they were."

16

LOVIE

Everybody had to run for Lovie Smith, at least in his first training camp. It was his new-sheriff-in-town moment. The Bears were his team now. There would be changes.

So everyone had to run to the ball. And he meant *everyone.*

"Lovie came in and had his ways of tearing us down and building us back up," long snapper Patrick Mannelly said. "And there were a lot of people that weren't happy. Just an example, during training camp, everybody had to run to the ball.

"You could see his practices where the defenses would fly to the ball. When he first started, the [offensive] linemen had to run to the ball. Ruben Brown was like, 'What is this stupid crap? Why am I running to the ball?' And he had a hard time with it, and he kind of mimicked running fast."

It was the start of a new era in Bears history, one that would go down as a good one, too.

"Lovie was just tearing us down and building us back up," Mannelly said.

It worked. Hired in 2004, Smith not only turned the Bears back into a consistent winner over his nine seasons with the organization, but became a beloved coach who oversaw a fun-loving team that featured some of the best players in team history.

"I think he brought us back to what Bears fan should have been and has always been known for, and that's defensive, physical football," Hall of Fame linebacker Brian Urlacher said. "We ran the football. We tried to run the football every year he was there. We won games because of our defense. I think that also endeared him to our fans, but what endeared him to us as players, was the way he treated us."

Challenging a Defense
Linebacker Lance Briggs remembers that Smith challenged the defense through numbers. And Smith would change them.

"We had started off at 20 points a game," Briggs said. "If we give up 20 points a game, we should win the game. Ron Rivera was a part of this team as well. He was our defensive coordinator. That point [total] dropped to about 13. I think maybe even close to 10."

It wasn't so much a goal, but an expectation. The better the Bears' defense got, the lower the number would go.

"He said, 'Hey listen, I know we're asking a lot of you, but if we want to win games, we need to give up 12 points or less—13 points or less,'" Briggs said. "And that says a lot about how he felt about that unit that was in that room."

Smith's defense was known for its simplicity, but the players he had in it is what made his version of the Tampa Two extraordinary. In nine years, Smith's defense ranked in the top five in scoring four times and in total yards three times. But no team was better at taking the ball away and scoring with it. They ranked first in takeaways in Smith's tenure. The Bears also scored a whopping 34 touchdowns.

"I think his legacy will be as a head coach who had a tremendous defense," cornerback Charles Tillman said. "He'll be known for taking the ball away. I think he'll be known as the coach that brought the Monsters of the Midway back to Chicago.

"His era, his time, when he was a head coach, that was a time that all Bears fans knew the entire team. They didn't just know who the quarterback was or Urlacher, they knew the entire defense, the entire team. I think he brought that back. Those were great years."

As Tillman said, it was the brand of football that Chicago came to love from their 1985 and 1963 championship-winning teams. Urlacher, in particular, was a game-changer on and off the field.

"The defense was loaded," Bears radio play-by-play broadcaster Jeff Joniak said. "Lovie knew how to press everybody's buttons and pull them all together. One time I was with Lovie and he went position by position in his coaching life in the Cover 2. Who were the best players? And he had some great options obviously from his Tampa and Rams days. But Brian revolutionized the middle linebacking position in that scheme because of his ability to drop and cover, and cover a lot of ground sideline to sideline [and] get everybody lined up."

But Urlacher wasn't alone. He would want you to know that. In Smith's nine years, he had nine players get into the Pro Bowl: Urlacher, Briggs, Tillman, safety Mike Brown, defensive end Julius Peppers, cornerbacks Tim Jennings and Nathan Vasher, and defensive tackles Tommie Harris and Henry Melton.

"The great thing about that group—and I think this stemmed from Lovie—there was a belief that it didn't matter what the offense was doing, they would find a way to win," said Zach Zaidman, the Bears' former sideline reporter. "There was never excuses. They would always find a way to win because they'd take the ball away. Or they'd do something dynamic on special teams. You never felt like they were out of the game because of how good that defense was."

The Offensive Struggles

When Smith was first introduced in 2004, the mild-mannered coach from Sandy, Texas, provided Chicago with his most famous quote.

"The No. 1 goal is to beat Green Bay," he said.

Okay, maybe that was his second most famous quote. Two years later, he said, "Rex is our quarterback" too many times to count.

But those two quotes are connected through time. The Bears had to catch the rival Packers because they had Brett Favre first at quarterback, then Aaron Rodgers. The Bears had Rex Grossman, Kyle Orton, Jay Cutler, and too many others to count.

As good as the Bears were on defense under Smith, they always struggled offensively. Smith, to use another famous quote of his, wanted to get off the bus running. But the problems at quarterback persisted.

In the end, trading for Cutler in 2009 didn't resolve them but expound them. He was good, but never became great enough. Smith changed offensive coordinators for Cutler, going from Ron Turner to Mike Martz to Mike Tice.

"Something just went off the rails with the offensive coordinator thing," said sportswriter John "Moon" Mullin, who covered the Bears for the *Daily Herald*, *Chicago Tribune* and NBC Sports Chicago. "I just don't mean how many there were, but the whole chemistry went weird."

Some coaches, including Turner, weren't too keen on Cutler. There were concerns about him off the field, but the Bears had a strong locker room at the time with center Olin Kreutz, Brown, Urlacher, and others. But the Bears' front office, which included Jerry Angelo and director of player personnel Bobby DePaul, were convinced in Cutler. His talent was worth any risks.

"It wasn't the kind of team that Lovie wanted," Mullin said. "So ultimately, it kind of trickled down off his head. Yeah, [it's] just kind of unfortunate. There were players who wanted to stay with Kyle Orton."

The best that Bears' offense ranked in total yards under Smith was during their Super Bowl run in 2006 when they were 15th.

Meanwhile, Smith's record against the Packers shifted. He won seven of his first 10 games against the Packers. But that changed after Rodgers replaced Favre in 2008. The Bears' lost eight of their last nine against their rivals with Smith. It included the NFC Championship Game at Soldier Field in January 2011. Rodgers led the Packers, while Cutler stood on the sideline with an injured knee.

"He should be remembered as a really, really good football coach," Kreutz said. "That's Lovie's legacy. He's got a good record. I know we were one short and that sucks for everybody that was there. And I know that's kind of his legacy. But he came in and there wasn't a lot of winning around here."

The Special 2006 Season

Under Smith, the Bears would watch a highlight tape during training camp to kickoff the season right way. But in 2006, it was different. Something else—something grand—was added by Smith for the video's conclusion.

"At the end of the highlight tape, he had a picture of the Lombardi Trophy and it had Miami, February 7, 2006, Chicago Bears and somebody else," Tillman said.

It was only the start, too.

"Every time we won the game, we would have a highlight tape and at the end of every highlight tape you would see the trophy," Tillman said. "I think, in his mind, he put it on our radar in July. We were going to the Super Bowl and we are winning this Lombardi Trophy and we're bringing it back to Chicago for our fans."

The Bears' 2006 season was Smith's best with the Bears. It ended with him and Tony Dungy becoming the first African American head coaches to lead their teams to the Super Bowl. Dungy's Colts, which had quarterback Peyton Manning, defeated the Bears 29–17 in Miami. But it's been seemingly forgotten that Smith's defense was short two of its stars. Brown and Harris didn't play because of injuries.

"I can't say one bad thing about [the season] except we lost the Super Bowl," Urlacher said.

It still was a memorable season, the best for the Bears in nearly two decades, from "The Bears are who we thought they were" game against the Cardinals to the emergence of star returner Devin Hester to owner Virginia McCaskey raising the Halas Trophy at Soldier Field in the snow after the Bears won the NFC Championship Game against the Saints.

"It was a blast," Urlacher said. "We truly expected to win every single game. You always believed that, but we thought we were going to win every game no matter what the situation was."

That started with Smith. A lot of games were won. He built a winning culture. His 84 victories (including playoffs) as coach trail only Mike Ditka and George Halas.

"You're talking about a coach who won a lot of football games here, coached here for a very long time, had several playoff appearances," kicker Robbie Gould said. "I feel bad that we didn't finish the season as well as we started it in his final season [in 2012].

"But he should be remembered as a guy who really started the trend of what Chicago Bears football is now. He's a guy who kind of put it back on the map.... He was a guy who made sure that everybody in our locker room appreciated what the city had to offer each guy."

A Fun-Lovie Team

Another fight in practice resulted in some stern words from Smith to Kreutz. It had to end. Kreutz wasn't just a Pro Bowl center, but one of Smith's leaders.

"For me with Lovie was, you never wondered what he wanted from you," Kreutz said. "He would tell you exactly, this is what I expect of you. I remember I got into a fight with somebody at practice and he was like, 'That's enough out of you. That's enough fighting guys.' He's like, 'You're supposed to be an older guy on our team. People look to you. That's enough.' And that's all he had to say, and that was enough for me."

The media and fans didn't always see that. Sure, there were issues that received public attention during Smith's day, including Kreutz's fight with Fred Miller at a shooting range in 2005 to the police raid of Tank Johnson's house in December 2006 to Briggs crashing his Lamborghini on a Chicago expressway in 2007.

But the players always had Smith. He was a father figure to many of them. Sometimes a look from Smith is all players needed to get back in line. But Smith listened to them, because he truly cared; and more often than not, players responded in the right ways.

"My experience with Lovie has always been a coach that you can always go to and tell the truth and always be honest about anything," Hester said. "And knowing at the end of the day, he's going to have your back regardless if you're right or if you're wrong. He's the type of coach that we built a relationship upon."

From headline-worthy problems to private issues, players confided in Smith. He was there for Tillman when his daughter, Tiana, required a heart transplant as an infant.

"It's just how he treated us," Tillman said. "He was a multi-tasker. He allowed us to do our jobs. And he challenged us. He challenged some more than others and he pushed me to the max. He pushed me to my capabilities. He saw something in me and he wanted me the best version of myself when it came to sports, when it came to being a dad off the field, when it came to taking care of my family when he had our incident with Tiana in the hospital with her heart."

When Smith was fired by general manager Phil Emery after going 10–6 in the 2012 season, players cried. It was the end of an era. Players loved playing for Lovie. His teams were fun. That was his culture. They played jokes on each other and had their own games—from dodgeball to their beloved "box game"—in the locker room. Urlacher was unbeatable at ping pong.

"The amount of games that we played, people would think that we were worst in the NFL," Briggs said. "They would think that the things we did, they would say, you guys have to be the worst defense in the NFL yearly. Lovie allowed us to do that because when we got on the field we were sharp, we were effective and we were producing. For us, he allowed us to create our own identity. That was the beauty of it. That was really, really the beauty of it. That's why those years were so precious and they were so much fun."

Without a championship, Smith's era might get shrugged off. But players insist it shouldn't be underappreciated. The best Bears' teams since the days of Ditka belong to Smith.

"We understand what's going on internally with him and what's expected of us," Urlacher said. "We appreciated that. We respected him. I think he returned Bears football to what it should have been. There's a few years there where it wasn't like it should have been, but he got us back to where we needed to be, the organization. And he did it the right way."

17

DOUG AND O.B.

Ed O'Bradovich was in the middle of explaining how exceptional the 1963 Bears were. That team had Bill George, who revolutionized the middle linebacker position, and Doug Atkins, a 6-foot-8 monster at defensive end.

With coordinator George Allen, an innovator who harped on the details of everything at practice, the Bears' defense was one of the best of their era.

"And, I'll tell you what, we dominated," O'Bradovich said.

Then the conversation shifted as fast as Atkins got off the line of scrimmage or as quickly as George identified what opposing offenses were trying to do.

"And, my God, since 1946, we've only won the world championship twice—twice," O'Bradovich said in a 2019 interview. "And it's been 34 years—Walter Payton's number—I mean, come on! It gets to the point where enough is enough.

"And I'm just telling you, when I look at it, from my perspective, what is the philosophy here. You've got to be so serious about this game. There is only 16 of them and you got basically eight to nine months to prepare."

It was vintage O.B. He wasn't done, either. He's never done. Questions about the good ol' days can quickly turn into rants about the current ones with Matt Nagy and Mitch Trubisky.

He's O.B. He was born and raised in the Chicago area. He went to Proviso East High School in Maywood, then the University of Illinois. He wore a Bears jersey as a defensive end for 10 years. He made an interception in the Bears' 1963 championship victory against the Giants. The team means so much to him. He cares. He wants to watch a winner.

"The whole point to me, I guess of me rambling on here and trying to tell you something is what I told you earlier in the beginning of this conversation, I know what the hell I'm talking about," O.B. blasted. "I've been there. As a matter of fact, I've seen too much and been through too much. I know what it is like to be through a 1–13 team. Are the coaches bad? Yes. Are the players bad? Yes.

"On the world championship team, the coaching was phenomenal; the players were great. And, you know, they say there is a fine line between winning and losing, not in the National Football League—not in the NFL. There is a huge difference. Guys have to be led."

Starting in 1992, Doug Buffone and O.B. became the voices of Bears fans in Chicago. In doing so, they left their own legacy after they left the field. They were teammates on it, and then teammates off it. Plenty of Bears players have joined the media in some fashion after their playing careers, but there will never be another "Doug and O.B." Their postgame shows on 670 The Score became therapy for fans during some very dark years for the franchise. Their rants became everyone's rants. Folks loved it.

Similar to O.B., Buffone's passion came through his own experiences. He was an underrated linebacker for the Bears from 1966 to 1979. He began his career playing next to Butkus and ended it as a teammate of Walter Payton's. Buffone knew toughness. He embodied it over his career. When he retired, he was the franchise's leader in games played.

"Let me tell ya why our show works," Buffone said in his autobiography *Monster of the Midway: My 50 years with the Chicago Bears*, which was written by Chet Coppock, an iconic broadcaster in Chicago.

"I didn't play trombone or tuba for 14 years; I played pro football. You can't bullshit me and you can't bullshit O.B.

"What we do is completely spontaneous. No one knows what we're going to say because we never know what we're going to say!"

The spontaneity made everything more real. Their dialogue was never prepared.

"I never knew if he was going to jump on offense right away or defense or special teams or jump on the coaches," O.B. said. "I had no idea. So every time when he said something or I said something, it was the first time."

But you could always count on their passion and their storytelling. It was fire with fun. They were an endearing combo—one that spanned 49 years, from teammates to broadcasters. Together, they took fans through the trying times of Dave Wannstedt and Dick Jauron before the Bears' fortunes turned under Lovie Smith. And then turned again under Marc Trestman.

"Doug was the same way that I talk about football and the way I do it," O.B. said. "And, again, I'll repeat it. If you do good, I'll tell you, 'You did good.' If you did bad, I'll tell you, 'You did bad.' And if you look like you don't care, I'm going to tell you, 'You don't care.' It's quite obvious. He was the same way."

In April 2015, Buffone passed away at 70 years old. There were touching tributes in print and ones shared on The Score. He would be dearly missed. And he still is.

Later that year, O.B. joined WGN Radio for a new show with Dan Hampton, an outspoken Hall of Famer from the Bears' beloved 1985 team. It would be full of fire and fun again. But what O.B. and Buffone built always will remain special.

"That show was unbelievable," O.B. said. "That show will never be repeated as far as I'm concerned. What you heard for those years, year after year, game after game, I think that show was like a one-and-done. I don't think there'll be another show like it. I was very proud to be with Doug. He played 15 years. He should have gotten more accolades than he did, and that didn't happen. I'm very proud of Doug."

O.B. always took note of all the notes that Buffone took during games. He still remembers Buffone's emotional challenge of the Bears after they were trounced by the Packers 55–14 in the second year Trestman in 2014. There also was the time that Buffone went after ownership. He "half-apologized" at first, but "took off after them pretty good," O.B. said.

"He had tears in his eyes saying it because all he wanted to do is have the Bears win."

Of course, the same is true O.B. That's why he might miss his arguments with Buffone most, especially the ones where Buffone was adamant about running the ball.

"All of a sudden, Doug opens up, 'Yeah, you got to start passing the ball,'" O.B. said. "I turned to him and I said, 'What?!' I said, 'What happened to this running? Running to daylight, running to victory. Running first. Run the ball, run the ball.' 'No, you got to pass the ball.'

"Oh, by the way, when we argued over the radio, what you heard was real. He'd say something to me and I'd say, 'Listen to me, you little twerp....'

O.B. couldn't help but laugh. That was their show. It was a real success because they were real. Every single show.

"We'd go back and forth with each other—and it worked," O.B said. "It worked for years and years and we developed quite a following. My God, we would take calls from Afghanistan, from Iraq, from soldiers. I mean, we'd get calls from all over."

18

THE TRADE FOR KHALIL MACK

The Bears had a preseason to conclude on a Thursday night against the Bills. But coach Matt Nagy, general manager Ryan Pace, and president/CEO Ted Phillips were preoccupied.

A more important matter had to be discussed on August 30, 2018. A dream could be turned into a reality for the Bears if Pace was aggressive and ownership was on board. It would take draft picks—high ones, too—and a lot of money to make it work.

If Pace and his staff could find common ground with the Raiders, then the Bears would acquire one of the NFL's best defensive players—outside linebacker Khalil Mack.

"Elite defensive players in their prime are rare, so when we knew we had a legit shot to acquire him, we did everything we thought necessary to get him," Pace said afterward.

The trade became official on September 1, 2018. It was another earth-shifting move made by Pace, the Bears' young GM who had traded up and selected quarterback Mitch Trubisky in the draft the previous year.

For the first time in the Pace era, which started in 2015, the Bears were all-in on their team. His rebuild, while not over, was on to the next stage. It was time to win. The Bears thought they had their quarterback in Trubisky with the right coach in Nagy. And now, Pace boldly acquired one of the best pass rushers in the NFL in Mack.

"I knew right then it had a chance to be a special season even though we lost the game [against the Packers in Week 1]," Bears radio play-by-play broadcaster Jeff Joniak said. "It does leave you speechless a little bit. It was a perfect storm."

Rumors, then conversations about Mack's potential availability intensified as the 2018 season approached. The Raiders—with new head coach Jon Gruden making a stand—weren't going to sign Mack to the massive extension that he was worth and deserved. His holdout was days away from entering the regular season.

The Bears weren't the only interested team. The rival Packers also had their eyes (and hearts) set on Mack. But Pace's tenure as GM has been defined by moments like this. He kept in continuous touch with Raiders GM Reggie McKenzie, who would later say that half of the league checked in about Mack's availability.

Being in the middle of contract negotiations with defensive tackle Eddie Goldman wouldn't deter the Bears, either. Pace wanted Mack.

Over 48 hours, Pace and Joey Laine, the Bears' director of football administration, secured a trade for Mack for first-round selections in 2019 and 2020, a sixth-rounder in 2019 and a third-rounder in 2020.

To make it work, the Bears held firm in receiving a 2020 second-round selection, and they got it, along with a late-round conditional pick. Phillips later would tell the *Chicago Sun-Times* that receiving that second-rounder in return was "critical" in making the deal workable from the Bears' end.

When two first-round picks and millions upon millions upon millions of dollars are involved, there needs to be a thumbs up from ownership. Pace got it quickly from Phillips and chairman George McCaskey. They were ready to go all in, too. The Bears made Mack the NFL's highest paid defender with a six-year, $141 million contract.

"There's a moment when there are windows to improve our team, and you've got to maximize those windows," Pace later said.

For those that cover the team, it was similar to other blockbuster moves made by the team—including the 2009 trade for quarterback Jay Cutler—but it also felt different. A former defensive player of the year had arrived in a city that loves defense.

At Mack's first practice inside the Walter Payton Center, the team blasted "Return of the Mack" by Mark Morrison. In his debut, Mack had a strip sack and a pick-six against the Packers at Lambeau Field.

"I give Pace a lot of credit because he hopped on that early and kept checking in [with the Raiders]," ESPN 1000 radio host Marc Silverman said. "It was like the Cutler trade on steroids and then he delivers. That was the thing. You're watching Jay and you're watching picks and everything. You're like, 'Oh, no. Is he not as good as I thought he was?'"

No one thought that about Mack during the 2018 season. The Bears won the NFC North, making their first playoff appearance since 2010, and boasted the league's best defense. He was voted to the Pro Bowl and named an All-Pro.

Joniak likened the acquisition of Mack to the Bears' trade for pass rusher Adewale Ogunleye from the Dolphins for receiver Marty Booker and a third-round pick in the 2004. The Bears' front office was backing up what they were saying about winning, and this time it acquired one of the most feared players in the league. This was Ogunleye times 10.

"That's important for a team when they know a front office has their back," Joniak said. "This one was a cannon shot."

For Bears players and coaches, it became their own "remember where you were" moment before what became a memorable, 12–4 season in 2018.

Trubisky's parents were in town and he was sleeping in on a day off for the team when his mother stormed into his room. He didn't believe what she was telling him.

"I said, 'No, you're making me mad, get out of here,'" Trubisky said after the trade. "You can't wake me up with that kind of news because you just don't believe it. But, he's here."

It was real. The Bears introduced Mack on September 2, 2018, at Halas Hall. Mack's parents were present.

"We'll remember this," Pace said that day, "for a long time."

19

DECEMBER 12, 1965

It's the final touchdown of the Bears' 61–20 rout of the San Francisco 49ers during a muddy, sloppy day at Wrigley Field on December 12, 1965, that offensive tackle Bob Wetoska remembers vividly from the game.

Late in the fourth quarter, Wetoska said that he and guard George Seals had opened a hole big enough to walk through for a two-yard touchdown.

The problem was that it was running back Jon Arnett who did the walking and subsequent scoring, and not Gale Sayers.

"Halas sent in Jon Arnett, and of course, Arnett didn't want to go in because he knew that if Sayers scored that touchdown that would be a new record," Wetoska said. "Nobody's ever scored seven touchdowns in a game. But Halas made him go in and so he did."

Why Arnett came in was questioned immediately and still debated. Halas said at that time that he feared that Sayers would get injured. Some players suspected that Halas didn't want a rookie getting that much attention or breaking old records.

Others, such as a Wetoska, suggested that money was a factor, especially knowing Halas' stingy reputation.

"I think it has something to do with a bonus or money in his contract for the next season," Wetoska said.

What could have been still shouldn't take away from what was that day was for Sayers. He totaled 336 all-purpose yards and scored six touchdowns. It's still a record for touchdowns in a single game by a rookie. It was an unbelievable performance—one of the best of all-time. The mud-filled conditions that Sayers played on—his touchdowns consisted of runs of 1, 7, 21, and 50 yards, an 85-yard punt return, and an 80-yard reception—only made it more impressive.

"He looked like he was gliding," said Mike Ditka, who played in the game. "The field was muddy. Everybody was slipping and sliding except him. It was the most unbelievable exhibition that I've ever seen in the history of the game."

Sayers' part in the Bears history was short-lived because of knee injuries. He appeared in only 68 games over seven seasons. But the "Kansas Comet" was and always will be one of the best players in Bears history. He was that good, that dynamic. "Give me 18 inches of daylight. That's all I need," Sayers said in the NFL Films' "The Great Ones" series. He played in only four full seasons because of his injuries, but was named an All-Pro five times. At 34 years old, he became the youngest player ever inducted into the Pro Football Hall of Fame.

"He was very sullen and he was very bitter after his career because he thought he would had been the greatest of all time if not for the knees," said Hub Arkush, the longtime publisher of *Pro Football Weekly* and the Bears' former radio broadcaster. "The truth is if he would have played in the 21st century, with the technology now, he would had been a much better football player because they would have fixed his knees."

The truth is that Sayers would had been good enough to be a star in today's NFL. He was transcendent. Packers coach Vince Lombardi once said, "He took you by surprise even when you knew he was coming." Sayers was just too difficult to stop.

"I would say that Gale was a runner that you had to witness to truly appreciate what he was able to do," said Fred Mitchell, the former *Chicago Tribune* reporter, who wrote Sayers' autobiography, *Sayers: My Life and Times*, in 2007.

"I think the only so-called modern-day running back who would be comparable would be Barry Sanders. And Gale told me that himself. Of the great running backs that he's seen since his day, that Barry Sanders most resembles his balance and his ability to change direction on a dime and speed, obviously. Gale was also a multi-purpose back in an era when you didn't have as much specialization. He returned kickoffs, he returned punts, and obviously ran from scrimmage, was flanked out on occasion as a receiver and even threw a few passes."

Part of Sayers' legacy lives on through Brian Piccolo's. The two were close friends after becoming what's believed to be the first interracial roommates in the NFL. Their connection became immortalized in the movie, *Brian's Song*. It came out after Piccolo died from cancer in June 1970.

Before Piccolo died, Sayers, who was known to be private and quiet, made a memorable speech when he received the George Halas Courage Award after coming back from a serious knee injury.

"I love Brian Piccolo, and I'd like all of you to love him, too," Sayers said. "Tonight, when you hit your knees to pray, please ask God to love him, too."

In March 2017, Sayers' family revealed that he had dementia. His arrival at the Bears' 100 celebration in June 2019 became emotional because of it. He was in a wheelchair and weighed 130 pounds, but he wore his Hall of Fame jacket and a baseball hat with his No. 40 on it. He was *the* superstar at a star-studded gathering for the franchise.

"He was unbelievable," Ditka said that day. "There's [nobody] like him."

Walter Payton would agree with that. Before every Bears running back was compared to Payton, it was Payton who had to play up to Sayers' legacy.

"It's an honor for me to be compared with Sayers, but there's really no comparison," Payton told the *Chicago Tribune* in 1975. "He was my idol. He's the man and he'll always be the man. There will never be another Gale Sayers."

20

AS GOOD AS GOOD AS GOULD

Patrick Mannelly knew Robbie Gould was different immediately. After being released by the Patriots and Ravens, Gould tried out for the Bears in 2005. Mannelly and punter/holder Brad Maynard had to be at Halas Hall for him and other kickers.

"I just remember that Tuesday workout—his first one," Mannelly said. "I didn't know who the heck Robbie was. Me and Maynard are out there, Robbie just looked and sounded different when he kicked the ball.

"The other guys were just getting it through the uprights, this way or that way, and it just didn't get the height. Robbie was very raw but had that trajectory, the boom, the rotation on the ball, that you're like, 'This kid can play.'"

Some of those "other guys" were veterans, too. But Martin Gramatica and Steve Christie didn't have what Gould had going, at least not anymore.

"Obviously, we made the right decision in bringing in him or keeping him," Mannelly said. "His growth was what impressed me the most. How hard he worked. How diligent he was at his craft. And then his mental makeup, how he dealt with misses, how he dealt with good days. Nothing changed. He got his routine. We figured out what made him good and tick and then it turned into making him great."

Gould, who went undrafted out of Penn State, officially signed with the Bears on October 8, 2005. His Bears tenure unceremoniously ended when he was released on September 4, 2016, a week before that season began.

But before he kicked for the Giants and 49ers, he became the all-time leading scorer in team history, surpassing a beloved member of the 1985 Bears, Kevin Butler. He became the best kicker in team history.

"I don't know what my legacy is," Gould said. "I've always told myself to stay in the moment and that you can let everybody else talk about you and your career and the things that you do."

* * *

Robbie Gould became "as Good as Gould" on January 14, 2007. On that day, Gould made a game-winning field goal in overtime of the Bears' 27–24 victory against the Seahawks in the divisional round of the playoffs.

It wasn't a gimme, either. It was a 49-yarder in the cold at Soldier Field. It also came after Gould made a game-tying field goal from 41 yards late in the fourth quarter to force overtime.

"As soon as it left my foot, I knew it was good," Gould later said on the broadcast.

The Bears got over the proverbial hump because of Gould's field goal, too. They advanced to their first NFC Championship Game since the 1988 season, when they were still run by Mike Ditka.

"Whew, best kicker I've ever seen, visiting or whatever," Bears radio play-by-play broadcaster Jeff Joniak said. "There is just no other way to put it. He made some really clutch kicks in Bears history. They would have never made it to the Super Bowl without him."

It starts with his two crucial field goals against the Seahawks. Overall, Gould went 6-for-6 on his field goals during the playoffs that year. He also made all nine of his point-after attempts. He made three field goals as the Bears routed the Saints 39–14 at Soldier Field in the NFC Championship Game. The Bears lost to quarterback Peyton Manning and the Colts 29–17 in Super Bowl XLI.

"There are just so many big kicks," Mannelly said. "He just made everything. You were always just so comfortable. When we ran out there and as an athlete you're confident in what you can do, and I'm like, 'Oh, we've got this made.'

"Maybe my Robbie moments that stick out the most are the ones he missed, that you're like, 'What! What just happened.' Like running off the field, 'We didn't do our job,' and those are very limited."

One of those was Gould's miss from 47 yards in overtime during a 23–20 loss at the Vikings on December 1, 2013. After the Bears blew a 10-point lead in the fourth quarter, coach Marc Trestman sent Gould out on second down for the game-winner.

"We're creatures of habits, routine or whatever," Mannelly said. "So we get into your routine before the fourth down. So we're starting on second down. I'm starting to snap. It was [punter] Adam Podlesh. So I'm starting to snap to him. Robbie is just starting his warm up in the net."

And then ...

"Boom," Mannelly said, "'You guys are in.'"

The specialists contested. But Trestman was absolute in his decision. Gould missed that kick. It sailed right and became another footnote in what eventually turned into a disastrous two-year run for Trestman.

"This isn't what we're used to," Mannelly said. "We've never practiced this. Like we do every Thursday, the two-minute drill on fourth down or knowing the time, a timeout, or it's a hurry field goal with no timeouts left."

Everyone was out of whack.

"I get the trust that Trestman had in Robbie but you've also got to understand that you're creatures of routine," Mannelly said. "Keep him in his routine. Let him understand. I did not understand that one."

It was all part of an emotional day for Gould. He flew to Minnesota separately from the team after being present for the birth of his son earlier that Sunday. Trestman also had Gould attempt a 66-yard field goal that day.

"There was no excuse," Gould said after the loss. "My wife did awesome. It was one of the greatest days in my life and I'm happy for my wife and my little boy. I'm sorry I couldn't do it for my teammates like I did for my wife this morning. That's hard to swallow. We're in a playoff hunt. I love my teammates just like I love my wife and baby and I just didn't do it today. It's on me."

* * *

On December 3, 2017, Robbie Gould single-footedly beat the Bears. As a member of the 49ers, Gould made five field goals—including the game-winner from 24 yards in the closing seconds—for a 15–14 victory at Soldier Field.

After making his game-winner, Gould stared down the Bears' sideline in his moment of revenge and triumph.

"I wanted this one really bad," Gould told reporters after the game.

Connor Barth, Cairo Santos, and Mike Nugent all kicked for the Bears during the 2017 season. Barth, who was Gould's first replacement, made only 68.8 percent of his kicks that season.

The Bears cut Gould for what they called "performance reasons" but he still was performing better than any kicker who replaced him.

"It motivated me," Gould said after the 49ers' victory. "It drives me every day. I have Ryan Pace and Jeff Rodgers and John Fox to thank for that.

"Because if I would've stayed here, who knows what my career would have ended like?"

Gould made kicking at Soldier Field—one of the toughest venues in the NFL for kickers—an art form but he also would study tape of all special teams. Mannelly called him a "special teams nerd." Gould would bring ideas to coordinators Dave Toub and Joe DeCamillis.

"While we're watching punt return, he's not sitting there scribbling in his notebook," said Mannelly, who was Gould's teammate for nine seasons.

"He's sitting there watching and kind of mentally grading his teammates, and he would go over there and talk to them. 'Hey, man, what do you think about this? Why aren't you playing well? Maybe, pick up here. Maybe, you should be doing something more at practice to get better.' But that was Robbie. He wanted to deal with everything, and he was great at doing it. And all the teammates respected the hell out of him."

Of course, that's also what made Gould different than your typical kicker. He was outspoken. His clashes with Rodgers prompted his departure. But, as teammates would say, that's also Robbie just being Robbie. He wasn't afraid to talk about league matters or contracts as a former NFLPA representative. He also wasn't shy about ripping the turf of Soldier Field when it needed to be.

Gould could do that. Again, he became more than a kicker. He was a fan favorite with an active foundation, Goulden Touch. He helped lead clean-up efforts in Washington, Illinois after a tornado ravaged the small town in November 2013.

"He was very enjoyable to talk to on all topics," Joniak said. "That's the side-bar stuff that I always appreciated as a play-by-play guy being able to get to know these guys at a different level. Being around so much and just finding out what makes them tick. What their lives are like and you can talk about things other than football, and he'd be one of those guys that you'd really enjoy."

It was all part of being the best kicker in Bears history. His preparation, work habits, and drive made him special.

"A lot of it has to do with being available," Gould said in 2019. "Because I knew that if I was hurt, somebody on the team had to get cut, because there can only be one kicker. So I prided [myself] on making sure that I stayed healthy, that I stayed available. Even when I was hurt, I would kick. The only way I didn't play is if there was truly a reason I couldn't play. And I think I took a lot of time to make sure that in practice that it was harder than the games."

Gould also was extremely hard on himself when he missed. He took certain challenges, especially from former coach Lovie Smith, to heart. He always wanted to be best. And he became the best in Bears history.

"You would always be bummed if you didn't make it happen, not only for yourself but for the guys," Gould said. "I think there was just a passion about how you fit into the team based on making your kicks."

21

THE BLACK 'N' BLUES BROTHERS

After a 45–10 dismantling of the Washington Redskins in Week 4 of the 1985 season, the entire offensive line for the Bears— starters and reserves—went downtown for a photoshoot.

For it, the linemen would have to wear black fedoras and dark sunglasses. But they would also be in their Bears uniforms and shoulder pads.

"They put a little dirt on us," center Jay Hilgenberg said.

This was the photoshoot for the famous "Black 'n' Blues Brothers" poster. Guard Tom Thayer called it an "all-day process." But before players danced and rapped in "The Super Bowl Shuffle," there was the poster. It was the unofficial start of a special season in Chicago, and fittingly, it started with the Bears' offensive line, a dominant but often underrated part of the team's success in the 1980s.

"Especially right on the cusp of an unforgettable season, too, to shoot a poster like that, we had a little chip on our shoulder with those pictures we had," said Hilgenberg, who, as the Bears' Pro Bowl center, is appropriately situated right in the middle of the it. "We showed a little swagger in those pictures."

Better yet, they backed up what the poster—an obvious reference to the popular, Chicago-based movie, *The Blues Brothers*—meant to the team and the city of Chicago.

"It was just like the tip of the iceberg actually of all the promotional opportunities throughout the course of the season that everybody was going to have an opportunity to take advantage of, if in fact, that we were successful," Thayer said.

* * *

In the first half of the Bears' divisional round playoff game against the Giants on January 5, 1986, a toss was called to the left. In this case, both guards, Thayer and Mark Bortz, had to pull, too. That meant left tackle Jim Covert would have to crash inside.

"Jimbo had to come down and block down," Hilgenberg said. "There was no one over Bortz, so the next guy would had been [nose tackle] Jim Burt, but then Jimbo's guy was the linebacker on the other side, and Burt was playing soft in the game."

So walking toward the line, Hilgenberg had a message for Covert.

"It just hit me right when they called that play," Hilgenberg said. "I was thinking, 'Well, Burt was playing so soft that it could be a tough block to get him cut off. On the way to the line of scrimmage, I look over at Jimbo and I go, 'Hey, Jimbo... knock Burt out, will ya?' He just looked at me. I see his eyes light up."

Covert did exactly that. It was another sign of how powerful and how imposing that Bears offensive line could be, and it came in a 21–0 victory in the playoffs. Giants quarterback Phil Simms was sacked six times that day; Jim McMahon wasn't sacked once. And Covert crushed a Pro Bowl–caliber nose tackle.

"He wiped him out unbelievably," Hilgenberg said. "He put him out of the game."

On January 15, 2020, Covert finally got his long-awaited call from the Pro Football Hall of Fame. It was an overdue individual honor for the Bears' starting left tackle, who earned the respect and words of praise from the Giants' Lawrence Taylor, the most feared pass rusher of their era. The former wrestler, who once prevailed in a practice scuffle against Steve "Mongo" McMichael, was headed to Canton.

"Our offensive line has never gotten the attention that it should have had," Hilgenberg said. "We dominated the rushing game in the 80s. Our offensive line, we played together for so long. And Jimbo was a dominant player. It's well-deserved."

In a way, it was an honor felt by an entire position group. Walter Payton was a superstar, but he doesn't shine week after week without Covert, Hilgenberg, Thayer, Bortz, and right tackle Keith Van Horne.

"[Offensive line coach] Dick Stanfel used to tell us almost every night before the game, he goes, 'All right guys, you go out there and you win this game. Those Bears, they're tough. They got a good defense. They're good. Their running back, he's really good. He's a great one. But guys, if we lose this game, they'll come out like, 'That offensive just didn't get it done,'" Hilgenberg said. "That's the way we played."

* * *

In the 1980s, it wasn't surprising if a mid-October practice turned into the intensity-filled showdowns that were more often seen in training camp. The Bears' defensive line of McMichael, Dan Hampton, and Richard Dent would walk to the line of scrimmage looking to raise hell.

"Mongo thought he was the greatest. Dent thought he was the greatest. I thought I was the greatest," Hampton said. "Well, in practice, we had to prove it. So for the offensive line to have any self-respect, they couldn't let us kill them. So every day almost escalated to a full-game tempo.

"And it was crazy for us to do that looking back now. I know for people, it's hard for you to believe. But we would almost play it like at game tempo, especially in August and September, all through training camp, all through September, until it started getting cold and the season started taking a toll. But for a lot of years, it was like a price of admission to watch us do drills, nine-on-seven and pass rush."

It was what the Bears' coaches wanted. Stanfel and defensive line coach Dale Haupt were old-school.

"They worked the hell out of us," Hampton said. "We hit sleds. We drove sleds. We did up downs. We ran. We did the ladder. We would do pass-rush drills every day. In Week 15, we'd be doing almost live pass rush drills because they had a belief if you don't use it, you lose it."

The coaching prowess of Stanfel, the Bears' line coach from 1981 to 1992, especially showed up in what Hilgenberg and Bortz became in their careers. Hilgenberg went undrafted out of Iowa in 1981 and became a seven-time Pro Bowl, two-time All-Pro center for the Bears.

Bortz was an eighth-round pick from the Bears' revered 1983 draft class with Covert (first round) and Thayer (fourth round), but he was a defensive lineman at Iowa. He went to Pro Bowls as an offensive guard in 1988 and 1990.

"Dick Stanfel happened to take this mold and work him and develop him into a Pro Bowl, long-term offensive lineman," said Thayer, who played in the USFL before joining the Bears in 1985. "Dick Stanfel he was the key element in our success."

Forget the games. It showed on the practice field against Hampton, McMichael, Dent and linebackers Otis Wilson and Wilber Marshall. It was a classic "iron sharpens iron" situation year after year. The Bears were built to win up front and it showed.

"A lot of what happened on that team was because of both the defensive and offensive lines," Hampton said. "Not only did we dominant the line of scrimmage, but we were expected to dominate it. Yeah, we had the great Walter Payton and we had some great linebackers. We had great pieces all over the place. But the true essence of that team in that five-year span—where people said we won more games than any team in history [and] we had five or six different quarterbacks, [where] it's not like the Patriots where they get one guy who is a Hall of Famer, playing every week, every down—it was because of the offensive line and the dominance."

* * *

In Hilgenberg's house, there is a frame on his wall of the outtakes of the "Black 'n' Blues Brothers" photoshoot. Thayer's nephew has a copy of the poster, which is signed by everyone in it. Thayer and Hilgenberg, who became part of the Bears' radio broadcasts after their playing careers, have more copies stored of the famous poster, too.

Thayer, though, is still surprised when and where he sees that poster decades after the offensive line traveled downtown together to shoot it.

"It's been fun because now, for as long as that poster has been around, it seems like every time you go to an appearance, you either sign one or talk to an older person who said they had one hanging in their bedroom or they still have one hanging in their garage," Thayer said. "It's had a lasting impression on Bears fans over the years, the Black 'n' Blues brothers poster did."

It did because of how good that offensive line as. Chicago always will appreciate blue-collar, tough guys and that's what that line was for years. Four of them were in place in 1984, with Thayer replacing Kurt Becker as a starter in 1985. There would be injuries to get through but the starting five of Covert, Thayer, Hilgenberg, Bortz and Van Horne would remain in place through the 1990 season. The 1991 season was Hilgenberg's last with the Bears.

From 1984 to 1991, no team ran the ball better than the Bears. In that time frame, they led the league with 20,872 rushing yards, 4,897 rushing attempts and 177 rushing touchdowns, which includes the playoffs. In the first three years of that run, the Bears led the NFL in rushing in each season. They also were consistent, ranking in the top five six times. The Bears had the second-best winning percentage in that span, trailing only the San Francisco 49ers.

It was dominance immortalized in a poster. There would be another one made of just the five starters later on. Hilgenberg, Bortz and Van Horne would also do a Chevrolet commercial in the same attire. But the original poster always will be sentimental.

From left to right, the poster featured: Tom Andrews, Bortz, Thayer, Van Horne, Hilgenberg, Kurt Becker, Andy Frederick, Stefan Humphries, and Covert.

"That was a fun day with those guys," Hilgenberg said. "I was happy about that because they included the whole offensive line in that poster, too. That was the good part of it."

22

"THE SUPER BOWL SHUFFLE"

Gary Fencik had to go. The video—all the dancing and rapping—was taking too long. The Bears' longtime safety had a hot date to get to.

"I was probably there for three to four hours, whatever," Fencik recalled. "I had a date with my wife. It was the first date I had with my wife. At some point, I go, 'Guys, I'm done. You can cut me out. But I got a date. I'm done with this thing.' Then that thing goes unbelievable."

It was December 3, 1985. The Bears had lost to quarterback Dan Marino and the Dolphins a night earlier in Miami. The Bears' proud defense, of which Fencik was one of the leaders, was torched in a 38-24 defeat on national television. But here Fencik was with a bunch of his teammates shooting the video for what would become "The Super Bowl Shuffle" at the Park West in downtown Chicago.

"We had come back and we had lost the game," Fencik said. "It's a *Monday Night* game, so we probably didn't get home until two or three in the morning and then we had bumps and bruises up at Halas Hall, then we had to go downtown to do this video, which nobody really wanted to do."

But the "Hitman" still did great. They all did, even though the producers were worried that no one would show. "The Super Bowl Shuffle"—which was originally called "The Shuffle"—started with receiver Willie Gault, who had non-football interests, including an acting career. The deal was with Red Label Records, with the idea that half of the proceeds would go to charity, which is why Fencik and others agreed to do it.

"The Shuffle" turned out to be so much more than that. It was part of the cultural phenomenon that the Bears turned into in 1985. It started as a recording that turned into a video that turned into a gold record and then a Grammy nomination. There was nothing like it—ever.

For Bears fans, it became a lasting memento—a reminder of the Bears' greatness that season and their confidence and bravado. It's passed down from generation to generation, from VHS tapes to replays on YouTube.

"It was so funny for so many different reasons," said longtime sportswriter Rick Telander, who chronicled the Bears of the 1980s for *Sports Illustrated*. "They kept saying it was for charity, but there was this kind of like, 'Guys, we can do anything we want. Let's fuck with reality.' All kinds of rules say you need to do this and you need to do that. 'We don't have to.' There was this rebellious element that had to come with huge amounts of confidence, and the arrogance came from the confidence. But if you're not confident—if you're an average team—you wouldn't even dream of doing anything like that."

Something Unique, Special

Inside the office of the old home of running back Walter Payton in South Barrington, Illinois, the gold record from "The Super Bowl Shuffle" hung for years.

"This is how I know it was special," said Jarrett Payton, his son and a sports broadcaster in Chicago. "It meant that much to him that he put it up in his office."

Walter Payton loved music and dancing. He was part of the Chicago 6 band with defensive linemen Dan Hampton and Steve "Mongo" McMichael.

"He played the drums; he played the bass guitar," Jarrett Payton said. "So for him, to be a part of that, he was all for it. You didn't have to ask him twice—and he was an entertainer."

The shuffle had Mike Singletary and Richard Dent, but it still needed more stars. Payton and quarterback Jim McMahon were a must. But Payton and McMahon didn't make it to the downtown video shoot. Instead, they were taped later at a racquetball court at old Halas Hall at Lake Forest College during a practice day. They had to be edited in.

The players recorded the audio weeks before the video was shot and produced. A dance routine wasn't choreographed until the day of, either. The contractual part of it was a process, too. Fencik said he didn't sign the contract for it until the Bears were en route to New Orleans for the Super Bowl against the Patriots.

"It's almost amazing that it actually turned out the way it did," Fencik said. "And it was kind of like when rap was first getting introduced. It became way, way beyond what any of us would have expected."

Lines were written to fit each player's personality—and this team had a lot of them. But that's what made the song work, too. Fans remembered them; they had their own favorites.

"They did say stuff that was personal to them like, 'I'm a rookie, I'm no dumb cookie,'" Telander said. "Fencik, Mr. Ivy League, he said something about, 'I'll ring your bell,' And [backup quarterback] Steve Fuller looks like a complete spaz but that's because if you look, his ankle is all wrapped up. I don't know if he's got a shoe on, so he can't dance really."

Again, it amazingly all worked. The choreography didn't really matter. The Bears, especially this team, were too beloved.

"I thought it was kind of silly," said longtime Bears writer Dan Pompei, who started covering the team in 1985. "It was kind of cocky, but it was reflective of who they were. They really didn't care. They were having fun. And they weren't concerned about the consequences of what they said or did. It was kind of befitting of the whole '85 team."

Sitting Out the Shuffle

In later interviews, Gault would say that convincing players such as Dent and Singletary was easy. But others, including Fencik, resisted.

"I'm from Chicago and no team had won any championship in Chicago since the 1963 Bears," Fencik said, "so to be so cocksure to have something called 'The Super Bowl Shuffle' during the regular season, I cringed at that."

While Fencik eventually relented, others didn't. Some were opposed to it, including Hampton, defensive tackle Steve McMichael, and center Jay Hilgenberg. They were starters, but didn't want lead roles in any such thing. Gault invited other teammates to join as the band in the days before the Bears played Dolphins.

"I said, 'You're crazy. We just got beat on national TV,'" Hilgenberg said. "I passed. I don't regret that I didn't do it. I'm fine that I didn't do it. I think it's really cool, the guys that did it. It's added to the whole '85—keeping us around, I guess—the memories."

Some players including Hampton, simply wanted to win it all first. There was a fear of looking foolish.

"We had to do certain things week after week after week for us to be successful," Hampton said. "If we're off doing some stupid video, then we were setting ourselves up for a downfall. Who's to say? A couple of guys break their arms and tear up their knees and we're not the same and we don't win the Super Bowl. We're going to look pretty stupid. So I made the decision. I just said, 'Hey, God bless you, do what you all want to do.'"

That was the beauty of the Bears in the 1980s, too. Coach Mike Ditka didn't know about "The Shuffle" until he and the team were informed of the video shoot. The McCaskey family obviously had their concerns. Later on, they were adamant that proceeds went to charities.

But under Ditka, if you worked hard, played hard, and won, he didn't seem to care what players did. They were everywhere. Ditka was a character himself—one who received endorsements and taped commercials, too.

"Every one of these guys were on the radio," Telander said. "They had restaurants. They were doing more stuff. They were doing ads. The weirdest part, I suppose, is that Ditka was leading the way after the Super Bowl, particularly. There's not anything on the planet that he hasn't endorsed."

But those were the Bears in the 1980s. "The Super Bowl Shuffle"—which only didn't win a Best R&B Performance Grammy because of Prince's "Kiss"—is part of their lore.

"There was something about them you just liked," said John "Moon" Mullin, a Bears writer for the *Daily Herald*, *Chicago Tribune*, and NBC Sports.

"Maybe it was the way they didn't take themselves too seriously. Like Richard Dent—who's in the shuffle—said, 'We didn't think much of it. It was our chance to put on a pair of tight pants and boogie or dance.' Even as they were making this, it wasn't even that big of a deal to them. Maybe that's uniquely American. We like our heroes to be regular guys. Be great and be a guy you want to have a beer with. I think everyone kind of felt that way. Again, it resonates."

23

NO. 46

With his time ending with the Bears following the 1982 season, safety Doug Plank stopped into the office of defensive coordinator Buddy Ryan at Halas Hall.

"I thanked him for being my coach and the great job that he did," Plank said.

In his response, Ryan made a promise that turned out to be an accurate prediction.

"Doug, I want to promise you something. I know you've had a hell of a career here in Chicago and there's a lot of people that like you," Plank recalled Ryan saying at the time. "I'm going to tell you something right now. I'm going to make you bigger and better after you've left."

Plank, who was a ruthless, hard-hitting safety for the Bears from 1975 to 1982, wanted to know how or why.

"Buddy, how are you going to do that?"

"The 46 defense," Ryan replied.

"Buddy, I believe it."

Everyone did, including owner George Halas. In 1982, Ryan was retained by the Bears for new coach Mike Ditka after safety Gary Fencik—along with the support of Plank, Dan Hampton, Steve McMichael, and others—wrote him a letter, stating the defense's belief in Ryan and his staff.

There was a sense that were great days ahead for the defense. They had great players, but also a great, innovative scheme that Plank said Ryan started formulating during the 1979 season. Plank, as No. 46, was an integral part of the process. Ryan had a habit of using numbers to name blitzes and the legendary defense was named after Plank's jersey number.

"I only saw parts of it," Plank said. "I only played in it for a few years, a couple years. But I could see where it is going. [Ryan] goes, 'I can't tell you exactly how it's going to happen, but you're going to be proud of this when it's all done.' I just gave him a big hug. That's the last time I saw him in Chicago."

Ryan's genius turned into the eighth-ranked unit in 1983, then No. 1 in 1984. A year after that, Ryan's defense was arguably the best ever, as the Bears went 15–1 and won Super Bowl XX by routing the Patriots 46–10. The Bears' defense hurt Patriots starting quarterback Steve Eason that night in New Orleans and finished with seven sacks.

Plank wasn't a part of those teams, but he still played an important role in the evolution of one of the best defenses of all time. He was moved from safety right into the middle of the action. He wouldn't only relay calls in the secondary, but now be in charge of everything that was happening in front of him. Plank handled the position that would eventually be filled by Hall of Famer Mike Singletary.

"Now I wasn't the only person obviously in the 46 defense," Plank said. "But I was the middle person. If you look at the bullseye of that defense, I was the bullseye. I was the guy in the middle."

At first, Plank admittedly didn't think much of the defensive scheme. Ryan, being Ryan, was always re-thinking his attacks.

"I didn't feel engrained or enshrined when Buddy gave it to me because I didn't know how long it was going to last," Plank said. "Maybe, it was just for that week. It might have been just a one-week defense. But it had so many different features, coverage features. To be a safety in the middle linebacker position, it gave you great appreciation for those guys that play up front."

Plank's appreciation would start with defensive lineman Dan Hampton. In many ways, the 46 would start with Hampton. Ryan wanted to overwhelm with numbers up front. But he needed a player—and got one in Hampton—who could consistently handle more than one blocker, which resulted in others having one-on-one opportunities or potentially free runs at quarterbacks.

Plank called it a "demanding" defense. Responsibilities would be swapped among players. But Ryan's hyper-aggressive attack always seemed to have answers for whatever the offense did. It was built to work that way. It took exceptional communication from exceptional players to make it click, and the Bears would reach that point in time.

"Now, all of sudden, we can do so many things," Plank said. "We can blitz. We can play two deep. I played deep half from middle linebacker many times. So I had to run out of there immediately. But I got really good at reading blockers—guards and centers. They'll tell you every time where the ball is going."

Plank retired after the 1982 season. He suffered a spinal contusion, which resulted in him missing every game but one. When he played, he hit hard all the time. Plank became known for it, which included the friendly fire that teammates endured.

"He's like a Butkus built to a quarter-inch scale," Ryan told the *Chicago Tribune* in 1980.

Dick Butkus, who is often considered the best linebacker of all time, has a college award named after him. But Plank, who was drafted by the Bears in the same year as Walter Payton, has the best defense ever. He gets asked about it all the time.

"[Ryan] was one of the few coaches that when he was done talking there was tears in people's eyes," Plank said. "If you looked around that room, you're going, 'Man I trust you guys. I'll do anything for you and I'll be held accountable.'

"I never in my life experienced the joy of getting back to the huddle like I did with Buddy. You went back there and it was like the greatest reunions of all time—each play. Guys would be like hugging each other, like during the game. This is insane. You wanted to play for Buddy and the Bears and each other like nothing I've ever done in my life."

24

THE
DANIMAL

Doug Plank remembers the days when Dan Hampton was told by defensive coordinator Buddy Ryan to go find "Susie" on the opposing offense. Then Hampton had to beat up "Susie" every single play, until the offense changed.

"We're looking for who Susie is," said Plank, who played for the Bears from 1975 to 1982. "Susie, a lot of times, was the weakest player, offensive lineman, and Dan sometimes would match up with that weakest player because we wanted a huge advantage. And it was funny watching other teams, when Dan would find the weakest link and he'd match up over top of that person, that person would jump to another spot, a tackle spot, or another guard, or flip over, it was hilarious. Dan basically was chasing the weakest link on their team."

Hampton's search for "Susie" didn't happen all the time in the infancy stages of Ryan's 46 defense. But it's a defense that would blossom into one of the most catastrophic for opposing offenses in the history of the NFL because of Hampton.

He was the heart and soul of it. The Bears' revered and feared 46 defense simply wouldn't have been what it was in the 1980s without the Hall of Famer in the middle of everything it did.

"Dan many times, he was the center," Plank said. "When you're at the center position, you're going to get double-teamed. You're going to get blocked by the centers and the guards, but what made it so much pressure on the offense was that the center couldn't help anyone out because he had somebody in his face.

"And as soon as he snapped that ball, he was just getting ran over because that defensive tackle—namely Dan Hampton—was going to force him right back into the pocket. It's hard to do multiple things. To try and take on Dan Hampton and hike the ball, that's almost an impossible task."

* * *

When it came to building the great Bears' defenses of the mid-1980s—particularly the Super Bowl–winning version of 1985—first came safety Gary Fencik, then came Hampton.

"Dan really changed the defense," said Fencik, who joined the Bears in 1976 after originally being a 10th-round selection of the Dolphins that same year.

"From the time that he was drafted and then came in as first-round defensive tackle, he changed everything. He made our offensive line better. He had an incredible motor and was just such a physical force that we got better the day that Dan Hampton became a defensive player for the Bears."

General manager Jim Finks selected Hampton, an All-American at Arkansas, with the fourth overall pick in the 1979 draft. As Plank explained, Hampton would move around the line of scrimmage. But over the center, Hampton essentially became the engine that made Ryan's 46 defense go. It wouldn't have been as feared or as dominant without him.

From 1983 to 1988, the Bears' defense ranked in the top five in scoring and in the top 10 in total yards every year. In those years, the defense sacked quarterbacks 397 times, which includes the playoffs and was by far the most in the league. Quarterbacks averaged a 60.0 passer rating in that time span, which also led the league.

Only 52 of those 397 sacks belonged to Hampton (46 in the regular season and six in the playoffs). Defensive end Richard Dent and defensive tackle Steve McMichael went on to be first and second in sacks, respectively, in franchise history because of the Bears' success in the 1980s. Linebackers Otis Wilson and Wilber Marshall also contributed to the pass rush.

But it all started with Hampton, a farmer's son from Arkansas. Hampton did the incredible and won Ryan over immediately as a rookie. Hampton didn't need a set position. He could do everything. Sometimes that resulted in less acclaim and attention. But Hampton didn't care.

"I don't want to get into comparing him, but nobody has played tackle better than Hampton," Ryan told *Sports Illustrated* in 1989. "And surely no one has played it with more heart. Dan's my hero."

That's high praise from a coach who rarely gave it. Hampton went to four Pro Bowls and was named a first-team All-Pro four times. But those accolades fall short of capturing Hampton's immense value. In 2002, former Bears defensive end Ed O'Bradovich tried to do it when he presented Hampton for the Pro Football Hall of Fame.

"This will tell you why he earned the respect of both his teammates and his opponents," O'Bradovich said during his speech. "From Dan's years of '79 to '90, the Bears defense led the league in each of the following categories: fewest rushing yards, fewest rushing touchdowns, most sacks, fewest points allowed, fewest total yards. Breaking down the Bears defense from '83 to '90 into 20 different categories, separate the games that Dan played from the games that he didn't play, and in every single category, the Bears defense improved dramatically with Dan on the line.... The Bears won 75 percent of their games when Dan played and only 33 percent when he didn't. Sacks: 3.6 with Dan; without him: 2.3. And, the one category that really stands out, the Bears only gave up 14 points per game with Dan, and without him, 23 points a game. Incredible."

Hampton, who was the highest-paid player on the Bears' roster at one point, often talks about there being "wreckers" and "catchers" in the NFL. He would know, too. He was the ultimate wrecker on arguably the best defense and team of all time.

"Buddy said, 'I'm putting you on the damn center. No center is going to block you one on one,'" Hampton explained. "If I started to wear the center's ass out, then they're going to have to start slide blocking and doubling down with the guard. Once they start doing that, then everything starts to get into a mathematical formula and simple. There's going to be somebody either open or single blocked, and a lot of times, Richard would get down on the guard, and he and Steve McMichael were All-Pro pass rushers and then you had Wilber and Otis outside."

The end result was devastation. Hampton's best individual season was in 1984, when he had 11.5 sacks. Winning mattered first to him. He always played hurt. He had 10 knee surgeries (five on each knee) during his playing career. His disfigured hands were featured in life-sized images over two pages in the Bears' centennial scrapbook, too.

"Again, my job was, I couldn't be blocked," Hampton said. "I couldn't be hooked, either way. If there was a run play, I couldn't be hooked. If it's a pass play, if I'm single blocked, I had to be able to get instant pressure, and if you do that a time or two earlier in the game, they're not going to be stupid and just let you wreck their game. There were a number of games that happened."

* * *

When it comes to working in the Chicago media, Hampton has some advice. After all, he's been a staple in it since his playing career ended, including roles on WGN Radio, NBC, and on *Pro Football Weekly*'s syndicated television show.

"The people of Chicago are smart," Hampton said. "They know sports. And they know a fraud when they see one. And so you've got to be honest and you've got to be yourself."

Hampton has never been afraid to do that. He's known for being the first player to ever dump Gatorade on a coach, which he did to Mike Ditka to celebrate the Bears clinching the NFC Central in 1984. He's also known for liking Jay Cutler and disliking Jim McMahon.

Hub Arkush, the publisher of *Pro Football Weekly*, said he sees Hampton's "old boy country charm" come through, too, whether it's on air or at live appearances.

"He's a very outspoken guy," said Arkush, who also was a radio broadcaster for the Bears. "He doesn't care what he says. It's if he believes it. He loves the Bears, but he hates what's wrong about the Bears, and he will come out and say it. That's pretty unusual for a guy who is able to still be a personality in the city he played in."

Because of it, Hampton is a lasting, endearing link to the great Bears teams of the 1980s. He's the Danimal.

"I see guys on the TV that never accomplished a damn thing," Hampton said. "Why do I want to listen to them? At least I felt like I had credibility. I played on the greatest teams of all time for some of the greatest coaches of all time. So I know the goods when I see it and people of Chicago always appreciate the fact that, hey, when it's good, that's fine. But when it's bad, you've got to tell them. You can't sugarcoat it, and you can't be an ass-kisser. That's one thing I will never be."

25

SAMURAI MIKE

When linebacker Mike Singletary first joined the Bears in 1981, he failed. General manager Jim Finks selected him in the second round out of Baylor, but he was undersized and overweight.

Safety Gary Fencik said there were two players that year who didn't finish their mile run in training camp in what he remembered to be a 12-minute mark.

"It was Jim McMahon and Mike Singletary," Fencik said.

There was more, too. Defensive coordinator Buddy Ryan had a reputation as being very unforgiving of rookie players. One of Singletary's jobs was being a messenger for Ryan's play calls. He had to run them in to safety-turned-linebacker Doug Plank, who wore No. 46 and for whom Ryan's beloved defensive scheme was named after.

"Mike, a lot of times, he would get so excited that by the time he got in the field he couldn't even tell you the defense," Plank said. "He sounded like a samurai warrior.... And I'm going, 'Please, tell me.' And that's where he got his name, 'Samurai.' I called him 'Samurai.'

"Buddy goes, 'Why did you call that defense, Doug?' Mike Singletary came into the huddle and I couldn't understand a word he said. It was like a samurai warrior talking to somebody who had no idea. I was like, 'Oh, my God. He's ramped up.'"

In time, that emotion and that passion would help Singletary transform into the next standard bearer at middle linebacker for the Bears. Singletary's seven All-Pro nods are the second most in team history, trailing only Bill George, who revolutionized the linebacker position decades earlier. Singletary was enshrined in the Pro Football Hall of Fame in 1998.

Singletary would fill the role that Plank once held in the middle of Ryan's 46 defense and take his game and that defense to another level. Fencik said that Singletary was "incredibly committed to being the best," which included dropping 20 pounds by his second season in the NFL.

"His accomplishments obviously speak for themselves," said defensive lineman Dan Hampton, who played with Singletary for 10 years. "Was he the prototypical middle linebacker? Probably not. What was he? 5'10", 225, 230 [pounds]? But he was able to run and cover. He was very smart in the sense that he could make adjustments. He had great study skills, where he would recognize things and recognize tendencies of an offense and not only use that to his advantage but call out certain things for the rest of us."

Singletary benefitted from playing behind Hampton, Steve McMichael, and Richard Dent. During the Bears 100 celebration, McMichael, always the gregarious one, poked fun at Singletary for that, too. But Singletary had the ability to organize the Bears' chaos—on and off the field.

"It's the fact that he was a true student of the game, worked hard, watched a lot of film, and created a work ethic that a lot of the younger players emulated and took pride in," said Fred Mitchell, who covered Singletary and the Bears for the *Chicago Tribune*.

"He wasn't physically imposing even in that era as a middle linebacker, but his intensity has been well-documented. It was the eyes and the concentration and the focus and the understanding of not only where he should be but where his teammates should be. If you switched sports and talked about baseball, I would compare it to a savvy catcher on a baseball team. He knows what everybody else is supposed to be doing defensively on the field and provides that extra little spark that all the teammates needed. That's what made Mike Singletary special, and he never got to the point where he rested on his laurels."

Singletary was a different brand of nasty. He hit like Dick Butkus, but didn't exactly snarl—or literally bite—like Dick Butkus. It's Singletary's wide eyes before the snap or him being captured by NFL Films barking at an opposing offense: "Hey baby, we're going to be here all day. We're going to be here all day, baby. I like this kind of party." He was still the type of relentless, hard-hitting, and hard-working linebacker who Chicago covets and adores.

Longtime sportswriter Rick Telander, who covered the Bears of the 1980s for *Sports Illustrated*, said talking to Singletary was like conversing with "a fire-and-brimstone minister." It showed on the field, too. The youngest of 10 children from a poor Texas family, Singletary always had perspective.

"The intensity level was the same between Dick and Mike," defensive tackle Jim Osborne, the only Bears player to play with Butkus and Singletary, told the *Chicago Tribune* in 1998. "But while Dick would be on the bottom of the pile trying to bite someone or twist an ankle, Mike would help you up. Dick was instinctive and knew offenses from limited film study. Mike watched more film than some of the coaches. He was something. He would knock your head off, and then kneel beside you and lead you in prayer."

Singletary's love of football turned into a coaching career, including two-plus years as the head coach of the San Francisco 49ers (2008–2010). His passion always was evident, particularly in his sideline interactions. But the best players don't always turn into the best coaches. Singletary's legacy is being the man in the middle of the legends that were the Bears of the 1980s.

"He was the glue of the defense," said longtime Bears writer Dan Pompei, who worked for the *Chicago Sun-Times*, *The Sporting News*, the *Chicago Tribune*, and The Athletic.

"When I think about him, I think about leadership and I think about a guy who was able to keep it all together because there were some wild personalities on that team. There were guys who just needed to be reined in. He had the ability to rein everybody in."

Pompei would turn to Singletary if he had a problem with a teammate that needed to be addressed. The wide-eyed linebacker always had an open ear.

"We'd talk about it and he might go and talk to that player," Pompei said. "He was just a great bridge for everyone on that defense. A stabilizing force, I would say. And then the other thing, he was all that, but he was also this electric, intense player that gave a charge— voltage—to the defense with the wide eyes, throwing around his body and being able to hit so hard that he cracked helmets. He helped on a number of fronts."

26

TED PHILLIPS AND THE McCASKEYS

On February 10, 1999, Virginia McCaskey was asked during a blockbuster news conference what the reaction of her father, George Halas, would be to her decision to name Ted Phillips the president of their beloved team.

"Go Bears!" she said then.

It was a monumental move, one wrought with emotion that showed that day at Halas Hall. McCaskey not only removed her son, Michael, from direct power, relegating him to chairman of the board, but she also named the first non-family member as president of the Bears.

"I never dreamed that I would be president of an NFL team," Phillips said that day. "It still blows me away."

Fully encapsulating Phillips' place in Bears history is difficult. In some cases, it's matter of whom you ask and what about. Simply put, he's been the organization's most powerful employee since that fateful day in 1999. He's not a McCaskey in blood, but official representation.

The Bears' business is football, but in regards to Phillips, it's important to separate the business from the actual football. Fair or not, Phillips often is painted as the ultimate villain—Public Enemy No. 1 when it comes to winning and losing for the Bears.

From the Dave McGinnis–hiring debacle to headline-worthy issues securing a deal for Soldier Field, what the Bears had in Michael McCaskey didn't work. Virginia McCaskey, his mother and the daughter of George Halas, recognized that. Phillips secured that elusive stadium deal in 2000. Soldier Field was renovated in 2002.

But the Bears are 163–173 over the first 21 regular seasons with Phillips in place as the franchise's president/chief executive officer. As of 2019, it included seven winning seasons, five playoff appearances, two NFC Championship Games, and one Super Bowl.

"The McCaskeys would be the first ones to tell you that they don't want to be public figures and they're not business students," said

Hub Arkush, the publisher of *Pro Football Weekly* and a former radio broadcaster for the Bears. "They inherited this business and Ted has made a fortune for them. He has been a very good accountant. He has been a good steward of the business of the Chicago Bears.

"As the director of business operations, the president of the team, and as a [chief financial officer], he should get tremendous credit. He's done an outstanding job. But anything related to football, from where I sit, he's always done more damage than he's done good."

* * *

On June 12, 2001, Phillips officially had enough of the Bears' old way of doing things. It's the day he hired Jerry Angelo as general manager—making him the first person in nearly 20 years to have final say on the draft and the Bears' head coach.

After Jim Finks left the Bears in 1983, Jerry Vainisi took over as general manager. But Vainisi was fired after the 1986 season, leaving the Bears with a different arrangement of decision-makers for years.

From 1987 to 1992, vice president of player personnel Bill Tobin and coach Mike Ditka were in charge of football operations. From 1993 to 1996, director of scouting Rod Graves handled personnel. From 1997 to 2001, it was vice president of player personnel Mark Hatley.

Through it all was Michael McCaskey, who was named team president in 1983 after Halas died. A year earlier, Halas briefly returned to fire coach Neill Armstrong and hire Ditka, which upset Finks, prompting his exit after the 1983 draft.

"The whole structure went awry once the Halases left and the McCaskeys took over," longtime *Chicago Sun-Times* sportswriter Mark Potash said.

Angelo was hired to change that structure. They needed a general manager.

With the help of Joe Bailey of the New York executive search firm of Russell Reynolds Associates, Phillips had a narrowed list of 11 candidates. He interviewed six, with the three finalists being the Buccaneers' Angelo, the Broncos' Ted Sundquist, and the Ravens' James Harris.

"I don't have an ego here; I want to win," Phillips said the day after hiring Angelo. "If I let my ego take over, I never would have brought in a GM."

It was a ground-breaking decision made by Phillips, one that the McCaskey family never will forget. Angelo became the fourth general manager in Bears history. Phillips joined the Bears in 1983 as their controller. He was promoted to director of finance in 1987 and then vice president of operations in 1993. As the Bears' lead negotiator in contract discussions, he always held a role in personnel. But he hired Angelo to run the team's football operations.

"It's an exciting day for the Bears and for me personally," Phillips said then. "I'm firmly convinced that we found the right man to lead the Bears back to their successful winning ways."

* * *

On January 21, 2007, Bears coach Lovie Smith handed Virginia McCaskey a trophy with her father's name on it to while standing on a stage in the snow at Soldier Field.

"We didn't have to say a lot—you could see it in her face how excited she was," Smith told reporters that night.

The Bears were headed to the Super Bowl XLI against the Indianapolis Colts—their first appearance since the team's revered 1985 season—after defeating the New Orleans Saints 39–14 in the NFC Championship Game.

The Bears not only were competitive again, but one of the NFL's best teams, with stars in Brian Urlacher, Lance Briggs, and Devin Hester. It was years in the making, but one still rooted in the McCaskey's decision to promote Phillips.

The Bears not only were stable under Angelo, they were competitive in nearly every season in his 11 years with the team. In Smith, the Bears found their most successful coach since Ditka. Smith had an 81–63 record in the regular season. The Bears didn't win the big one against the Colts, but they were 3–3 in the postseason. They were relevant.

"I still say that's a huge mistake to fire him after a 10–6 season with a group that was loyal to him and you knew that, not all of them, but some of those guys were not going to play for anybody but Lovie," said Bob LeGere, who covered the Bears for the *Daily Herald* from 1992 to 2018. "That started the demise."

Angelo didn't fire Smith. It was general manager Phil Emery, who replaced Angelo in 2012. In 2001, the Bears made Angelo inherit Dick Jauron for a year. A 13–3 season full of memorable defensive plays resulted in a contract extension. The same happened to Emery, but a 10–6 season by Smith in 2012—which also was full of memorable plays on defense—didn't turn into a playoff berth. Not that Emery needed it, but the reality that the Bears weren't in the playoffs for the fifth time in six seasons served as another impetus for change.

Phillips led the search that resulted in Emery. He cited a talent deficiency for the change. Angelo acquired quarterback Jay Cutler in 2009 and later signed defensive end Julius Peppers, but there still were first-round picks that missed, from running back Cedric Benson to offensive tackle Gabe Carimi.

When Emery was introduced on January 30, 2012, Phillips said that the depth of Emery's plan was appealing. "Nobody had a negative thing to say about Phil Emery," Phillips said then. The time would come for that.

* * *

On April 21, 2010, the Bears passed their internal torch. It was announced that George McCaskey would replace his older brother, Michael, as chairman of the board. Michael McCaskey has been in that role since Phillips was promoted to president in 1999. Before him, Ed McCaskey, his father and husband of Virginia, was the chairman. Michael McCaskey passed away on May 16, 2020, after a long battle with leukemia.

"It's a privilege to continue George Halas' legacy," George McCaskey said then about his grandfather. "That's one of the goals of the Halas/McCaskey family."

George McCaskey still had Phillips at his side. That wouldn't change. But McCaskey, who had been the Bears' director of ticket operations since 1991, was different than his brother and even this father.

"He knows enough to stay out of the way—Michael didn't," said Potash, who had multiple stints covering the Bears. "Michael thought that he was an actual team president and had to be told that he wasn't."

It was a rejuvenating change for a team that needed it. Under Phillips and McCaskey, the team finally rid itself of its cheap stigma. The Bears signed quarterback Jay Cutler to the richest contract in franchise history in 2014 and then beat it when the team made outside linebacker Khalil Mack the highest paid defender in the league in 2018. Others were signed to lucrative contracts, too. Halas Hall also was remodeled and expanded twice under McCaskey and Phillips. McCaskey also was willing to move training camp to Halas Hall because of their significant improvements.

"If you look at [the Bears'] record since George Halas passed away, it's not good," said longtime Bears writer Dan Pompei, who is in the Pro Football Hall of Fame as a Dick McCann Award winner. "I think they have some winning to do in order to rectify their opinion in the public court. And it's understandable.

"But I think they're a family that is ultimately very committed to the Bears, and they want to do the right thing. I think sometimes they haven't been able to figure out how to do that. They're obviously in somewhat of a new era now with George being in control. He's definitely different than Michael. They obviously hope this is going to be something that makes them a better organization."

* * *

On December 29, 2014, Phillips sat next to McCaskey inside the Bears' new media room at Halas Hall.

Together, they discussed their decision to fire coach Marc Trestman and Emery after a season filled with tumult and embarrassing conflict. Virginia McCaskey and her feelings about what transpired during that 5–11 season were discussed.

"She's been very supportive," George McCaskey said that day. "She agrees with the decisions that we've made. She's pissed off. I can't think of a 91-year-old woman that that description would apply, but in this case, I can't think of a more accurate description."

It was an appropriate way to encapsulate the emotions of Bears' fans at the time. Emery's hiring of Trestman began with optimism and ended in flames. There was conflict. An overwhelming amount.

The worst of it came in Week 16 of the 2014 season, when Trestman decided to bench Cutler—whom Emery signed to a massive extension in the previous off-season—against the Detroit Lions in favor of Jimmy Clausen. It came two weeks after offensive coordinator Aaron Kromer became known as one of the sources behind an NFL Network report that was critical of Cutler.

"Every coach, to a certain extent, will shift blame around behind the scenes," said Jeff Dickerson, who started covering the Bears for ESPN radio in 2004. "Marc, from what I could gather, did that a lot. He liked to move the blame around. It was very obvious it just wasn't working."

For those like Dickerson who closely covered Smith's team, it was major break from the past. The locker room lacked structure and leadership. Even worse, Emery's Bears said goodbye to Urlacher—the face of the team—with a press release.

"There were very few games [under Lovie Smith] where they showed up and you're like, 'They're not ready to play,'" Dickerson said. "Literally, there was only a couple or a handful of those. Under Trestman—*holy cow*. Remember that string of games where it was Green Bay, it was New England? They were not ready to play, and it was so obvious. They were just getting absolutely decimated."

Emery and Trestman were both fired a day after the 2014 season ended. In two seasons together, they had more controversies in the headlines than they did victories, with only 13. Another search would commence.

This time, Phillips and McCaskey would turn to consultant Ernie Accorsi, the former general manager of the New York Giants, for assistance. He would remain in place as an advisor until general manager Ryan Pace and coach John Fox were hired.

"[Phillips] was responsible for the Phil Emery and Marc Trestman nightmare," Arkush said. "That couldn't have happened anywhere else. That never should have happened and that's completely on him."

* * *

On August 30, 2018, Phillips joined Pace and coach Matt Nagy in Nagy's office in Soldier Field before the Bears concluded the preseason against the Buffalo Bills. There was a more pressing, important matter to discuss: Khalil Mack was available via trade and the Bears potentially had a deal in place.

"I don't need to have four committee meetings and let's discuss it all," Phillips told the *Chicago Sun-Times* during a 2019 interview. "That's why you have to have the right people in place....

"You have to be decisive. It wasn't a long, drawn-out, lengthy discussion. Once I understood it all—because [Pace] never leaves a stone unturned, he's very thorough—and when I hear it all, it's, 'Go get him.'"

Acquiring Mack from the Oakland Raiders meant parting with multiple first-round picks, but also signing him to a six-year, $141 million contract. Phillips not only had to give a thumbs up to Pace, but he needed to get one form McCaskey. But they were happy to give it. It was time to win; Mack would undoubtedly help with that.

It's one of the best examples of how Phillips and McCaskey trusted their "football guys." Sometimes it works. Mack is an example of that. And sometimes it doesn't. That would include the firing of Smith and hiring of Trestman.

"Here's the thing I always struggled with," LeGere said, "if Ted Phillips is not a football guy, then why is he allowed to hire the football guy who is going to hire the football guy."

27

GEORGE ALLEN

In 1963, the Bears replaced an innovative assistant coach by promoting another one. It was the year that George Allen was promoted to defensive coordinator in place of Clark Shaughnessy, whom, according to the February 13 edition of the *Chicago Daily Tribune*, "resigned somewhat mysteriously in the last month of the 1962 season."

It's said that Shaughnessy, who is considered the father of the Bears' revolutionary T formation offense, had another quarrel with Bears owner/head coach George Halas. This time he had enough.

In time, Allen, who was hired as the Bears' primary scout in 1958, would have his own spats with Halas that would garner headlines. But Allen's impact on the 1963 season and other facets of the Bears' organization was, in some ways, immeasurable.

Defensive end Ed O'Bradovich saw it in the scouting report that Allen handed out. It was no longer the typical two or three pages.

"I'll never forget it," O'Bradovich said. "The day that George Allen was named the defensive coordinator for us, the head man there, we got a thing that was about an inch thick on the opponent. He would break it all down. It was unbelievable. He was the right coach at the right time with the right guys. And I'll tell you, we dominated."

The Bears did, winning their first championship since the 1940s. In that era, the 1963 defense was as good, if not better than the Bears' 1985 version. Mike Ditka, who played for '63 team and coached the '85 team, said as much during the Bears 100 centennial celebration. It started with Allen, whom he remembers as being as driven as he was.

"They call me a Class A [personality]. He was really a classic A," Ditka said in an interview with the *Chicago Tribune* in 1991. "I mean, he was a go, go, go person. He didn't get mad. He didn't explode that way. But he was A. A hyper go, go, go, got-to-be-working, got-to-be-doing something, got-to-be-talking, got-to-be-motivating. He had to be involved in everything. That is not bad. I think we need more people that way."

With linebackers Bill George and Joe Fortunato, safety Richie Petitbon, defensive end Doug Atkins, and others, the Bears' defense allowed only 10 points per game during the 1963 season. The Bears handled the Giants 14–10 in the championship at Wrigley Field, intercepting quarterback Y.A Tittle five times.

Afterward in the Bears' locker room, Fortunato stood up on a chair and made a speech with a game ball in his hand.

"I want to announce, as one of the co-captains, that the game ball goes to the man who played such a great part in our fine defense— coach George Allen," Fortunato said, according to the *Chicago Tribune*.

But the celebration wasn't done yet. Television broadcast cameras and radio stations then captured the Bears' song for Allen: "Hooray for George! Hooray at last! Hooray for George! He's a horse's ass!"

It was a joke that was a sign of their affection. Allen was said to be an extremely determined and intense coach. He was known for his neatness and his preparation. He was innovative on and off the field. He changed how the Bears practiced. Everything was based on the details.

"He changed everything," O'Bradovich said. "His main thing was, No. 1, don't make mental mistakes. Mental mistakes will kill you more than physical, especially for the defensive backs. We were doing things that nobody knew what the hell we were doing. We were taking out the tight end. We were taking out the wide outs right at the line of scrimmage."

Certain legends wouldn't be Bears without Allen, either. He was in charge of the Bears' draft, not Halas. In 1965, the Bears selected linebacker Dick Butkus and running back Gale Sayers with the third and fourth overall selections, respectively.

"He's the one that drafted Butkus and Sayers," said O'Bradovich, who had an interception in the 1963 championship and also was brought in by Allen in 1962. "[It's] probably the greatest draft in the history of football. How the hell do you draft two kids in one year, both No. 1s and both of them are in the Hall of Fame? How does that happen?"

It all ended after 1965, though. He left the Bears to be the head coach of Los Angeles Rams, prompting Halas to sue him for breach of contract. Halas continuously bemoaned Allen's decision, which, according to the *Los Angeles Times*, included making a speech to fellow owners during a winter meeting in Los Angeles.

Packers owner Vince Lombardi was apparently amused by Halas' words and actions and loudly whispered his own thoughts to Rams owner Dan Reeves: "Sounds as if you've got yourself a hell of a coach."

It's true. Halas, who eventually dropped his lawsuit, knew it, too. Allen never won another title, but he never had a losing season in 12 as a head coach. He had a 118–54–6 career record (including playoffs), coaching the Rams for five years and the Redskins for seven. He earned Coach of the Year honors in 1967 and 1971. He was known for his knack for trades—131 of them—and for coining the phrase "the future is now." He was the first coach to hire an assistant to coach special teams. Allen, who coached the Chicago Blitz of the USFL in 1983, passed away in 1990, but was voted into the Pro Football Hall of Fame in 2002.

"We practiced until we covered every plan and every eventuality, until we did it in our sleep during our leisure time," Hall of Fame defensive end Deacon Jones said during Allen's enshrinement speech.

"Often times, it's best to describe someone in their own words. And I can find none better that exemplified coach George Allen than those words he said, 'In sports, the only measure of success is victory. We must sacrifice everything to this end. The man who can accept defeat and take his salary without feeling guilty is a thief.'"

The Bears players whom Allen coached know that well, too. They had a special coach in Allen, even if he was only their defensive coordinator.

"That's why George Allen was so special," O'Bradovich said. "He endeared himself to the ballplayers and if we didn't have George Allen, we would not have won a world championship in 1963."

28

JERRY ANGELO

Jerry Angelo pushed all of his chips in when he traded for quarterback Jay Cutler in April 2009. But the Bears general manager didn't say the proverbial "all in" until 11 months later.

In free agency in 2010, Angelo swung for the fences again and signed defensive end Julius Peppers to a six-year, $95 million contract with $42 million guaranteed.

Nearly a decade later, Hall of Fame linebacker Brian Urlacher can still feel the excitement of that moment. He remembered facing Peppers and the Carolina Panthers in the playoffs in January 2006.

"The [2005] team, we lost in the playoffs to them, and that was probably the first time I saw him on the field where I paid attention," Urlacher said. "The things that he could do at his size and with his athletic ability, you talk to some of the offensive linemen on our team, you're like, 'Oh, my goodness. This dude is the man.' Just getting a player of his caliber to come play with us was exciting as hell."

For Angelo, it was the final piece to figuring out his Super Bowl puzzle. He had his quarterback and now he had his prized pass rusher who revitalized a once-great defense. The Bears were built to win on both sides of the ball in 2010.

"He has been billed as advertised not just as a player, but as a person," Angelo told the *Chicago Tribune* that year. "And it goes one in the same with us."

It was a master plan that unraveled in the NFC Championship Game against the rival Packers at Soldier Field. Cutler suffered a Grade 2 MCL sprain in his knee, but his inaction set off a firestorm on social media.

In the end, it was Angelo's backup plan that spelled his end. Caleb Hanie, the Bears' backup to Cutler, threw two interceptions against the Packers. The following season, Cutler was lost to a broken thumb, leaving Hanie and Josh McCown to struggle in his place. The Bears started 7–3, but finished 8–8.

Team president Ted Phillips fired Angelo after that season, which was his 11th in charge of the team. Angelo's backup plan at quarterback behind Cutler was faulted, along with an overall talent deficiency, but the Bears in 2011 still were one or two plays away from being 10–6 without Cutler.

"If Marion Barber doesn't run out of bounds—which was like unbelievable that he did that—they win that game in Denver," said Jeff Dickerson, who has covered the team for ESPN Radio since 2004. "If Roy Williams catches a pass that literally hits him in the chest for a touchdown, they beat the Chiefs. Roy Williams, he had a famous quote: 'I saw a big brown thing in my face.' That was the ball."

Phillips would later hire Phil Emery, who would fire Angelo's coach in Smith, after the Bears went 10–6, but failed to advance to the postseason during the 2012 season. Then came the short-lived, but controversial two-year era of coach Marc Trestman.

Angelo's legacy isn't as tarnished as Emery's three-year run. Far from it. The Bears went 95–81 in the regular season under Angelo, which included three seasons with Dick Jauron. The Bears went 13–3 in 2001. Angelo gave Jauron an extension because of it. But in 2004, Angelo hired his own coach in Smith, who led the Bears to the playoffs in his second season and to Super Bowl XLI against the Colts in his third. Overall, Angelo's teams went 3–4 in postseason.

Angelo's legacy includes assembling some of the best defenses in franchise history. He drafted Pro Bowl players in cornerback Charles Tillman and Lance Briggs in 2003, defensive tackle Tommie Harris and cornerback Nathan Vasher in 2004, and defensive tackle Henry Melton in 2009.

His best draft pick was arguably taking returner Devin Hester in the second round in 2006 after listening to area scout Mark Sadowski, who is from the South Side of Chicago. Angelo also drafted tight end Greg Olsen in 2007 and running back Matt Forte in 2008.

But there also were too many first-round misses for Angelo: wide receiver David Terrell (2001), offensive tackle Marc Colombo (2002), defensive end Michael Haynes and quarterback Rex Grossman (2003), running back Cedric Benson (2005), offensive tackle Chris Williams (2008), and offensive tackle Gabe Carimi (2011).

"He wasn't perfect," said Mark Potash, who covered Angelo's career and the Bears for the *Chicago Sun-Times*. "But he was a good GM. He just needed too many things going right. He really couldn't get the quarterback right, including Cutler.... It was two things, really. Too many misses on first-round picks. That was the biggest thing. But also, he jumped on Cutler because I guess he had to, but I don't feel like he really researched what he had there, the kind of guy he was."

Pro Bowl center Olin Kreutz was a stalwart of the teams run by Angelo and Smith. He remembers those teams as ones built to win with defense but always with questions and holes on offense.

"People used to ask me for years, like, 'Olin, what's wrong with the O line?'" Kreutz said. "I wouldn't say it because you're trying to be a teammate, but I would be like, 'Have you seen the fucking draft picks since I got drafted? From 1998 to 2011, they didn't hit once.' It was always Fred Miller, Ruben Brown, John Tait. It was always free agents that would come in [to start]."

Smith's problems on offense also were Angelo's. There were changes made at offensive coordinator and the July 2011 trade that sent Olsen, a first-round pick in 2007, to the Panthers for a 2012 third-round selection. It was the result of then–offensive coordinator Mike Martz's preferences at tight end, but it also infuriated Cutler. Martz was fired after the 2011 season, while Olsen went on to have a career with the Panthers that some consider Hall of Fame worthy.

Angelo's selection of Benson in 2005 was a curious one because they already had Thomas Jones. It was made in the same year that the Packers drafted Aaron Rodgers, even though they already had Brett Favre. Bob LeGere, who covered the Bears from 1993 to 2018 for the *Daily Herald*, said the Bears had "many, many other needs" at the time of Benson's selection. Plus, there were off-the-field concerns with the running back from Texas, some of which played out at the NFL level.

"They took a running back fourth overall when they had their guy [Jones] and everybody on the team felt like he was their guy, especially the offensive line felt like he was their guy," LeGere said. "But they used the No. 4 pick, which they could have used on a million other things. And they brought in a guy they didn't need and it created a problem in the locker room—and it prevented them from addressing other needs."

There were other issues that Angelo and Smith had to get through, including the arrests of defensive lineman Tank Johnson and receiver Sam Hurd, and also a botched draft trade with the Ravens.

All that said, Angelo's 11-year run should still be viewed as successful, especially when compared to what transpired after him. He brought in some of the best Bears of all time and his teams won four divisional titles.

Angelo's hiring itself was a significant step in the right direction for a franchise that once was directionless. Angelo, who spent 14 seasons with the Buccaneers, was hired after Phillips used the help of Russell Reynolds Associates, a New York executive search firm. He became the Bears' first official general manager in title since Jerry Vainisi, who was fired in January 1987.

"He brings a proven football philosophy to our organization," Phillips said when the Bears announced Angelo's hiring. "Jerry's credentials and enthusiasm made him the best person to lead our football operations."

It wasn't always perfect. Angelo had his failures. He didn't win the Super Bowl. But Angelo still accomplished part of what the Bears hoped he would do. The Bears won more than they lost. He led their football operations well, and his era should be remembered well because of it.

"That Angelo era was the first time since [Mike] Ditka in the heyday where the Bears every year were in the mix," Dickerson said. "You went into every year knowing that they're not going to be bad. They're going to be right there. And they were right there."

29

MARC AND PHIL

There was nothing that Marc Trestman could say on December 18, 2014, that could fully explain the weight of his decision to bench Jay Cutler in favor of backup Jimmy Clausen in Week 16 against the Detroit Lions.

"I think this is in the best interest of the team," Trestman said that day at Halas Hall. "I think we need a lift at quarterback. I think we need a spark. The weight of the world should not be on Jimmy Clausen.

"He's going to get an opportunity to play and I'm hoping that our team, against a very, very good defense, there will be some response from our football team."

Of course, Trestman's team was a mess then. They were 5–9. In the same room at Halas Hall nearly a year ago, the Bears celebrated their signing of Cutler. He signed a seven-year, $126.7 million extension—the largest in franchise history at the time. And now, Trestman was benching him.

On the same day, Cutler was asked if he thought if he played his last game for the Bears. Sitting him certainly required having conversations with, at the very least, general manager Phil Emery, right?

"This was a coaching decision," Trestman said. "And the people that I work with in the building all said, 'This is a coaching decision, make the coaching decision that you think is appropriate for this time.'"

It was the coach's last stand. A tenure that started with seemingly boundless optimism was bottoming out as an endless failure. Turning to Clausen didn't work. He was just as bad as Cutler was that season. He suffered a concussion, too, leaving Cutler to start the season finale in Minnesota against the Vikings. A day later, on December 29, Trestman and Emery were both fired by the Bears. Cutler remained with his massive contract for the next GM and coach.

"It's got to be one of the most dysfunctional teams in Chicago sports history," ESPN 1000 radio host Marc Silverman said.

Silverman experienced that firsthand during "The Jay Cutler Show" on ESPN 1000. Cutler and receiver Brandon Marshall rotated weeks during the 2014 season. On air and in worse ways off it, Cutler and Marshall ripped each other.

That was Marshall, though. In Week 7 of that season, Marshall was overheard yelling in the locker room—including at veteran kicker Robbie Gould—after the Bears lost 27–14 against the Miami Dolphins—Marshall's former team. In September of that season, Marshall also called his own news conference without consulting the media relations staff as a response to an ESPN documentary that detailed his troubled past. Marshall handed out paperwork to reporters.

It was all part of Marshall's turbulent three-year run with the Bears, which started well under Lovie Smith in 2012 but ended in turmoil under Trestman. He produced big plays on the field, but he also produced too many big stories off it. There is almost too much to fully detail, but it also included fighting with Chris Harris, an assistant defensive coach, at practice.

The problem—a major one—was that Marshall wasn't alone. The 2014 season began with tight end Martellus Bennett throwing rookie cornerback Kyle Fuller, their first-round pick, to the ground in camp, and getting yelled at by Marshall. Bennett was defiant in a subsequent interview, which was overheard by Emery, and later suspended.

But there was a lot more. This can go on and on. The dysfunction, the angst, and the frustrations were widespread. Trestman's ship— one built by Emery—sunk fast. Everyone abandoned ship.

Before Trestman benched Cutler—which was widely viewed as his swing at saving his job—the lowest of all the low points was the team's discovery that offensive coordinator Aaron Kromer was one of the sources behind an NFL Network story that was critical of Cutler after the Bears were routed by the Dallas Cowboys 41–28 on *Thursday Night Football* in Week 14.

In the last week of the season, defensive tackle Jeremiah Ratliff had a major blowup in practice. The coaching staff tried to send him off, but he refused. Instead, an assistant was shoved to the ground and a play clock was damaged. Ratliff was finally escorted from practice, but he still was a starter in the season finale against the Vikings.

"Fair or not, I got the impression from players and from other people saying that Trestman was not a leader," said Bob LeGere, who covered the Bears for the *Daily Herald* from 1992 to 2018. "He could not walk into an NFL locker room and lead men. And he couldn't get them to follow him in tough times. As long as he was winning and offense was performing, he was a good hire. But he could not rally the troops. He was not a leader. Guys would not follow him, like they did with Lovie."

In many respects, whomever replaced Smith in 2013 would have issues. Smith was there for nine years and went 10–6 in 2012 before Emery, who replaced Jerry Angelo in 2011, fired him.

To be fair, Emery was praised for making an offensive hire and one with Cutler in mind. Trestman had success as the Raiders' offensive coordinator and quarterbacks coach from 2001 to 2003 and earlier in the same positions for the 49ers during the 1990s. Former NFL quarterbacks Steve Young and Rich Gannon were among the many who commended the Bears for his hiring.

Before joining the Bears, he was the head coach of the Montreal Alouettes, winning back-to-back Grey Cup titles. Trestman also was endearing from a media perspective at first, providing long, insightful answers to nearly everything asked. Trestman's story—a long-winding one that took him from the NFL to the college ranks and to the CFL—became easy to root for.

"He was a breath of fresh air at the beginning," said Mark Potash, who covered Trestman's two years for the *Chicago Sun-Times*. "His ideas not only sounded good, but they were good. That team was 3–0 [in 2013] and beat the Steelers pretty good at Heinz Field his first year. To me, this was the biggest indicator of the impact of Trestman, because his message really resonated. Players loved him. They loved everything about him. In the first nine weeks of that season, they had like no false starts. The focus was fantastic."

And then it dissipated. In the end, Emery still chose Trestman over Bruce Arians, a former coach of the year with the Colts who later won the honor again with the Cardinals in 2014—the same season everything imploded for Trestman's Bears.

"It was a bad culture," said long snapper Patrick Mannelly, the all-time leader in games played for the Bears. "Wrong fit, wrong players at the wrong time with the wrong head coach. Just a bad mix from top to bottom. It just didn't work. Marc let things go on that probably shouldn't. He let people, like Brandon Marshall, be too much, too loud, too opinionated when we shouldn't be hearing his opinion. We should probably be hearing another player's opinion.

"I don't think it helped to have the carryover that we did from Lovie to Marc. It didn't transition well with Lance Briggs and Charles Tillman. That's tough. They respected the hell out of Marc when he comes in as a head coach. But it just was not a good mix between head coach and that locker room."

Cutler didn't become an All-Pro under Trestman. But the worst of it was the demise of the defense. After being one of the NFL's best in 2012, the Bears had their two worst statistical defenses of all time in 2013 and 2014 under defensive coordinator Mel Tucker, who was forced to run Smith's Cover 2 defense.

"We still had a lot of talent," said Mannelly, who played for Trestman in 2013. "That's the one thing. We had a lot of talent and we went what 8–8 [in 2013] and lost in the final game and got our asses kicked by the Eagles in the second to last game, and then knowing we had to win one of two to get in, and we didn't. That was disappointing. We should had been a lot better than we were. Then it just went downhill. That mix of player and coaching different just didn't work."

Briggs, a holdover from Smiths' era, played coach after practices in an effort to correct what linebackers coach Tim Tibesar was installing. It was just another sign of the mixed messages. It was all off. It started with Emery's decision to end negotiations with future Hall of Fame linebacker Brian Urlacher by sending out a press release during the NFL owners meetings on March 21, 2013. It not only infuriated players but staff members.

Overall, Trestman and Emery had a different way of dealing with veterans. For some players, the shock and feelings from Smith's firing never wore off, because it was never addressed. Instead, the locker room was reorganized; the music was turned off. Many of the fun games that players enjoyed amongst themselves under Smith were no more.

"There's a way that guys grew up in the NFL," said kicker Robbie Gould, who spent both seasons under Trestman. "I think Lovie and Marc were two completely different guys, had two completely different philosophies on football. Obviously, one was on offense, one was a defensive-minded guy. Not to say that either of those were the right way. But I think guys grew up in an atmosphere of having fun and we had a lot of success early on. The next thing you know, you can't get your haircut in the building. There is no music in the locker room. There was just all these rules that came into play that had really nothing to do with how were successful.

"But you had to respect the rules because that was their locker room. It's their regime, right? I think change is difficult for people. And I think at times it was hard to understand why until you could kind of see the whole story and understand why we're doing what we were doing. I think that took a little bit of time for people to get adjusted, from Marc to Lovie and from Phil to Jerry."

The absence of Urlacher loomed. He was the leader of Smith's Bears and the beloved face of the franchise. Instead, Marshall, Bennett, and others were given a voice. It would have been tough for any coach to handle, but close observers clearly saw Trestman struggle with it.

"His message resonated at the beginning and then the more strong-willed players like Brandon Marshall, all of a sudden they took over and they saw what they can do and they saw that they could run over this guy," Potash said. "He built the wrong culture because he just wasn't strong enough. Everything dissipated."

A once-proud franchise was no longer that. In the news conference announcing the firings of Trestman and Emery, chairman

George McCaskey said that his mother, team owner Virginia, was "pissed off" by what transpired during the 2014 season. Everything had to change. Some players realized from the start that it wouldn't work.

"We were forced fed somebody who had a different type of leadership style for who we had in the locker room," Mannelly said. "I think a Bruce Arians, with the way he's kind of straightforward, would have fit perfect. But it was just not a good mix. Marc is a super nice man, and I respect him as a human and all that stuff, but it was just not a good fit for him or us."

30

MATT AND RYAN

The itinerary that general manager Ryan Pace set for his coaching search was jam-packed. With chairman George McCaskey and team president Ted Phillips as Pace's company, the Bears would meet with six coaches in five days.

It would start on January 3, 2018, two days after John Fox was officially fired after three disappointing and uninspiring seasons. Bears defensive coordinator Vic Fangio—who had become close with Pace because of their work ethic—would be first in the Wrigley Room of Halas Hall.

After that, it became a whirlwind—literally.

Thursday: Vikings defensive coordinator George Edwards at the Westin Edina Galleria in Minnesota.

Friday: Vikings offensive coordinator Pat Shurmur at the same Westin in the morning; Patriots offensive coordinator Josh McDaniels at the Renaissance Patriot Place Hotel in Foxborough, Massachusetts, in the afternoon.

Saturday: Eagles quarterbacks coach John DeFilippo at the Rittenhouse Hotel in Philadelphia.

Sunday: Chiefs offensive coordinator Matt Nagy at the Raphael Hotel in Kansas City, Missouri.

In order to make it all work, the Bears chartered a jet. Getting from Minneapolis to Foxborough had its difficulties. The winter storm known as the "Bomb Cyclone" that winter limited their options to a small airfield in New Hampshire. Pace was a seasoned scout. Traveling wasn't a problem for him, but this was the worst flight Pace had ever been on. Phillips glasses flew from his face as the plan shook. But the Bears—specifically Pace—had a plan to keep, a new coach to find.

"As the plane is coming to a halt, Ted yells at me, 'Ryan, this better be worth it!'" Pace said in a story in the *Chicago Sun-Times*.

It was. The Bears didn't hire McDaniels; their search continued. It eventually ended in Kansas City, where Pace and Nagy—who was

Pace's main target from the beginning because of extensive research—hit it off immediately.

A long interview at the Raphael Hotel turned into a long dinner at Stock Hill steakhouse with their wives, then a long night of negotiations that concluded with a long-term deal of five years.

Pace had his coach for his quarterback in Mitch Trubisky. McCaskey woke up to a text message from Phillips, who negotiated Nagy's contract with his agent, Trace Armstrong, a former defensive end for the Bears.

"Monday, January 8, 2:19 AM: Just agreed to a five-year deal for Matt Nagy," McCaskey told the *Chicago Sun-Times*. "Getting contract draft to him in [the] morning. Go Bears."

* * *

When Pace took over as the new 37-year-old face of their football operation on January 9, 2015, he asked for patience and time.

Pace would go on to hire John Fox, whom McCaskey and Phillips were interested in after working with consultant Ernie Accorsi, the former Giants general manager who worked with Fox in New York. Fox would be expected to spark a quick turnaround. But the talent just wasn't there.

"There will be a major emphasis on character, toughness, instincts, and intelligence," Pace said when he was introduced. "The most important thing is that we have an aggressive plan and we're improving."

It was a major hint of what was to come, except no one took it from Pace then.

In time, Pace's aggressive approach would turn into trades up during the draft for Trubisky, outside linebacker Leonard Floyd, safety Eddie Jackson, and running back David Montgomery. He traded two first-round picks and more to the Oakland Raiders for outside linebacker Khalil Mack a week before the 2018 season.

Pace instituted a "no regrets" way of operation. Phillips and McCaskey not only respected it because of Pace's research, but loved it. It was a bold way to run a team. It led to questions but also praise. It was just different. Some outsiders saw it as a refreshing, others as risky and disconcerting.

"It got off to obviously a rocky start," said ESPN 1000 radio host Tom Waddle, who played receiver for the Bears during the 1990s. "I'm not ashamed to say that I was critical of a lot Ryan's decisions early in his tenure."

It started with Pace's selection of receiver Kevin White in the first round in 2015. Injuries limited him to five starts over three seasons. There were a lot of swings and misses in free agency. Signing quarterback Mike Glennon, while cover for Trubisky in the draft, turned into four starts for $18.5 million during the 2017 season. He never gave Trubisky the time that Pace wanted his young quarterback to have as a rookie.

But the conversation about the Bears changed in 2018 after the acquisition of Mack. A young, up-and-coming defense had a superstar now. It was a bold move for Pace in a tenure that was full of them.

"I think the balls to make the trade for Khalil Mack was outstanding and it was in character as far as I'm concerned," said Waddle, who began his career playing for Mike Ditka. "He's a guy that if he sees and likes it—whether it's Mitchell Trubisky or it's a more proven commodity in Khalil Mack—he's going to make the big deal."

But Pace's process always required time, and he was promised it by McCaskey and Phillips after general manager Phil Emery's quick fix approach imploded into mayhem. Pace's first two years were spent getting rid of talented players who also were problems. The Bears had one of the oldest rosters in the league. Receiver Brandon Marshall and tight end Martellus Bennett were traded. Defensive tackle Jeremiah Ratliff was cut after a blowup full of threats to staff members at Halas Hall. After the guaranteed portions of Jay Cutler's contract were up after the 2016 season, the Bears quarterback was released after eight seasons, too.

It was an overdue house-cleaning. Fox was needed for it, too. He was the first coach hired by the Bears with previous head coaching experience. He took the Carolina Panthers and Denver Broncos to Super Bowls.

But Fox's tenure soon became marred by conflicts, especially when the wins weren't there after his first two seasons. Longtime observers saw Fox have a falling out with Pace and Fangio. Players and other staff members did, too. Fox had an endearing charm, but he wasn't putting in the same work as others.

"He was a bridge coach," said John "Moon" Mullin, who covered the Bears for NBC Sports Chicago at the time. "It didn't end well, obviously. Things went sideways with Pace and Fangio."

Fox was on the hotseat during the 2017, especially after Pace drafted Trubisky. Pace didn't tell Fox about his intention to select Trubisky until the day of the draft. Fox was known for his socializing, especially during the NFL scouting combine. Pace wasn't going to let anyone blow his cover and true goals for the 2017 draft. He wanted to find his quarterback. In a matter of months, it would be time for Pace to find his next coach through his own search—an opportunity he always was going to get from McCaskey and Phillips.

As Fox's tenure played out, spats with media members who had covered the team for years before him became commonplace. The conflict felt instantaneous, too. He changed long-standing rules for covering his team starting in training camp.

"I lost my love of football covering John Fox," said ESPN 1000 reporter Jeff Dickerson, who started covering the Bears in 2004. "I love football. I loved being around people who played the game at the highest level. It was so interesting to learn the game. I was so thankful that there were people along the way that would take the time, not just to me, but everyone, to explain the game of football. Then that guy showed up. And honest to God, I never felt like that our job was a nine-to-five job until that guy took over. He ruined it for everybody. He ruined any sort of love of the game."

Those are harsh words, but Dickerson wasn't alone in his sentiments. Those who worked at Halas Hall experienced it as well. For some, getting past the two-year run of coach Marc Trestman and general manager Phil Emery would require even more time and someone more than Fox. Halas Hall lacked buzz and inspiration. The Bears need a coach who could provide it.

"I look at his tenure as a colossal waste of everyone's time," Dickerson said "As crazy as it was under Trestman and Phil, that was the worst it has ever been, when John Fox was here. I think the dwindling attendance shows you the fans felt the same exact way. If we could have stayed home, we would have stayed home, too. Because you learned nothing, you gained nothing, he built nothing, he stood for nothing."

* * *

Two days after the 2019 regular season, Phillips and McCaskey were standing in familiar spots in the PNC Center at Halas Hall.

While McCaskey answered questions in front of a collage of photographs that formed the Bears logo, Phillips did the same near a lighted Bears sign. It's close to where Phillips answered questions about Fox's hiring and then Fox's firing.

"We were 12–4 just a year ago," Phillips said that day. "We had the Coach of the Year, the Executive of the Year. They haven't lost their abilities, and we haven't lost the talent level. We've just got to be able to maximize it better this coming season."

The 2018 season was a special one. The Bears had the NFL's best defense and quarterback Mitch Trubisky showed considerable progress in his second season with Nagy as his coach. As Pace hoped, their connection worked. The Bears made the playoffs for the first time since 2010.

"The hope was there," McCaskey said then. "The Bears were back."

They weren't, though, at least not fully. The Bears went 8–8 in 2019. Nagy's 20 wins still are the most in the first two years for any coach in franchise history. But Nagy's offense was significantly worse in 2019—so was Trubisky. He was a rollercoaster with more downs than ups. He suffered a torn labrum in Week 4 against the Vikings in his non-throwing shoulder, but he regressed overall as Nagy's extension on the field. Trubisky went from having a 95.4 passer rating in 2018 to 83.0 in 2019. Other statistics showed the same regression, too.

Pace's tenure ultimately will be defined by what Nagy is able to get out of the quarterback position—the Bears traded for veteran Nick Foles during the 2020 off-season—but Pace built the Bears' defense into one of the best in 2018 and 2019. It includes acquiring Mack; signing defensive lineman Akiem Hicks, linebacker Danny Trevathan, and cornerbacks Kyle Fuller and Prince Amukamara; and drafting Floyd, Jackson, defensive tackle Eddie Goldman, and linebacker Roquan Smith. Pace's connection with Fangio was the primary reason that Nagy was able to retain him for one season before he left to be the Denver Broncos' head coach in 2019.

Beyond the wins and playoff appearance against the Eagles, Nagy's first two years already felt considerably different than Fox's and Trestman's to those who covered the team. The Bears fell well short of their own expectations, but Nagy never lost his locker room during their 8–8 season.

"He wants to relate to the players, but he can also be in charge," Dickerson said. "I think he's a great people person. I think people genuinely like him. That's important. People in the building like him. It wasn't as smooth [in 2019] as it was the year before. But the guy is smart. If there is a guy who I would think to myself, if I had a multi-billion dollar business and I've set up all my rules where I've got one person who is the public spokesperson for the company, he's a great choice for that."

In Nagy, Pace saw the perfect leader for his young, overhauled team. A new culture started with the players that Pace acquired, then improved because of Nagy. "Club Dub" was an example of it during the 2018 season as the Bears celebrated their victories. It was organic. But not everybody is going to fit into it, player or coach. And the odds are, any additions to it you won't see coming from Pace.

"He's a silent assassin," Bears radio play-by-play broadcaster Jeff Joniak said. "He's got that big smile on his face. He wants the building to be positive. He doesn't want long faces around the building. It doesn't matter what department you're in. But you talk about competitive, holy smokes. That guy is competitive—and he's just going for it. He goes for it all the time. It took him awhile to get the types of people he wants in that organization and he has never varied on what he wants. Everything hasn't worked, but he's looking for very specific people."

31

BRETT AND AARON

The Detroit Lions have their curse of Bobby Layne, but so do the Bears. It's how longtime beat writer John "Moon" Mullin would describe the disparity in quarterback play between the Bears and Green Bay Packers.

In 1948, Bears owner George Halas traded Layne, a record-setting quarterback in college who was originally acquired from the Steelers, to the New York Bulldogs for two draft picks and $50,000.

Layne would eventually end up with Lions; win championships in 1952, 1953, and 1957; and become a Hall of Famer before being traded to the Steelers in 1958—which started the Lions' own version of the curse.

But at least, the Lions drafted Matthew Stafford. Instead of having an heir apparent for Sid Luckman, the Bears entered quarterback purgatory, regardless of who was running the team, and essentially never left it.

"This is not a new problem," said Mullin, who had a long career covering the Bears for *Daily Herald*, *Chicago Tribune*, and NBC Sports Chicago. "Maybe, this is a curse of Bobby Layne. They gave him away basically for fifty-grand because they needed some money. The Red Sox had the curse of the Bambino. Maybe this is the curse of Bobby Layne. You'll be sorry and I mean forever."

Halas would later describe the trade as "my biggest blunder" in his own autobiography, *Halas by Halas*. But he's not alone when it comes to quarterbacks. More blunders—or call them swings and misses— would occur for the Bears after Halas stepped away and let others run his team.

"It's the hardest position in all of sports to play at a high level," said former Bears receiver Tom Waddle, now a radio host for ESPN 1000 in Chicago. "It's hard to find that guy. It's hard to find that guy and then have that guy excel."

"It's night and day"

On fourth-and-8 from the Bears' 48 with 46 seconds remaining in what was essentially a playoff game in Week 17 against the Bears at Soldier Field, Packers quarterback Aaron Rodgers took advantage of a blown coverage in the secondary.

Safety Chris Conte didn't stick with receiver Randall Cobb in man coverage, instead he settled at the first down marker in zone coverage. With defensive end Julius Peppers in his face, Rodgers hit Cobb for a 48-yard touchdown and a 33–28 lead. Bears quarterback Jay Cutler threw an interception to Packers cornerback Sam Shields as time expired to end the game.

It was almost poetic. The Bears fired Lovie Smith before that season and hired Marc Trestman. The franchise was finally going to morph from a defensive-oriented team into an offensive one. Better late than never in the era of quarterbacks.

But it didn't work. In that season, the Bears also had the "Shea McClellin Game." In Week 9 at Lambeau Field, McClellin sacked Rodgers on the Packers' opening possession and broke his collarbone. The Packers went 2–4–1 without Rodgers, but he returned in Week 17 against the Bears and led his team back into the postseason for the fifth consecutive year.

The Bears' history isn't complete without mentioning the Packers, who likely wouldn't exist without Halas' foresight and willingness to share money with them. The rivalry between the two teams has evolved over generations. But everything shifted in Green Bay's favor starting in 1992. That's when Brett Favre took over under center.

"It's not that Favre was better, that Aaron Rodgers was better than the Bears quarterbacks," said Bob LeGere, who started covering the Bears for the *Daily Herald* in 1992. "It's night and day. It's the string of horrible quarterbacks that [the Bears] had, guys who started games. There were guys who literally that we could tell from watching them play that they didn't deserve to be in the NFL, let alone starting at quarterback for the Chicago Bears."

In Green Bay, the Packers replaced a Hall of Fame quarterback with another one. With a sweep of the Bears during the 2019 season, the

Packers increased their lead in the all-time series to 99–95–6, which includes splitting two playoff games.

The Bears previously had a sizable advantage in the rivalry. But that changed with Favre, who went 23–13 against the Bears. Rodgers has been even better, posting a 19–5 mark from 2008 to 2019. The most bitter loss for the Bears is Rodgers' 21–14 victory in the NFC Championship Game in January 2011 at Soldier Field. Cutler, as everyone remembers, suffered a knee injury in the NFC Championship Game and didn't return. Rodgers went on to win Super Bowl XLV against the Pittsburgh Steelers.

"It's tough because the Packers are in your division and they go from Favre to Rodgers and you're like, 'Shit, what are we doing?'" Waddle said. "It's been frustrating. It really has.

"It's hard to explain. But... you can argue that it's the biggest reason why the Bears have not had sustainable and consistent success over the last couple of decades."

"Like a franchise malaise"

The Bears surprised the entire NFL world by trading up to draft quarterback Mitch Trubisky with the second overall pick on April 27, 2017. It was the franchise's latest attempt—this time by general manager Ryan Pace—to fix the quarterback position.

Television graphics still show the list of quarterbacks that the Bears have had, while the Packers have had Favre and Rodgers.

But forget the Henry Burrises, Craig Krenzels, Jim Millers, Chris Chandlers, and Chad Hutchinsons of the NFL world. Trubisky joined Jim McMahon (1982), Jim Harbaugh (1987), Cade McNown (1999), and Rex Grossman (2003) as a first-round draft pick by the Bears. His predecessors all failed for various reasons.

"It's almost like a franchise malaise," Mullin said. "How did the 49ers get it right with [Joe] Montana and then Steve Young? I think it's more than just luck in the draft. [Former general manager] Jerry Angelo always had self-deprecating humor about it. 'I always had trouble. I couldn't figure out offensive linemen,' because he was a [defensive] linemen. Maybe that was his way of saying I can't figure these guys out—and quarterback."

Philosophy does matter. To Mark Potash, a longtime sportswriter for the *Chicago Sun-Times*, the Packers' success started with Ron Wolf, the general manager who traded a first-round pick for Favre in February 1992. It still didn't preclude Wolf from drafting Ty Detmer in the ninth round.

Wolf made selections of quarterbacks a habit. It was his philosophical belief to keep adding them. Quarterbacks always had value, whether they became backups or trade bait. Wolf had Favre, but he also drafted Mark Brunell, Jay Barker, Kyle Wachholtz, Ronnie McAda, Matt Hasselbeck, and Aaron Brooks. Brunell and Hasselbeck went on to be Pro Bowl quarterbacks for the Jacksonville Jaguars and Seattle Seahawks, respectively. Brooks was the Saints' starter for 84 games, including two in the postseason.

"It's an organizational thing," Potash said. "The disparity between the Bears and the Packers is an organizational thing."

Of course, the Packers found their true heir for Favre in 2005 when general manager Ted Thompson selected Rodgers with the 24th overall pick. Rodgers sat for three seasons behind Favre before becoming their starter.

Angelo, the Bears' GM, drafted running back Cedric Benson fourth overall that year and quarterback Kyle Orton in the fourth round. Orton started 15 games that season for an injured Rex Grossman, the 22nd overall pick in 2003.

"Just their, whatever you want to call it, gumption to take Aaron Rodgers when they had Favre going pretty strong," Potash said. "Those are the things that the Bears don't do—literally, not what they do. They wouldn't even pick a quarterback if they had a bad quarterback."

Those swings add up. Angelo acquired Cutler in a blockbuster trade with the Denver Broncos in 2009. But the only quarterback drafted with Cutler on the roster was David Fales in the sixth round in 2014. Angelo didn't make it, either. His replacement, Phil Emery, did.

"It was always frustrating," Bears radio play-by-play broadcaster Jeff Joniak said. "You had a lot of great players come through, really impressive players. But that position is still one. That's the one that still makes the biggest difference in the entire sports world.

"Yeah, there were some very rough years. Even Rex, he had a great start to that '06 season, and I just remember the times that he got injured over the course of his career, just the fear, the disbelief and anger a little bit from the front office as they put a lot on his shoulders to be the guy. Same with Jay. It just never materialized like you thought it would."

32

SID LUCKMAN

For 10 years, Sid Luckman was more than a former Bears quarterback and local celebrity to Larry Mayer. Luckman was Mayer's "in"—as in *into* Soldier Field to watch Bears games.

"Right across the street from Oak Street Beach, right on the curve there, there is a building called the Carlyle, really fancy condos," Mayer said. "[*Chicago Sun-Times* columnist] Irv Kupcinet lived there. John Johnson, who started Johnson Publishing Company, lived there and Sid Luckman lived there. He became friends with my grandmother. She was the building manager. That was her title. He got me season tickets."

Luckman didn't put Mayer and his family in the nosebleeds for the some of the best years in team history, either.

"It was great years," Mayer said. "We started when we were actually on folding chairs on the field. I sat on the 10-yard line literally on the field."

There were unforgettable parties in Luckman's condo, too. As a teenager, Mayer made sure to stop in his grandmother's building to see who was coming and going.

"You'd see ex-Bears there," Mayer said. "I remember Ed Vrdolyak walking in. Anybody who was anybody in Chicago knew [the party]. Sid Luckman was a great guy."

Luckman was a great quarterback, too. Mayer knew that then because his father would tell him all about it. But Mayer also has covered the Bears since 1992. He started writing and working for the Bears' official website in 2000.

"I obviously never saw him play," Mayer said. "But I was very into research. I knew he was the best quarterback. And he wasn't just a great quarterback. He revolutionized the NFL. I don't think he gets enough credit for it. Back in the [1930s], the quarterback didn't touch the ball as much as the running back. When they would get the snap, the running back would get the ball and either run or pass."

It changed with Luckman, whom Bears owner/coach George Halas envisioned as a game-changing player for the T formation offense that Halas and assistant Clark Shaughnessy designed. Halas traded end Edgar "Eggs" Manske to the Pittsburgh Steelers [then known as the Pittsburgh Pirates] for the second overall pick in 1939, which was used on Luckman, a star tailback at Columbia University in New York. The only problem was that Luckman was considering a life without football at the time. He was interested in the trucking business.

During his recruitment of Luckman, Halas had dinner with him and his wife in New York, where he presented a $5,500 contract.

"You and Jesus Christ are the only two people I would ever pay this to," Halas told Luckman, according to the Bears' centennial scrapbook.

It worked. On July 24, 1939, Halas signed Luckman in Chicago. The *Chicago Daily Tribune* called it "Luckman's Lucky Day" the following day. Luckman also was named to the college all-star team which would play an exhibition against the New York Giants, the reigning NFL champions.

"I'm going to like Chicago," Luckman said then. "You do big things in a hurry around here. Take a young drug store cowboy from Brooklyn and in one short day sign him to an attractive contract with one of the best big league teams, sell him the city and then wind up inviting him to take part in football's greatest game. I'm not being kidded, am I?"

It took years for Luckman to transform into the quarterback he's remembered as. Stories about his diligence and work habits were included in his own autobiography and ones about Halas. But that day in 1939 truly was the start of something special.

Luckman became the most valuable player in 1943 and led the Bears to four championships in 1940, 1941, 1943, and 1946. The Bears became known as the Monsters of the Midway during that decade of dominance, and Luckman became the greatest of them all. He was the Bears' quarterback during their 73–0 victory—arguably the famous final score in all of sports—against the Washington Redskins in the 1940 title game. Luckman's career average of 8.4 yards per passing attempt is the second-best mark in NFL history.

"He revolutionized football with the way he could throw the ball and run the ball," Mayer said. "He won four championships in seven years. Imagine if a Bears quarterback had done that at any other point in team history. He'd be revered. It's sacrilegious to say he'd be more popular than Walter Payton but think if any big quarterback could have done what he did."

* * *

On November 9, 2015, quarterback Jay Cutler rolled to his right on a play-action play from the San Diego Chargers' 1 on a first-down play in the second quarter on *Monday Night Football*. Tight end Martellus Bennett was wide open for the touchdown.

"That touchdown pass just put Jay Cutler ahead of Sid Luckman as the all-time touchdown passing machine in Bears history," ESPN analyst Jon Gruden said during the broadcast.

It was Cutler's 138th touchdown pass for the Bears. Luckman retired after the 1950 season with 137 after 11 years in the NFL.

"A record has been on the books for 72 years, the all-time leader in passing touchdowns," ESPN broadcaster Mike Tirico said. "Certainly, the eras have changed significantly. But the Bears haven't had somebody that long to throw that many scores."

As special as Luckman was for the Bears, the problem is that his legacy has endured. Cutler did what Jim McMahon, Jim Harbaugh, Cade McNown, and Rex Grossman weren't able to do. He had enough longevity to rewrite the Bears' record books. But that's also part of the problem. Cutler left the Bears with 52–52 record, including the playoffs. He didn't win anything.

"The Bears leader in yards, touchdowns, everything, is one of the most, I wouldn't say reviled… it's Jay Cutler, one of the most maligned quarterbacks in Bears history," said longtime *Chicago Sun-Times* sportswriter Mark Potash.

"It's not some guy who is idolized, revered by the fanbase, and that just says it all. The Bears' quarterback is maligned."

The Bears are known for their stars at linebacker and running back but also their failures in finding their quarterback—a longstanding issue that spans different general managers and coaches and different eras and generations. The rival Packers had their Luckman in Bart Starr, but later found Brett Favre and Aaron Rodgers. Erik Kramer holds the Bears' single-season records for passing yards and touchdowns with 3,838 and 29 in 1995. But the Bears still didn't advance to the postseason that season.

"How often does that happen?" Potash said. "Their single-season record of 29 touchdowns and 3,800 yards was not only a non-playoff year but a disappointing year. That was just where they couldn't finish. They were in all sorts of games and they finished 9–7."

* * *

On May 24, 1983, Halas wrote Luckman a letter. In it, he said he loved Luckman with all his heart. The two had formed a father-son relationship over their years together. It included Luckman being a quarterbacks coach for the Bears and later a team executive. In October of that year, Halas passed away.

"You added a luster to my life that can never tarnish," Halas said in the letter which is in the Bears' centennial scrapbook. "My devoted friend, you have a spot in my heart that NO ONE else can claim."

Luckman was more than a quarterback. He was an enduring and endearing team legend. It's always been that way, too. It will take a quarterback who is truly special to match what he means in the long history of the Bears. It will take winning more than one championship. McMahon already did that.

Luckman even fit the Bears' history of playing great defense. He was a standout defensive back in an era in which players played both ways. But Luckman was so good, so valuable, and so beloved by Halas and his family that his defensive success remains a mere footnote is his story.

"He had 17 interceptions as a defensive back," Mayer said. "He has the same number of interceptions as Mike Brown. Think about that. [Safety] Mike Brown is considered one of the best defensive playmakers in Bears history. No one ever says a word about Sid Luckman playing defense, but he had some important interceptions. You could make an argument that he was one of the best all-time, all-around players ever."

33

THE PUNKY QB

During the dog days of training camp in Platteville, Wisconsin—when coach Mike Ditka berated and barked at all his players to get after it on hot days—members of the Bears' offensive line felt fortunate that they had quarterback Jim McMahon.

"For me, he was kind of a nice distraction during training camp," center Jay Hilgenberg said. "We were getting screamed at a lot by Ditka and stuff like that where McMahon could just do something to really bug Ditka just so easily. It all kind of made us all kind of happy. It was kind of a circle, too."

As in, it always happened. It was McMahon. One of his greatest gifts was his ability to poke and prod Ditka, his mercurial coach and the former star tight end for the Bears' last title-winning team in 1963. No one did it better than the self-proclaimed "Punky QB." It took an icon to take on an icon.

"He was kind of the most unique guy that I ever played with up until that point," said guard Tom Thayer, who became the Bears' radio analyst after his playing career. "All the quarterbacks that I played with, they had this serious demeanor, just total football dedication, no nonsense style to them....

"Now all of a sudden I got Jim McMahon, who comes in with a big dip underneath his lip, is kind of a sarcastic personality about him but is not afraid to have uber amounts of fun and challenge the coach's personality and say fun things to him."

On McMahon's first day as a Bear, he arrived in a black limousine, an open beer in his hand, the rest of his six-pack under his arm, and a wad of chewing tobacco in his bottom lip.

In the coming years, McMahon would moon a television helicopter and wear a headband that said "Rozelle" after NFL commissioner Pete Rozelle said he couldn't wear one that said "Adidas." There would be more, too. He came out with his own autobiography in 1986 in which he ripped the Bears' ownership when he was still playing for the Bears.

But all of fit the wildness of the Bears of the 1980s.

"Wearing stuff. Defying the commissioner. I see echoes of it in all these athletes are doing now," said longtime sportswriter Rick Telander, who covered McMahon's Bears teams for *Sports Illustrated*. "Even though the Bears didn't necessarily have a cause, they were tugging at the reins of responsibility and of the man and the organization and the things you were supposed to do—authority. They were not going to just let authority tell them what to do. If we win, screw you."

In many ways, McMahon was the eye of the storm. It worked for the Bears, who had plenty of different characters, starting with Ditka, during those days.

* * *

On page 161 of the Bears' centennial scrapbook, the greatest draft miss in team history is explained. In 1979, the Bears planned to take Notre Dame quarterback Joe Montana with their third-round pick. Jerry Vainisi, the Bears' treasurer at the time, even moved Montana's name to their draft board once the 66th overall pick came up.

But general manager Jim Finks—the chief architect of the 1985 Bears—had second thoughts. The Bears had Mike Phipps, Bob Avellini, and Vince Evans at quarterback. The Bears, it was argued, needed depth at running back behind Walter Payton

So Montana's name was removed from the Bears' draft board. Instead, Georgia running back Willie McClendon was selected. The 49ers later drafted Montana with the final pick in the third round. As everyone knows, he went one to be one of the greatest quarterbacks of all time.

"I was stunned," Vainisi said, according to the scrapbook.

Three years later, the Bears took McMahon with the fifth overall pick out of Brigham Young.

"I wanted to be known as the best college quarterback ever, and now I want to be known as the best quarterback who ever played in the NFL," McMahon said when the team introduced him after the draft that year.

Over the years, McMahon's antics became more memorable than his play, but they shouldn't be. He didn't get along with every teammate—far from it—but they still remember the confidence they all felt when McMahon was in their huddle. He didn't become the Bears' long-term answer at quarterback, but the Bears still were better when he played, winning 46 of the 61 games that he started. He'll forever be the quarterback from the Bears' first Super Bowl–winning team.

"He brought a certain attitude and brashness and leadership to the offense that the quarterback position has to have," said safety Gary Fencik, "and that we were so sorely lacking in that from the time I came in 1976 to really Jim became the quarterback in '82. He was very confident. Players really liked him on both sides of the ball. You just believed that this guy was going to win. And he was really competitive in trying to do that."

It showed on the field, perhaps too much. His style, while effective and endearing to the fan base, was still considered reckless by Ditka and even those who covered the team. McMahon never completed a full 16-game season. During the Bears' Super Bowl–winning season in 1985, he appeared in 13 games in the regular season, starting 11 of them. It also the only season that McMahon was named to the Pro Bowl.

McMahon's injuries and lack of availability are often considered the top reasons why the Bears didn't become a dynasty during the 1980s. Hall of Fame defensive lineman Dan Hampton became an outspoken critic of McMahon when they played together and especially later after their careers ended. The Bears needed McMahon, who threw for 11,203 yards, 67 touchdowns, and 56 interceptions over his seven seasons with the Bears.

"I don't want to disparage all the quarterbacks that we had before because all in their own ways, they obviously wanted to win and they were talented," Fencik said. "But there was just something, when you see a special player, whether it's defensively or offensively—like a Walter Payton—you recognize it. For myself, when you're on that sideline in the fourth quarter and you need a touchdown, you really had a belief that Jim and that offense was going to come through."

* * *

In the years since his father died from cancer in 1999, Jarrett Payton routinely hears from members of the '85 Bears. They check in on him and his sister, Brittney, as if they were their own flesh-and-blood family. It's especially true around the anniversary of Walter Payton's death on November 1.

"Jim McMahon, he's another one," said Jarrett Payton, who became a sports broadcaster for WGN in Chicago after his own playing career. "He's one of the best guys that keeps up with me. And people are like, 'What?' If you would had told me that when my dad passed, I'd be like 'Jim's going to hit me up? And call me? And make sure I'm good?' Anytime that he switches his phone, he sends me his new phone number. We connect through Instagram and Twitter. We're always going back and forth. So I'm very grateful for him as well."

Once a Bear, always a Bear. When Mitch Trubisky made reservations for his secret dinner with the Bears brass before the 2017 draft, he did so under the name of "James McMahon."

"Most people don't realize, but [McMahon] got another ring with the Packers," said Hub Arkush, the publisher of *Pro Football Weekly* and former Bears radio broadcaster. "But once they traded him inside of a year or two, he became a 10-year backup."

The Bears traded him to the Chargers on August 18. 1989, turning to Mike Tomczak (and Jim Harbaugh) that season, but ultimately kicking off the franchise's next quarterback search. It was the end result of his deteriorating relationship with Ditka.

"He believes he can win with anybody. It's his coaching that gets it done," McMahon said after the trade, according to the *Chicago Tribune*. "Now I don't have to deal with that anymore and I feel very relieved. I feel sorry for the rest of the guys who have got to put up with it."

It was a fitting end. On the same day, teammates bemoaned what would be missed. Great times—parties, headlines, antics—were remembered. And decades later, it still continues. No quarterback played better for Ditka or got to him more. It's truly a unique legacy to have.

"He was not controversial, but he was just not afraid to bring fun in the locker room," said Thayer, who was McMahon's teammate for four seasons. "And I think it was important for us because we needed the levity. We were a super-serious football team and Jim kind of showed us that it was okay to have a little fun along with the preparation."

McMahon had a little fun at the very end, too. He was Brett Favre's backup during the 1996 season, when the Packers fittingly defeated the New England Patriots in Super Bowl XXXI. It was 11 years to the day of the Bears' own Super Bowl win.

When the Packers were invited to the White House to celebrate, McMahon showed up in his Bears jersey. The "Punky QB" struck again. The '85 Bears weren't honored until President Barack Obama was in office.

"We were the team that had the most fun that won—we did," McMahon said during the Bears' centennial celebration. "We had a great time. We had a great time together."

34

TOM WADDLE

Tom Waddle can still remember the play and throw from quarterback Jim Harbaugh in Week 1 of the 1991 season against the Vikings at Soldier Field.

"Later in the first half, there were thirty-some seconds left," Waddle said. "I was in and Harbaugh threw me a deep pass and I caught it and bounced into the end zone for a touchdown. We ended up winning the game 10–6. So it was really a meaningful play. It was my first real contribution to the organization in a meaningful way."

During the celebration and in the middle of all handshakes afterward on the field, Waddle ran into coach Mike Ditka. It was the perfect time to share a moment with the Super Bowl–winning coach.

Waddle had first joined the team in 1989 as an undrafted free agent after he became the all-time leading receiver at Boston College. It took Waddle years to earn playing time and now he'd just scored his first touchdown in the NFL—a highlight-reel, full-extension diving score down the right sideline in a tight game against a rival.

"I remember Coach Ditka came over to me and kind of put his hand on my shoulder and after cutting me three or four times and said, 'I always knew you could do it, kid. Way to go,'" Waddle said. "I still remember it being really emotional. I kind of ducked my head in this kind of sappy way and started to say, 'Coach, thank you so much for giving me this opportunity. You're the only guy in the league that believed in me. I promise you that if you continue to believe in me, I'll keep playing hard for you. I don't know how much I could do for you but you know...'

"I went through this 30-second diatribe of pledging my heart and soul to Ditka. I looked up and he was like 30 yards away running into the locker room. I'm spilling my guts to somebody who I thought was still there and wasn't there."

That is Waddle's "Mike Ditka story," and Waddle has plenty of them from playing for the Bears legend. You might have heard several of them on the radio airwaves of ESPN 1000 as Waddle became a legend in his own right in Chicago after his playing career.

"You know why? Because Tom is one of the most genuine, sincere persons I've ever met," said Jeff Dickerson, who started covering the Bears for ESPN Radio since 2004. "Tom is a friend to everyone. I don't think Tom Waddle has an enemy, not that I'm aware of. I just think the guy is so relatable. He sort of laughs about his career, which there is nothing to laugh about. He was a very good player."

* * *

Marc Silverman once received a Tom Waddle No. 87 jersey as a birthday present. So even though, it might sound as if the ESPN 1000 radio host is patronizing his longtime on-air partner, he's not. Silverman grew up in the Chicago suburbs rooting for Waddle and the Bears.

"He was, at that time, my favorite player," Silverman said. "He represented all of us. It's so cliché but he wasn't the biggest, he wasn't the strongest. He was cut all the time; he kept coming back. He was just symbolically Chicago."

It was Waddle's blue-collar demeanor that endeared him to fans, to Ditka and the remaining members of the Bears' beloved 1985 team. Waddle didn't start a game until this third season, but he worked and developed. He led the Bears with 44 catches and 552 receiving yards in 1993, which was the first season with coach Dave Wannstedt.

The only reason that Waddle was signed by the Bears in the first place was because the team wanted North Carolina receiver Randy Marriott. Waddle's agent, Brad Blank, represented them both. Blank forced Bill Tobin, the Bears' director of player personnel, into a multi-player deal.

"He said to Bill Tobin, I'll make sure Randy Marriott signs with you if you take Waddle," Waddle recalled. "We were kind of like this package deal."

Marriott never played in a regular season game for the Bears. Waddle, on the other hand, caught 185 passes for 2,262 yards and 10 touchdowns (including playoffs) over six seasons. It included making a team-best nine catches for 104 yards and a touchdown in the Bears'

17–13 loss against the Cowboys in the wild-card round on December 29, 1991.

When Waddle first joined the Bears in 1989, he walked into a locker room full of legends. Jim McMahon was still the quarterback. The offensive line still had Jay Hilgenberg, Mark Bortz, Tom Thayer, and Keith Van Horne. The defense was still led by linebacker Mike Singletary and linemen Richard Dent, Dan Hampton, and Steve "Mongo" McMichael.

"These were all guys who were obviously Bears superstars and stars that were recognizable," Waddle said. "You talk about a surreal experience. Walking into that meeting room the first time in '89 with all those accomplished famous people was pretty unbelievable.

"Especially for me as an undrafted free agent, it was purely speak when spoken to. I was scared death to even say a word. I didn't say much. That was nothing really for me to say other than yes sir, no sir."

But with all of them and Ditka, there was a hard-working, demanding culture, one that fit Waddle well, even if he began his career on the practice squad.

"What was really cool for me is the one thing that I could guarantee was no one was ever going to outwork me," Waddle said. "I mean everyone was going to outrun me and outjump and out-other stuff. But I practiced really hard and I earned the respect of all of those guys, especially the defense. The offense as well, but [it was] going against those guys."

Practicing against a defense led by the three future Hall of Famers in Singletary, Dent, and Hampton made Waddle more than battle-tested.

"I earned the respect of those guys because of how hard I played and how I practiced," Waddle said. "They became advocates of mine, too, which is something I'm always going to be very proud of."

* * *

On June 7, 2012, ESPN 1000 announced that Bears quarterback Jay Cutler would be joining their popular *Waddle & Silvy* show.

It not only was an indication of the show's success, but the appeal of Waddle through generations. Cutler was from nearby Santa Claus, Indiana.

"He grew up a big Waddle/Harbaugh fan," Silverman said. "That sort of got us in the door."

But when that door shut years later and Cutler moved on, *Waddle & Silvy* still worked—and worked well, like it always has. Waddle wasn't like other former Bears players who entered the media after their playing careers. He told it how it was but didn't go over-the-top bonkers.

"Waddle is the guy if you go to a party, he's the guy you want to be hanging around with," Dickerson said. "Everyone gravitates towards him because he's so much fun. He's a fun guy and he works super hard."

When Waddle played, he had a great relationship with the media, naming writers Dan Pompei, Fred Mitchell and Melissa Isaacson. By his final season, he was already on WBBM-TV/Chicago (CBS). Then came WFLD-Fox 32, WLS-TV (ABC), *Sports Central* with David Kaplan and then ESPN 1000.

Because of Waddle, Bears fans got to know Cutler—arguably the most mercurial player in organization history—better. Cutler changed off the field because of his marriage with Kristin Cavallari and the family they started—and it showed live on the air. That started with Waddle.

"I kind of decided that A: I don't have all the answers, [and] B: We ain't curing cancer," Waddle said. "We're not reinventing the wheel. And while I can be critical of the play of certain people, regardless of sport, I'm not going to veer into the world of personal criticism or get personal with it. It's been a good formula for me."

It's obviously worked. *Waddle & Silvy* is one of the most successful sports shows in Chicago radio history.

"I think [being a former player] only gets you in the door," Silverman said. "Then you have to be really good. And Waddle is really good and he's really funny. He's just naturally funny. He's got a great personality. He's one of those guys that when you go out at night that you just want to hang out with and have drinks with. And he'll out-drink you."

Waddles raised his family in the northern suburbs. For Silverman, there is now a strong friendship with one of his favorite players as a kid. Waddle once got mad at Silverman after Silverman told him about his engagement on air.

"He's sort of like my big brother in all these life moments," Silverman said.

Having been paired together with Waddle for more than a decade, Silverman, who described himself as a "typical sports dork," saw the former Bears receiver expand his knowledge of all Chicago sports. It's why he can host an everyday sports shows, while other former Bears remain relegated to football segments. Waddle can talk about everything and make it entertaining and enlightening.

"It gets you in the door being a fan favorite, but there's lots of fan favorites who tried to be in the media who don't make it," Silverman said. "I think Waddle is a great example of where hard work and what an unbelievable personality can take you."

It's the story of Waddle's professional life, which started by winning over Ditka and revered stars from the 1985 team, even if Ditka ran away from him after he scored his first touchdown.

"I'm so very blessed and fortunate to be so well received by the Chicago Bears fanbase," Waddle said. "It's a blue-collar fanbase. They appreciate a hard day's work. I think the fan base identified with me because I was an Average Joe. So I had a natural relationship with Bears fans."

35

2001

The Bears were driving in the second quarter of their first playoff game in seven years. On third-and-4 from the Eagles' 25, quarterback Jim Miller went for it. He lofted a pass into the end zone for receiver Dez White.

What happened after that essentially ended the Bears' magical 2001 season.

Eagles safety Damon Moore intercepted Miller's throw. The veteran Bears quarterback then found himself in a tussle with Hugh Douglas, a brash, physical defensive end. As Moore took off down the field, Douglas drove Miller into the frozen turf of Soldier Field, separating his throwing shoulder.

"Jim, to me, was the one quarterback who could bring the entire room together that we played with—offense, defense, special teams, coaches, the entire building," long snapper Patrick Mannelly said. "What I saw is what leadership for the quarterback should be like.

"And when he went down, it was like, 'Ohhhhh.' Jim wasn't the greatest quarterback. He'll tell you that. But he had all those intangibles—one of the smartest guys behind center that we've ever had. And when he went down. That's your star leader. You're like, 'What are we going to do? You better pick it up back up. Let's go.'"

It didn't happen. The Bears trailed by six points at the time and it eventually turned into a 33–19 loss against the Eagles in the divisional round of the playoffs. A memorable 13–3 season was over, unofficially ending when Miller was injured. He was replaced by Shane Matthews, who completed 8 of 17 passes for 66 yards and two interceptions.

"They weren't good," said Marc Silverman, a host for ESPN 1000 and former Bears reporter. "But that '01 team was one of my most favorite Bears teams of all time. It was just so fun. They had the mojo working."

It was the dramatic touchdowns that safety Mike Brown scored against the 49ers and the Browns, Matthews' Hail Mary touchdown to running back James Allen, and defensive lineman Keith Traylor's interception and long return. It was the second year of linebacker Brian Urlacher's Hall of Fame career.

"The dynamic that they had up front to let Brian sort of go to the ball and not worry about setting blocks, that defense was awesome," Silverman said. "The lucky bounces. The back-to-back San Francisco, Cleveland games. Ted Washington in the middle. The Keith Traylor interception. I have more memorable plays from that team.

"But It was Shane Matthews and Jim Miller for God's sake quarterbacking that team. We had legit hopes that they could ride that defense to the Super Bowl until Donovan McNabb sort of took them out."

In a way, it was so Bears. They won with their defense and by running the ball with Allen and rookie Anthony Thomas. But they still didn't have a quarterback.

In the 11 years that the Bears were coached by Dave Wannstedt and Dick Jauron, the 2001 season was only the second time that they advanced to the playoffs. But their magic wasn't a formula for long-term success. They were the proverbial flash in the pan. In 2004, Jauron was replaced by Lovie Smith.

"It was like magical season, but to me, it felt like a one-off season," said Mark Potash, who covered the Bears for the *Chicago Sun-Times*. "At the time it was happening, even then people knew, it was just one of those magical seasons. The victories were just so unbelievable."

The Renovation Process

As Bob LeGere, the beat writer for the *Daily Herald* from 1992 to 2018, and Larry Mayer, the Bears' longtime team website reporter, wrapped up their game stories from January 19, 2002, a wrecking ball waited for them. With the Bears now out of the playoffs, the renovation process of Soldier Field would commence—immediately.

"That was the last game at Soldier Field," Mayer said. "They had such a tight window to build the new stadium. The second that game ended, there was a ball, like a demolition ball, hitting the walls behind us. That's how fast."

"You could hear it from the press box," LeGere added. "There was a crew ripping out carpeting and taking chairs away."

The 2002 season would be spent at the University of Illinois' Memorial Stadium in Champaign. The looming renovation of Soldier Field only added to special feelings of the 2001 season. But their final sendoff was ruined by Douglas, a human wrecking ball.

"Hugh Douglas just basically picked him up by the shoulders and slammed him to the ground," Mayer said. "Now he would probably get kicked out of the game for that."

In 2019 interview with the *Philadelphia Inquirer*, Douglas essentially said the same. The NFL has changed since then. Quarterbacks are protected at great lengths nowadays.

"At the time, even Troy Aikman said in the broadcast that I did nothing illegal, because you're taught as a defensive lineman to get after the quarterback," Douglas told the *Inquirer*. "When a quarterback throws a pick... he should get off the field. I did what I was told to do, what [defensive coordinator] Jim Johnson coached us to do. Go get the quarterback. Make sure he didn't make the play."

In a way, Douglas sounded surprised that Miller was jostling with him.

"He shouldn't have tried to resist," Douglas told the *Inquirer*. "Resistance is futile."

It should be remembered as a day that the Bears were outcoached, too. Eagles coach Andy Reid's staff was loaded on the defensive side. It started with Johnson, but he also had future head coaches in Sean McDermott, Ron Rivera, Leslie Frazier, and Steve Spagnuolo as assistants. Bears first-year offensive coordinator John Shoop was outmatched.

"There was a reason we were getting out-schemed that day," center Olin Kreutz said. "It felt like they knew what we were doing. Well, it's because they knew what the hell we were doing."

Searching for *That* QB

In December 1999, Miller was suspended four games for taking an over-the-counter supplement that contained a banned substance—and it came on the heels of the best three-game stretch of his career. The

Bears went 1–2 against the Vikings, Chargers, and Lions, but he threw for 983 yards and six touchdowns and had a 101.8 passer rating in them.

"He was holding a press conference and the first thing he said is, 'You know what? I had no idea. If they say it was in there, it was in there. It's on me to know what I put in my body. They tell us to ask the trainer if we don't know,'" said LeGere, who started to laugh.

"But he said, 'You guys have seen me in the locker room. Nobody's stuffing dollar bills in my underwear.'"

Even when the Bears appeared to have a quarterback—one they liked on and off the field—they didn't. Miller, who became a radio analyst for Sirius XM after his career, was only playing because Cade McCown floundered as a first-round pick. Matthews, his backup, wasn't much better.

"Jim was cerebral," Kreutz said. "He studied the game. When you listened to him talk now, that's how Jim was. I remember Jim on the airplane. He was just taking notes, going through his book. He could see things that were coming."

But for one season in 2001, the Bears' endless search for quarterback didn't matter. Miller's stats weren't exceptional, but the Bears went 11–2 with him as their starter. The Bears won with Matthews, too.

In Week 8, Matthews threw two touchdowns in the final minute against the Browns, including his Hail Mary that was tipped by receiver David Terrell and caught by a lunging Allen as time expired to tie the game. In overtime, Brown intercepted a tipped pass from quarterback Tim Couch for a pick-six. A week earlier, he did the same against the 49ers, taking advantage of tipped pass off of the hands of receiver Terrell Owens. Urlacher was heading his way.

"It wasn't just what Mike Brown accomplished being the only player to ever do that in NFL history," Mayer said. "It was that the two games were such incredible comebacks. They were like down 27–9 in the third quarter in one game. The Cleveland game they were down 21–7 with a minute left in the game."

The second week of the 2001 season also was postponed because the terrorist attacks of 9/11. The Bears' matchup against the Jaguars was moved to January. That game's most memorable moment was Traylor tipping a pass, intercepting it, and making a thunderous 67-yard run. It helped seal the NFC Central for the Bears. The rival Packers were right behind them at 12–4.

"That culture really plays a part of a team and when you start winning and people talk about winning streaks, it makes a difference," Mannelly said. "It makes you more confident. I enjoyed going to work more. And I think when you enjoy going to work more, you work harder. And I think guys kept buying in and working harder and harder and harder. That's kind of the first time that I realized when you enjoy going to work, you're going to be a better team. That's kind of what happened then."

36

MIKE BROWN

The Bears wouldn't be who we all thought they were in 2006 without safety Mike Brown. The Bears' near-miraculous comeback against the Cardinals—the one that set off Arizona coach Dennis Green—started with him.

On second-and-10 from the Bears' 15 in the waning seconds of the third quarter, defensive end Mark Anderson had an unblocked run at quarterback Matt Leinart, sacked him, and forced a fumble.

The loose ball bounced and bounced until Brown scooped it up and walked right into the end zone. He fired the ball into the stands. It was the first touchdown scored in what ultimately became one of the most memorable victories by a Bears team in this generation.

"That was as close to the '85 Bears that I've ever seen," said longtime Bears reporter John "Moon" Mullin, who covered the Bears for the *Daily Herald*, *Chicago Tribune*, and NBC Sports Chicago.

It was an easy score, but it also was a vintage Mike Brown play. No one was surprised to see Brown in the right spot at the right time again for the Bears defense. It's what he did. When Brown was healthy, he was one of the most exciting players ever in team history.

"There's some football players who live in the matrix," longtime Bears center Olin Kreutz said. "Mike does. He sees it. You line up in a formation and he sees your play in his head. That's how fast he's playing. You can see him moving before snaps, like where's he going? That's not his responsibility. Well, he's going to the play."

The pick-sixes he scored in back-to-back games in 2001 to beat the 49ers and Browns are examples of that. So was Brown's scoop-and-score against the Cardinals five seasons later in the Bears' uncanny 24–23 victory.

It was all part of an exciting comeback on *Monday Night Football* that featured one very somber moment for the franchise. On the Cardinals' next possession after Brown's touchdown, the Bears' star suffered a tear to the Lisfranc ligament in his right foot.

It's been seemingly forgotten by outsiders that Brown and Pro Bowl defensive tackle Tommie Harris didn't play in the Super Bowl that season for the Bears against the Colts because of their injuries.

"We started to worry if we were going to make it to the Super Bowl," Kreutz said. "How many teams lose two All-Pros and make it to the Super Bowl? Tommie Harris was the best [defensive] tackle in the NFL at that time. Mike Brown was the best safety. We lost both of them. That's how talented that team was."

But everyone knows it was even better with Brown. Kreutz and linebackers Brian Urlacher and Lance Briggs would be the first to explain that to you at length. He was a second-round pick out of Nebraska in 2000, the same year that the organization took Urlacher with No. 9 overall selection. But unlike Urlacher, Brown started immediately. Brown was that good immediately, that darn smart.

"I felt like I'm pretty smart, too," Urlacher said. "Uh-uh. Mike Brown was the smartest guy on the field when he was on the field. And I'm slighting myself because I felt I'm a pretty damn smart guy on the football field. But Mike Brown knew everything that was going on all the time from Day 1 when he got there. Not Week 1. Not Week 2. From Day 1, he knew exactly what was going on all the time."

Brown was named a first-team All-Pro in only his second season, making five interceptions, which included his two pick-sixes. But injuries became part of his story starting in 2004 when he ruptured the Achilles tendon in his right leg in the second game of the season. He missed the final four games of the 2005 season because of a calf injury but was still voted to the Pro Bowl. Brown had his Lisfranc injury in 2006 and then suffered a torn ACL in the season opener in 2007 against the San Diego Chargers. He had an interception and a 27-yard return in the game, too.

"Sad is the word—and for him," Kreutz said. "That guy, no one had more passion."

In recent years, Brown has talked openly about how he still struggles with missing Super Bowl XLI.

"You play for the 'ship," Brown said during a panel discussion at the Bears 100 celebration in 2019. "You play for the ring. Our team made it and I couldn't be out there. It's the game. It's the one sport, it's one game for a championship. It's not a series. It's a game. And it's the biggest game in the world. I still struggle with it, especially when I get around all you folks [fans and media]. Like I said, now that I have children, it makes it a lot different. The past is the past and now I am looking forward to watching my children grow and be solid citizens. I am trying to teach them the right way to do things."

The best way to view Brown's place in Bears history and his impact on the teams he played for is through the lens of his teammates. He was special to them—one and off the field.

Brown was released after playing in 15 games in the 2008 season. When he left, his seven total defensive touchdowns was a team record. It was later broken by cornerback Charles Tillman. Brown's three fumble returns for scores still are the most in team history. Urlacher called Brown the Bears' best player when he was healthy.

"Always in position to make plays—always made plays," Urlacher said. "A great tackler. That dude would knock the piss out of you for 5'9", 5'10", whatever he was, he would knock the piss out of you. Good athlete. I can go on and on about Mike Brown. He was very underrated in my opinion. Our team realized how good he was, but people outside don't really understand how good he was."

Instead of seeing the star that faded because of injuries, Brown's teammates see the teammate who helped his own replacements learn and improve. They remember how he held his teammates accountable. And they remember his brilliance on the field when he played.

"He's one of the best safeties I've ever played with," Briggs said. "Smart. Physical at the point of attack. He understood angles really well. He understood where he needed to be. He understood where everybody else needed to be. He'd get you lined up. There were things about his game that are uncoachable. I wish I would've had more time with him. I wish he would've been able to play the type of career without being plagued by injuries because he would've had a Hall of Fame type of career."

But more importantly, Brown's teammates remember his passion. He was different. Everyone felt it. That's on and off the field.

"I think the best compliment you can get is when a guy walks into a room, and you're like, 'That guy is a football player, man,'" Kreutz said. "That's Mike Brown. When Mike Brown walks into the room, I tell my kids, that's a football player—there he is."

37

LANCE BRIGGS

Before the Bears played the Chargers in Week 8 of the 2019 season, the organization honored players from 2000s. And for those players, it meant hearing linebacker Lance Briggs' battle cry one more time before taking the field together.

"Lord, look at Susie," Briggs said. "She's so sweet. She got everything that Uncle John needs. Oh, I'm going to have me some fun. I'm going to have me some fun."

It's an improvised line from actor Bill Duke's character, Mac, in the movie, *Predator*. Briggs said it when his Bears took the field under coach Lovie Smith. It was a tradition.

"It's really cool," Hall of Fame linebacker Brian Urlacher said. "We did it every game. It's dumb but it's funny to us. That's all that matters."

It mattered plenty to Urlacher and other teammates because Briggs mattered plenty to the Bears' best teams from the 2000s. Most would describe Briggs as the "Robin" to Urlacher's "Batman." But that's unfair. Urlacher would argue that he wouldn't have had the same storied career without Briggs at his side for most of it. They were a dynamic duo but more like Iron Man and Captain America.

"No. 1, he's a great friend and a great teammate," Urlacher said. "Just, overall, a great guy. I think he's one of the most well-liked guys not just by me but the whole team over my career there. I mean, everyone liked Lance. He's just a good fun guy to be around. I think he was endearing to the city because of the way he played.

"That dude played hard as hell. He made plays more importantly and he did it the right way. He didn't really pop off in the media. He didn't pop off to anyone. He just went out there and played football. And he played hard. That was endearing to our fans, his teammates as well and also our coaches."

Built to Play in Chicago

Long snapper Patrick Mannelly remembers thinking that Briggs was going to mess up as one of the guards next to him on the punt team. Briggs was a rookie and seemingly out of place.

"I tell Mike Sweatman, our special teams coach, I'm like, 'This guy is going to get a punt blocked,'" Mannelly recalled. "And he goes, Patrick, it doesn't matter. This kid is going to be a hell of a linebacker and we got to get him on the field.' Low and behold, we get a punt blocked because of Lance. But Coach Sweatman was right. He became a hell of a player."

Briggs, a third-round pick from Arizona in 2003, did it rather quickly, too. He took over as a starter in Week 4 of his first season and didn't stop. He started 13 games as a rookie. By Briggs' third year—which was his second under coach Lovie Smith—he went to his first Pro Bowl and was named first-team All-Pro. He became a star as a punishing Will linebacker in Smith's defense. He went to seven consecutive Pro Bowls and also was named a second-team All-Pro in 2006 and 2009.

"He played like he never thought about the consequences of playing football," center Olin Kreutz said. "Even if you meet Lance now, he just sits there in the room and he has that look: 'If you want to do this, we can do it.' He just has that. And I think that's who he is.

"I heard someone said that [former general manager] Jerry Angelo said that he was the best short-yardage linebacker to ever play the game or in his era, and I wouldn't argue. He would just take on anybody. A lot of times you'd see the defense make a stop and Lance would have like two or three guys on him that he took on in this short-yardage situation."

Urlacher often gets mentioned in the same breath as Bill George, Dick Butkus, and Mike Singletary, but Briggs carried on the team's linebacker tradition, too. He was arguably the harder hitter of the two.

"God, dog, he could knock the daylight out of you," said cornerback Charles Tillman, who also was drafted in 2003. "He could make daylight evaporate. [Defensive coordinator Rod Marinelli] used to say, 'Make daylight evaporate' and that was something Lance Briggs had a damn PhD in. He was making daylight evaporate, separating the man from the ball."

It showed in the 16 fumbles that Briggs forced in his career. But Kreutz said everyone forgets how great of an athlete Briggs actually was because of how physical he was. Just watch him in coverage. Briggs not only broke up 84 passes in his career but had five pick-sixes.

"The thing I remember about Lance is that every game he made plays, man," Urlacher said. "Always in the right spot. He stressed me out a bunch because he didn't always start out in the right spot but he always ended up in the right spot and he always made a ton of plays for our defense."

Briggs had knack for it, even though he didn't always perform like it in practice. His teammates will tell those stories with smiles and laughter. Tillman said that linebackers coach Bob Babich often got after Briggs during practices for his mistakes.

"I say this in a kind way, not trying to diss him, but I don't think Lance was the best practice player," Tillman said. "'Bullet Bob' would be like, 'Dang it, Lance you've got to make this play' in practice. And he'd be like 'Alright, alright, I know.'

"Bullet Bob would mess Lance up with a different fake or a sneak or something like that. Sure as shit, Bullet would get him on the play and Bullet's all mad. 'Lance, come on, we just talked about this'— 'Alright, Bullet, I know.'"

Briggs simply was different when the stakes were real.

"He rarely messed up in game time," Tillman said. "He could get beat 10 times in practice and he'd be like, 'Alright, I'll get it. I'll get it.' But game time would come, you're like, 'Dang, why didn't you do that in practice?' He was a gamer. He was like a 100 percent gamer all the time. My first pick, I'm taking Lance every time. He is a true gamer. When the game is on the line and you want someone to come through a 100 percent a 100 of the time, yeah, it's Lance, man. He's coming through. That what he does."

For as hard as Briggs hit on game days, he rarely missed a game— or even snaps. From 2004 to 2012, Briggs missed only four starts. He was remarkably durable. He believed that he should be that way.

"He would come out and be stung," former Bears radio sideline reporter Zach Zaidman said. "It was almost as though he hated when the trainers came to him. It was a mark of weakness for him because he wanted to go out there. Just the relentless nature and when your best players are like that—because Urlacher was that way, too—when your two best players are like that, everyone else is going to give you that much more. That's the essence of that group."

A Fun-Loving, Smiling Force

During training camp, linebackers always had to be on guard when photographs were taken. Babich was fair game, too. But Briggs often was the target.

"He could take it as much as he could give it," Zaidman said. "Lance, he didn't look like your prototypical NFL linebacker and almost all the guys would make fun of him. They would post pictures of him at training camp when you wear the short jerseys, if you were photographed."

Teammates looked for Briggs' gut.

"If you ever went into the linebacking room at Halas Hall or in Bourbonnais back during the day, there would be all these disgusting, unflattering pictures, because Lance never looked like he was really in the best shape." Zaidman said, "and they would accentuate it."

Tilman called Briggs the "comic relief" in the Bears locker room. Kick returner Devin Hester called him "free minded." And kicker Robbie Gould said that every good team needs that. The radio belonged to Briggs in the locker room.

"He was the life of the party," Gould said. "He always kept guys in the locker room relaxed. Not only was he the deejay, but he was a guy who was always joking around, having a good time, laughing. But I think that every team has a theme or a group of guys that kind of set the stage. I would say that those guys were serious when they needed to be. But they were also able to have some fun along the way."

What Gould is getting at is that the Bears wouldn't have been the same or as good during the 2005, 2006, and 2010 seasons without Briggs. Smith's Bears always had fun—it's one way that they should be remembered—and Briggs was an integral part of it.

Briggs and Tillman shared a pregame routine of running around the field together, while it was Urlacher who told Briggs to keep calling out for "Susie" before the team took the field.

"I shredded the lines because they're not the actual lines," Briggs said. "But our guys, when I said it, they're like, 'Forget those lines. You just use your own. I remember saying it the first time and Lach was like, 'I like it. I like it, Boogie. I like it, Boogie. You're going to have to keep doing it.'"

Other players, including Tillman and defensive end Alex Brown, would be sure to get close to Briggs. In time, Smith, as modest and reserved as a coach he seemed to be, got within an earshot of Briggs, too. He would later address Briggs' beloved war call in a meeting.

"He said, 'I know when it's time to play when somebody's talking to Susie—he's talking to Susie and he's ready to have some fun,'" Briggs recalled. "It was a lot of fun."

So was Briggs' 12-year career.

38

OLIN KREUTZ

Sometimes an "Olin story" gets to Olin Kreutz. The former Bears center said he'll leave the room when some of them are brought up. He doesn't want to hear them.

"When you're some place for 13 years, like I was, there is good and bad stories about you," Kreutz said. "I understand my personality. I understand what I'm like. I understand.

"And there's some things that you do that bluntly, when you get older like me and you're 42 with six kids, that you're kind of ashamed of now. Like, 'Holy shit, I can't believe I did that stuff.' And there's things that you're proud of. But that's life."

But his teammates have different stories to share. None of them start by mentioning Kreutz' fight with fellow offensive linemen Fred Miller at a gun range that left Miller with a broken jaw. Instead, they remember the softer, human side of Kreutz. Believe it or not, he had one.

For cornerback Charles Tillman, it's how Kreutz treated him when his infant daughter, Tiana, was hospitalized because of a rare heart condition and later underwent surgery in 2008.

"Olin Kreutz is like one of the main guys checking in: 'Hey, we got our team chaplain aside. So whoever ya'll pray to. Or whatever your God is. I think we need to pray for Peanut's daughter.'

"This is Olin orchestrating all this," Tillman said. "These are the stories that you don't hear about Olin. In my opinion, Olin is one the best teammates I've ever had."

* * *

With the Bears trailing by 20 points at halftime against the Cardinals on October 16, 2006, Kreutz made a speech that even linebacker Brian Urlacher struggled with at first. The Bears began the day as undefeated, but they were in the middle of playing their worst game of the season. Urlacher not only knew it, but felt it.

"He said we're going to win this game," Urlacher said "I remember it. He goes, 'We're going to win this game! We're going to come back and we're going to win this football game!' I was like, 'Shut the fuck up.' We're down 20–0 and hopefully we can make it close and make a game out of it."

But Kreutz had a way of making you believe that you could win any game. The more Urlacher heard from Kreutz, the more prepared he became.

"We're like, 'Yeah, fuck yeah we are,'" Urlacher said. "And then [coach Lovie Smith] got on board and we went out there in the second half and we made some plays."

As every Bears fan should remember, the Bears defeated the Cardinals 24–23 that night. It became known as the "Brian Urlacher Game" because of all his tackles and his forced fumble on Cardinals running back Edgerrin James, which cornerback Charles Tillman returned for a touchdown.

Safety Mike Brown and returner Devin Hester also scored in the second half. Afterward, Cardinals coach Dennis Green went off with his "the Bears are who we thought they were" tirade.

When the Bears became Super Bowl contenders against in the 2000s under coach Lovie Smith, it was because of Urlacher, the face of the team, but also because Kreutz' leadership. The offense was never great under Smith, but the coach had someone great in Kreutz.

"In my opinion, he was the leader of our team my whole career there," Urlacher said. "He was the guy that I looked up to and I'm pretty sure most of the guys on our team looked up to. I mean, he practiced hurt. He played hurt. He was in the weight room every day. He was the first one in the building, last one to leave. Not a super vocal guy. None of our guys were really vocal when it came to getting people jacked up to play. But you knew when he said something, that you needed to respond."

* * *

An interview from Kreutz from the Bears' 25–7 loss against the Vikings on October 27, 2002 can still be found on YouTube.

In a postgame show with Dan Jiggetts, Tom Waddle, and Corey McPherrin on WFLD-Fox 32, Kreutz went through the Vikings' blitzes and his failures at center, but also was asked about his injuries and others on the offensive line.

"I'm going to be completely honest with you," Kreutz said. "I feel like 100 percent. I've got no excuse for you. I just played like shit today."

Even on live television, Kreutz had a way with words. He had standards that he held himself and his teammates to during his career. Drafted in the third round in 1998 draft, Kreutz was voted to six consecutive Pro Bowls from 2001 to 2006. He was a first-team All-Pro in 2006, the Bears' Super Bowl season, after being second-team selection a season earlier.

"He just told it how it was, and it was honest," Tillman said. "He didn't sugarcoat anything. Some people they're too sensitive, especially nowadays. People are too sensitive. They can't take that. He just told it how it was. You knew what you got when you dealt with Olin. You're going to get the brutal honest truth. I respected that. But more importantly, I respected him."

At times, Kreutz's blunt style ruffled the feathers of some teammates. He was known to get after the media, too. He read everything.

"He was truly about his players," Tillman said. "He was about those 53 guys in that locker room. If you were outside the locker room, well, yeah, I'm not going to say he didn't care about you, but he put his team first and you've got to respect that. You got to respect that. And, if you weren't pulling your weight, he didn't mind calling you out. I didn't have a problem with that. I respect that."

Smith did, too. He needed it. Smith always connected with his best players and Kreutz was no different. There were certain lines that Kreutz couldn't cross, but he was allowed to do what he did because his own mistakes were few. His work ethic was respected by his peers. Kreutz played the bully at times, but he was a beloved one.

"He's probably one of my favorite people in the locker room—my favorite teammate," fullback Jason McKie said. "He would get on you. But he would get on you, I think, to test you to make you better. I think a lot of people who couldn't understand that, they were scared of him or didn't last long, but people who understood that he was getting on you, cracking jokes or was trying to intimidate you, [it] was to make you better. His leadership role was without question. He was the bonified leader of our team. He was the heartbeat of our team by far. He demanded everybody to be great."

There were wins to celebrate and games to be had. Smith's Bears played all sorts of games that were rarely featured in print or on air.

"We had a good ass time in the locker room, man," Urlacher said. "[Kreutz] was one of the ring leaders of all the stupid games we played.

"He was a fun guy. There were sometimes that it got a little sketchy at times. But Olin was a fun, fun guy. He was one of my favorite teammates in my whole career."

* * *

On September 18, 2011, Kreutz was no longer a Bear, but he was playing them for the time as a new member of the New Orleans Saints. He remembers running into Urlacher and Lance Briggs during the game. But Larry Mayer, who has covered the Bears for their own website since 2000, vividly remembers what Kreutz did right before it.

"He gets introduced as their starting center," Mayer said. "Down in the Superdome, all their starters run out of the tunnel, run to the middle of the field, and stop. Well, Olin runs out of the tunnel and he sees at the opposite end of the field that Robbie Gould is warming up. No one is holding for him. He's got that little metal [holder] with the ball. So Olin runs the length of the field and before Robbie can kick it, he just kicks the ball away. The ball goes like flying into the wall. And Robbie is just like, 'What are you doing?' And Olin is just dying laughing. It was great."

Or there was the time that Bears and Vikings got into a large fight in 2004 in the Metrodome. It began with safety Todd Johnson's unnecessary roughness penalty for a hit on receiver Nate Burleson and ended with 15 players getting fined.

"The officials are finally breaking it up and restoring order and I'm looking down at the Bears huddle," Mayer said. "All of a sudden, I see

Olin walking on the 50-yard line by himself towards the Vikings bench and he stops about 10 feet in front of the bench and does the *Karate Kid* crane pose like he's going to kill everyone on the other team."

Now that's an "Olin story"—a good, clean, and fun one. He was one of the most colorful and beloved players from the best Bears' teams during the 2000s.

"The funny thing about the stories is that when you're telling stories about an old player or a former player, people usually exaggerate to make it funny or interesting," Mayer said. "With Olin, you almost have to go in the opposite direction so people actually believed it happened, because he did some of most outrageous, funny things that I've ever seen on the field, off the field."

His *Karate Kid* pose against the Vikings is just an example.

"I've never seen a video tape of that," Mayer said. "I don't think they got it on TV. But I saw it with my own eyes. That's just so Olin. He would take on the whole team if they wanted it. Trust me."

If you want to go, Kreutz, to this day, would be happy to oblige. It could be with his helmet back on or grappling on a mat or in the media. Kreutz became an analyst for NBC Sports Chicago and 670 The Score after his career.

"For me, it was never about like the history or Pro Bowls or the Hall of Fame," Kreutz said. "I really just liked the war. I liked the competition. I really liked really showing up. I like it now. If somebody wants to tie up now, I'd be happy to do it. Win or lose."

It's part of who Kreutz is. It's how he was raised. But there's more to him. He wasn't all fire. Sometimes he was merely supportive. That's what kicker Robbie Gould remembered about him when he missed three field goals late during the 2006 season.

"You always needed a guy that was kind of hard in the locker room because I think there are times when there are bumps and bruises, and the mentality is, 'Pack it in. I don't need to practice today,'" said Gould, the all-time leader in points. "But I also think that there was a point to him if you did screw up, he'd be the first guy to put his arm around you and be like, 'Hey, forget about it. Let's go to the next one.' I think it was my second year. I had missed a couple in a row and Olin's like,

'Who cares. Worry about the next one. That one's over with.' It really changed my mentality."

His lesser-known soft side is what some of his longest teammates will remember most and best about him. It was helping Tillman and many others. Those are stories about Kreutz that would probably make him leave the room but for different reasons. He cared. A lot.

"He was our true leader," long snapper Patrick Mannelly said. "Brian was our face and leader. Brian led by just being the most-humble superstar that I've ever been around, where Olin would lead with iron fists. But people don't know or realize that he'd pull them back in the meeting room and talk like this.

"If you had a family issue going on, people felt comfortable to go to him, to talk to him, to ask him for advice and he would take all that on. People don't realize what he did inside of that building and outside of the building with people's lives."

39

MONGO

Having spent more than 10 years together on ESPN's radio airwaves in Chicago, Jeff Dickerson has learned a few things about Steve "Mongo" McMichael. For starters, the former defensive tackle from the Bears' revered 1985 team is extremely fan-friendly.

"He said that he wants to flood the market with his autograph so when he dies it's not worth anything," said Dickerson, who has covered the Bears for ESPN radio since 2004. "The guy will sign anything for anybody anywhere anytime."

McMichael openly cheers for the Bears.

"What I like about Mongo is that Mongo isn't one of these '85 Bears that roots against the team because he just wants his appearance money to keep rolling in," Dickerson said. "He wants them to be good. He wants to share the spotlight. He's very different in that regard."

Better yet, Dickerson knows what's real and what's schtick. Sure, Mongo has seen and lived some things. Just ask him about Thailand or his professional wrestling career. But as a player for the Bears, some of the craziness was an act. The son of a schoolteacher, McMichael was highly intelligent.

"The most underrated player from the '85 Bears," Dickerson said. "Talk to anybody about Mongo, talk to all those offensive linemen about Mongo, he was the smartest defensive lineman. He knew your plays. He tried to act crazy so the other team would underestimate his intelligence.

"Don't let the act fool you. Some of it's an act. When he was playing, he'd be grunting and growling and barking like a dog and saying all kinds of crazy things and threatening your livelihood, but he did that so they would think that he was an idiot. In the meantime, he's literally calling out where these guys are going to be blocking you before the play started."

There isn't a more underrated player from the best Bears team of all time. Ask McMichael's teammates, and they'd tell you that McMichael deserves to be in the Hall of Fame. He's second in sacks in team history, trailing only defensive end Richard Dent, who was voted into the Hall of Fame in 2011. Dent has 124½ career sacks; McMichael has 92½, which is significantly more than Hall of Famer Dan Hampton, who is third with 57.

McMichael was an ideal fit for the Bears of the 1980s. It was his brashness and his bravado. It was his toughness and his talent. He played hard and you can bet that he partied hard. All of it made him a perfect fit for the Bears of the 1980s.

But he wasn't an instant success in the middle of Buddy Ryan's 46 defense. He was drafted by the Patriots in the third round in 1980, but he was cut after one season because they didn't like his choices off the field or how he tormented some of their best offensive linemen when he was on it during practices.

"They knew there were some practices where I didn't get any sleep the night before," McMichael told the *Chicago Tribune* in 1991.

"So they called me up to the office and said, 'We're releasing you because we think you are the criminal element of the league.' But it was not a bad thing, because then I came to the Bears."

Paired with Hampton in the trenches, Ryan had a nearly unstoppable tandem. They took pride in being tone-setters during practices and games. Coach Mike Ditka wanted everything to be earned in practices, and Hampton and McMichael were happy to oblige. They relished it over 10 seasons together.

Hampton was the one who gave McMichael his two long-lasting nicknames: "Mongo," after Alex Karras' character in *Blazing Saddles* and "Ming" after Ming the Merciless from the television show, *Flash Gordon*.

"Nobody laughed more than we did," Hampton said. "We wanted to be like the bad asses of the team, and in a way, we ran that team. Sometimes if we had a game where we didn't play as well as we wanted or even God forbid, we lost one, Ditka would kind of come to me and say, we need to crank it up in practice. We need to get something out of it. So Steve and I would crank it up in practice, and then the rest of the team, the next thing you know, it's like training camp. Everybody's knocking the hell out of each other. So in a way, we kind of run the team. We were kind of like the heartbeat in the sense that we felt like we were the caretakers of the team, but not only the caretakers but kind of like the enforcers. And it was cool.

"Self perception is what it is, but there is no question in my mind that Dick Butkus knew he was the king badass of all time. When he played, that's what he wanted to project. Well, we wanted to be like that, too. We wanted to project that, 'Hey, when you came in here, you had three hours of hell.' And we were going to be the tip of the spear that you're going to have to deal with, and Steve and I did that for a long time."

It worked so well. McMichael, of course, got his revenge on the Patriots in the Bears' 46–10 pummeling of them in Super Bowl XX. McMichael had one of the Bears' seven sacks on the Patriots two quarterbacks. Talk about "criminal." McMichael was voted to the Pro Bowl and named first-team All-Pro in 1985 and 1987. He was a second-team All-Pro in 1986, 1988, and 1991.

"I think Steve McMichael is the most underrated player in Bears history," said former Bears receiver Tom Waddle, who played with McMichael for five years. "If you're a defensive tackle in that league and you sack almost a hundred quarterbacks over the course of your career, I think you can make a good case to being Hall of Fame worthy."

McMichael's interviews were Hall of Fame worthy, too. He was can't miss. McMichael's postgame show on WMAQ-Ch. 5 with sportscaster Mark Giangreco became must-watch television in the late 1990s. It was entertaining and unpredictable. His Texas drawl made it only better.

"McMichael would say some things that would be censored nowadays and probably get him off the air," said Fred Mitchell, who covered the Bears for the *Chicago Tribune*. "We didn't have Twitter to follow like you guys do now and all the social media, but we certainly had to monitor television and radio comments. We'd get a call from the sports editor, who said, 'Did you hear what McMichael said on Giangreco's postgame show?'"

It's why becoming a pro wrestler was the perfect career move for McMichael after football. His last NFL season was spent with the rival Packers in 1994 and then after that came nearly five years in wrestling. He had a long run with World Championship Wrestling. McMichael was always a natural showman, a natural bad ass.

"He was a really intimidating, great player," Waddle said. "Tough as nails. Never missed a practice. I don't think I was ever around him when he ever missed a game. He was one of the best leaders both verbally and by example. [But] you could tell that there was a teddy bear inside of him. He's a really sweet guy. He loved being the center of attention. But he was also a heart of gold kind of guy."

40

THE SACKMAN

During the 1980s, defensive coordinator Buddy Ryan and other staff members confided in star Dan Hampton. They wanted to know how he felt about certain players.

So in 1983, they asked for his thoughts on Richard Dent, a defensive end from Tennessee State who was drafted with the 203rd pick in the eighth round.

"Richard, he was a low draft-pick rookie," Hampton said. "That means you should do everything possible to try to make the team, which means being the first in the lines of all the drills, being the first one in running sprints—and he was lazy. You almost had to force him to do things.

"And I said, 'No. 95, are you kidding me? That damn kid is the laziest kid we've ever had.'"

But Ryan wanted Hampton to look more closely at the tall, skinny kid from the small school. There was something more there, something potentially great for the Bears' 46 defense.

"Buddy laughs," Hampton recalled, "and he goes, 'Yeah, but watch him. He always makes the right decision.'"

Hampton started to watch Dent all the time. The Bears' defense was already formidable, but a productive defensive end could make it truly devastating for the opposition. The Bears were being built to overwhelm teams on both lines of scrimmage.

"Certain people can play defensive line," Hampton said. "You have to have this kind of bizarre awareness of knowing how to fight pressure because they're blocking you a certain way for a reason. Your job is to react instantaneously. You can't sit there and think, 'If I do this...' No, you're already blocked. You have to have like a sixth sense. Richard had that. He would always take the right angle on a trap block or a reach block. If a tight end was trying to overhook him, he would go underneath and make the play."

It's what the "Sackman" did over his first 11 seasons with the Bears. For a team that prides itself on defense, Dent holds the honor of being the franchise's all-time leader in sacks with a 124½. Dent was inducted into the Hall of Fame in 2011. He was named first-team All-Pro and voted to the Pro Bowl four times each.

The Bears' 1983 draft is arguably their best ever because they selected Dent so late, in addition to six other starters. But without scout Bill Tobin, it would have never happened. General manager Jim Finks wasn't keen on Dent, even though Dent was a three-time Division I-AA All-American. Tobin, though, did his research and went to bat for the pass rusher. To Tobin, the solution for the next step was straightforward: Dent needed dental work.

"We had a combine that year, but he weighed 227 pounds and he had poor teeth," Tobin told the *Chicago Tribune* in 2015. "He couldn't retain weight or anything and the first thing we did after we drafted him is we took him to a dentist and they corrected all that and, hell, he started developing and gaining weight. And Richard is one of the few guys who actually grew height-wise. He was a little over 6'3" but he grew probably an inch and a half in my estimation. He got bigger and he kept his quickness."

In his second season, Dent had a team-best 17½ sacks and was voted to his first Pro Bowl. In his third, he led the entire NFL with 17 sacks, was named an All-Pro and voted the Most Valuable Player in Super Bowl XX. He was the fifth defensive player to receive the honor at the time. Dent had six sacks during the Bears' Super Bowl run.

"He was the big playmaker on the team," longtime Bears/NFL writer Dan Pompei said. "[Hampton] often says that, 'I was the wrecker and Richard was the catcher.' They needed each other. They made each other great. Without a great pass rusher, they're just another defense. And [Dent] was a great pass rusher. He was a shark. He had instincts that were unbelievable. Instincts to be able to get to the quarterback. Instincts to be able to get the ball out. Instincts to make the play at just the right time when it was needed."

Pompei presented Dent for the Hall of Fame in 2011, taking over for Don Pierson, who also wrote for the *Chicago Tribune*. Pompei and Pierson are both in the Hall of Fame as Dick McCann Award winners.

"He was a special, special player, and probably underrated in terms of historical accomplishments," Pompei said.

When Dent first arrived, he had his obvious limitations. It's why he was given the nickname, "The Colonel," after Colonel Sanders, founder of Kentucky Fried Chicken, who, like Dent, did only one thing well. But his defensive teammates remember how quickly that seemed to change under Ryan and his staff.

"Richard came in as a skinny defensive end from Tennessee State who had a great move, who had a great pass rush, but really needed to become more of a complete player and Buddy Ryan was just on him Day 1," safety Gary Fencik said. "And the reason they were calling him the 'Colonel' was because he had one good move or one good thing and that was a pass rush.

"But to his credit, he gained weight; he got better. It just made our defensive line so much better to have not one, not two, but probably three really good pass rushers on the defensive front. It makes it a lot easier to play safety and a lot better to be in the secondary when you have a pass rush that was effective. We certainly had one for a number of years when all those guys matured together."

Dent, Hampton, and Steve "Mongo" McMichael played together from 1983 to 1990. In that time frame, the trio combined for a whopping 205.5 sacks. They were the NFL's best wrecking crew. Hampton might have had his doubts at first, but Dent fit right in. His talents allowed the Bears to do even more up front with their stunts, twists and zone blitzes.

"It was almost perfect that Richard kind of materialized right on the scene," Hampton said. "Not only did he have a certain chutzpah, where he thought he was a badass in his second year—I had been the defensive player of the year, Mongo had made a Pro Bowl, [and] he thought he was the man. And in a way, we kind of laughed at him, but the next thing you know, eight sacks, 10 sacks, 12, 15."

In Super Bowl XX, Dent forced a fumble against Patriots running back Craig James in the first quarter that was recovered on New England's 13-yard line. Two plays later, fullback Matt Suhey scored. Dent set the tone. It's what Hampton and McMichael wanted to do, too. It was a competition to make big plays at big moments in big games—

and the Bears played in a lot of them during the 1980s. But in their biggest game it was Dent who is remembered as doing it—hence the MVP award.

"He was special so much of the time, especially in big games," Hampton said. "In 1988, one of the best games we ever played on defense was against Joe Montana and the 49ers and we played in the championship game two months later. We had home-field advantage because we beat them here in Chicago in a huge defensive must-win showdown. Richard played a great game in that contest as well."

It was a 10–9 win for the Bears against the 49ers at Soldier Field. The "Sackman" did what no other player has done better for the Bears in their storied history: he sacked Montana twice.

41

BRIAN'S SONG

Brian Piccolo died in the early morning of June 16, 1970 in a New York City hospital. His fight with cancer, which started in the middle of the 1969 season, was over. The Bears fullback was only 26 years old.

"He was so young to die, with a future that held so much for him," Bears owner George Halas said that day. "But Brian made the most of the brief 26 years allotted to him, and he will never be forgotten."

Halas, a founding father of the NFL, had never been more right about anything. Piccolo was survived by his wife, Joy, and their three young daughters, Lori, Traci, and Kristi.

But Piccolo's story would continue. To the Bears, his legacy would become just as vital and integral to the fabric of what they are and what they were going to be as a franchise as some of the legends he played with in the 1960s, if not more so. Piccolo was that revered, that beloved as a teammate and as a man.

On October 1, 1971, the book *Brian Piccolo: A Short Season*, which was written by popular Chicago sports broadcaster Jeannie Morris, was released. On November 30, 1971, the country would learn more about Piccolo. The made-for-television movie, *Brian's Song*, debuted that night on ABC. The movie was inspired by a chapter in the autobiography of running back Gale Sayers, *I Am Third*, which was released in 1970.

The film, which starred James Caan as Piccolo, was a resounding success, winning four Emmy Awards and more. The movie's theme song, "The Hands of Time," earned a Grammy. The film was centered around the relationship that Sayers and Piccolo shared. As rookies in 1965, they became what's believed to be the first interracial teammates in the NFL. Their story only made them more revered, more beloved.

An Enduring Friendship

Before *Brian's Song* debuted on television, there was a private showing for Bears players and their families in a theater in downtown Chicago.

"We, as players, our wives and our kids, everybody, there wasn't a dry eye in that theater," said Ed O'Bradovich, a defensive end who played with both players. "What a great picture that was. Was someone of it a little Hollywood-ishey? Yeah. But the majority of it was pretty much right on."

It would include the bond that Piccolo and Sayers shared. Ed McCaskey, the son-in-law of Halas, suggested that two players of the opposite race room together. Halas was on board with it. Sayers, the fourth overall pick from Kansas, asked that it be Piccolo, an undrafted signee who starred at Wake Forest.

"Those two guys had a fabulous relationship," said O'Bradovich, who, along with Dick Butkus, played himself in *Brian's Song*.

"Brian Piccolo was a practical joker and so was Gale. Those guys were always pulling pranks. They always were."

Sayers became an instant superstar, scoring 22 touchdowns as a rookie. Piccolo, on the other hand, took two years to become a regular on offense, despite being college football's leading rusher in his final season at Wake Forest. Piccolo's breakthrough came in the 1968 season after Sayers suffered a serious knee injury. He ran for a career-best 450 yards that season. In 1969, Piccolo was Sayers' fullback.

"He actually was an impressive football player," said Hub Arkush, a former Bears radio broadcaster and the publisher of *Pro Football Weekly*. "He was a grinder. He didn't have the talent but on dedication, toughness and hard work, he became a decent NFL running back for a year or two."

In the process, Piccolo endeared himself to those he played with and for. He embodied certain qualities that the franchise believed in under Halas. He worked for it. O'Bradovich remembered former Redskins/Rams linebacker Myron Pottios telling him that the hardest hit he ever took was from Piccolo. When Ed McCaskey's responsibilities increased within the organization in the 1960s, Piccolo became his middle man to the locker room.

"On his first day on the job, Brian Piccolo said, 'Don't worry about a thing, Big Ed. I'll square you away with the players,'" said Patrick McCaskey, a grandson of Halas and a Bears board member. "And he did. My parents thought highly of him and really adopted him."

Together, Sayers and Piccolo became a symbol for more off the field during a trying, soul-searching time for the entire country.

"The real story is understanding what was going on in America in '67, '68, and '69, the summer of '69, and for the Chicago Bears to be having this racial awakening at that time," Arkush said. "I know my reaction to it was being so impressed that George Halas understood. All we hear about is this crusty, old last guy in the world.... He saw where the game was going. He saw the importance of integrating it, and he went out of his way to make this happen."

What Sayers, the fleet-footed NFL superstar, and Piccolo, the role model for NFL perseverance, had was real. Their story wouldn't be an enduring one if it wasn't. They truly deeply cared for each other.

"It was a racial turning point in Chicago in some respects," Arkush said. "Obviously, we're still fighting it 50 years later but the fact that it was happening with the Chicago Bears. It became a positive story here in Chicago.... Once the story came out, it was far more about the impact it had on race relations in the city than it did on the football team."

An Enduring Honor

In Week 9 of the 1969 season on November 16, Piccolo scored on a one-yard run in the fourth quarter against the Atlanta Falcons and immediately removed himself from the game. His teammates were stunned. It wasn't like Piccolo to do that. But he was coughing too much, too hard. And his chest was in too much pain.

Two days later, a spot was found on his lung. He had embryonal carcinoma, which is usually testicular cancer. A malignant mass was removed from his lung. The fight for his life was on.

At one point, those close to Piccolo thought he would persevere. It's what he did. In December that year, Piccolo told everyone that he expected to return. But chemotherapy wore on him. His once-strong appearance changed. There would be more surgeries. Parts of his chest muscle were removed, then his left lung. He would lose this fight.

"We loved the kid," said O'Bradovich, who visited him in the hospital with Mike Ditka. "Everybody loved Brian Piccolo."

Especially Sayers.

"Brian was a very, very close friend," Sayers said on the day that Piccolo passed away. "I put him in the same category as my family. I felt as close to him as I did to my wife and children and I'll miss him."

The Bears, though, make it a point that Piccolo is remembered every year through the Brian Piccolo Award. It's announced at Halas Hall during a news conference. It's led by Patrick McCaskey, whose mother, team owner Virginia, was very close to Piccolo. Members of the Piccolo family are in attendance.

"Brian Piccolo was very special," Patrick McCaskey said.

Since 1970, the Bears have honored rookie players who "best exemplify the courage, loyalty, teamwork, dedication and sense of humor of the late Brian Piccolo." Guard Glen Holloway was the first award winner. In 1992, it expanded to include one veteran player.

Piccolo's No. 41 was retired after his death, while a room was named after him inside Halas Hall, which was renovated in 2018. To the Bears, they're honoring not only a former player, but a family member.

"[Piccolo's legacy] definitely means everything to the organization and to the McCaskey family—Virginia on down," said radio play-by-play broadcaster Jeff Joniak. "It's not for show. It's the real deal. It does underscore that within the billion-dollar industry of professional sports and in particular the National Football League and what is a dying breed of pure family-run organizations that made their money on one thing and that was football, that family remains extremely important and valuable to that franchise."

There are schools in New York City and Chicago that are named after Piccolo as well as a park in south Florida, where he was born and raised. At Wake Forest, Piccolo's No. 31 will never be worn again and there is a dormitory that bears his name. The Atlantic Coast Conference has had its own Piccolo Award since 1970, which honors a player for their courage.

Halas, McCaskey, and Billy DeCicco, a family friend of Piccolo's, founded the Brian Piccolo Fund not long after his death to support cancer research. Proceeds initially went to Sloan Kettering in New York, where Piccolo was treated. They later were shifted to Rush University Medical Center in Chicago. Millions have been raised, which includes help from Wake Forest's annual Brian Piccolo Cancer Fund Drive.

In other words, Piccolo lives on. He was a great man and a great teammate who became even greater in death.

"He was a below-average player whose impact was as great as any Bears player in 100 years," longtime Bears writer Dan Pompei said. "That impact went well beyond football, with about $12 million being raised in his name, and many people surviving testicular cancer because of him. Between *Brian's Song*, *A Short Season*, The Brian Piccolo Award, Brian Piccolo Middle School 53, Brian Piccolo Stadium, Piccolo Residence Hall at Wake Forest, and the Brian Piccolo Park and Velodrome, his spirit is alive and well."

42

73-0

Caught up in the jubilation of a 7–3 win against the Bears, Washington Redskins owner George Preston Marshall provided the Bears with their most famous bulletin-board material ever.

"The Bears are front-runners, quitters," Marshall told reporters, according to the *Chicago Tribune*. "They're not a second-half team, just a bunch of crybabies. They fold up when the going gets tough."

It was a shot fired at the Bears after the controversial finish to an intense game on November 17, 1940. A Bears' rally reached the end zone as time expired. But quarterback Sid Luckman's pass went off the chest of fullback Bill Osmanski. The Redskins' Bob Titchenal prevented the catch.

"There was time for only one more play," *Chicago Tribune* sportswriter Arch Ward wrote in his story in the following edition. "Luckman passed to Osmanski in the end zone, but the former Holy Cross star couldn't lift his arms because of what appeared to be interference on the part of Titchenal, Washington's center."

The final play was protested by Bears owner/coach George Halas, which prompted Marshall's response. It was all part of an emotional, dramatic finish against their rivals at the time. With 20 seconds remaining, Luckman's throw from midfield to halfback George McAfee put the Bears on the 1-yard line. Halas tried to substitute in players, but it resulted in a penalty. All of it set the stage for Luckman's final throw to Osmanski, Halas' protest to officials and then Marshall's fiery retort.

Over the years, Marshall's words were tweaked or shared in bits and pieces. But the context and message behind it always has remained the same for the Bears in their history: an opposing owner ripped them. The Bears would get an opportunity to shut Marshall up in the championship game after each team won their respective divisions.

When the Bears arrived in Washington for the championship game on December 8, there were local newspapers headlines that still played off Marshall's now-famous critique of the Bears. Halas being Halas, he used it to motivate his team.

"Coach Halas had gotten those papers blown up, and they were hanging in the dressing room when we came in the next morning," Luckman recalled 40 years later in a story for the *Tribune*. "Then he gave us the greatest pep talk we ever heard.

"He told us: 'You fellas know you are the greatest football team in America. Now go out there and prove it not only to yourselves but the football fans of America. Prove it to the Redskins. Look what their owner thinks of you.' It's not easy to motivate people who have played for a long time, but we couldn't get out the door fast enough."

The Bears ran over the Redskins that day. Ten Bears players combined to score 11 touchdowns in a 73–0 rout. A subhead in the *Tribune* the following day called it a massacre. The Bears were so dominant that day that they didn't even need Luckman. Halas sat him for the entire second half of the drubbing of the Redskins. The Bears led 28–0 at halftime and 54–0 after three quarters. At one point, the Bears, who made eight interceptions, were told they could no longer kick extra points into the stands because only one ball was left for the game.

"Not since the British sacked this city more than 100 years ago has Washington seen such a rout," *Chicago Tribune* sportswriter Wildred Smith wrote. "The thousands of loyal Redskins rooters, who had come to boo the Bears, stayed to roar bravos in spontaneous tribute to the incredible Chicago eleven. And finally, in resentment at the pitiful collapse of the Redskins, these fans booed the men who had been their heroes."

The Bears became the new Monsters of Midway during that decade. It was once a nickname for the Maroons from the University of Chicago because of the Midway Plaisance, a remnant of Chicago's World's Fair, on its campus. It now belonged to the Bears because of their dominance. Their title in 1940 was their first since 1933, but also the first of four championships won during that decade (1940, 1941, 1943, and 1946). The Bears were undefeated during the regular season in 1942, but lost to the Redskins 14–6 in the title game, furthering enhancing their rivalry in that era.

It was a legendary game that was full of Bears legends that came during a difficult time for the United States. Halas and others left the Bears at points during the 1940s to serve during World War II. But it also was the start of the Monsters of the Midway. That decade belonged to the Bears. It was the most resounding win in a title game in NFL history. The Bears have the full game on tape, too. It's been shared and storied on their own website.

"I'll give you one interesting stat: both teams had the same number of first downs in the game—17," said Larry Mayer, a writer for the Bears' website since 2001. "So that's kind of funny to me. Another interesting thing is that they only had four officials back then, and one of the officials was Irv Kupcinet, the *Sun-Times* writer. He was an official first."

Four members of those Bears teams had their numbers retired by the franchise, starting with Luckman (No. 42), McAfee (No. 5), and center/linebacker Clyde "Bulldog" Turner (No. 66).

With Halas and other players serving during World War II, Bronko Nagurski returned to play tackle during the 1943 season, which ended with the Bears' 41–21 victory against the Redskins for the title. Nagurski's No. 3 is retired, as well as Halas' No. 7. All five are in the Pro Football Hall of Fame.

"Just like you call the Steelers the team of the 1970s or the Patriots the team of this decade, the Bears were definitely the team of the decade in the '40s," said Mayer, who has covered the Bears for 28 years. "They were dominant."

43

THE RED GRANGE TOUR

By today's playing standards in the NFL, what the Bears did during the winter of 1925–1926 with Harold "Red" Grange would be very unacceptable and outrageous. The players' union simply wouldn't allow it.

There were 19 games played in 66 days—which included a grueling eight games in a 12-day span. But the NFL had to grow somehow, some way, right?

Grange was the NFL's first superstar and he played for the Bears. It was time to spread his stardom and the allure of the Bears across the county.

"Red Grange was very important to the survival of not only the Bears, but the league," said Patrick McCaskey, the grandson of George Halas, a Bears board member and a team historian. "When they went on that tour, coast to coast, it drew many fans and it helped the teams that they played survive."

Grange arrived in Chicago on November 22, 1925, a day after playing his last collegiate game for the University of Illinois against Ohio State. Despite the wishes of his own father and legendary Illini coach Bill Zuppke, Grange left school early, too. Grange was represented by C.C. Pyle, a theater owner from Champaign, Illinois.

Pyle knew he had a star attraction in Grange, who was considered the greatest college player at the time. The Bears and especially the NFL needed one at the time—and Grange would be paid like it.

On the same day as Grange's arrival and signing in Chicago, Halas, who owned the Bears with the Ed Sternaman at the time, announced that box seats at Wrigley Field were sold out for the Bears' Thanksgiving game against the rival Cardinals.

"The Bears and the Cardinals are great pro teams," *Chicago Daily Tribune* sportswriter Don Maxwell wrote in the November 27 edition. "They have thousands of enthusiastic followers. But the more than 36,000 folk who made the turkey wait until the game was over weren't there to see their teams play. They were there to see the red head of Wheaton."

The game ended in a 0–0 tie, which, according to Maxwell, should be viewed as a success because the Bears lost to the Cardinals 9–0 earlier in the season. But it was the bank accounts of the Bears and Grange (with Pyle, who was known as "Cold Cash" or "Cash and Carry") that benefited the most.

Pyle convinced Halas to have two promotional tours for the Bears, starring Grange. With more than 20 franchises coming and then quickly going over the first four years of the NFL, Halas agreed. Grange's stardom could help. It was important to share the wealth that Grange produced. It became known as the barnstorming tour. Some of the Bears' opposition would consist of local pick-up teams.

The first part of the tour was in the Midwest and on the East Coast.
December 2: St. Louis, MO
December 5: Philadelphia, PA
December 6: New York, NY
December 8: Washington, D.C.
December 9: Boston, MA
December 10: Pittsburgh, PA
December 12: Detroit, MI
December 13: Chicago, IL

The second part took the Bears from Florida to Louisiana to the West Coast.
December 25: Coral Gables, FL
January 1: Tampa, FL
January 2: Jacksonville, FL
January 10: New Orleans, LA
January 16: Los Angeles, CA
January 17: San Diego, CA
January 24: San Francisco, CA
January 30: Portland, OR
January 31: Seattle, WA

In front of 5,000 spectators, the Bears defeated the Washington All-Stars 34–0 in Seattle to finish their tour. Grange ran for 99 yards and threw a 31-yard touchdown pass in the victory.

It wasn't always that easy. Grange didn't play in Detroit during the first leg of the trip after getting injured in Pittsburgh. It resulted in some fans demanding refunds. Quarterback Joey Sternaman also remained the best player on the Bears. The *Chicago Daily Tribune* wasn't that impressed with Grange.

"As a football player, heralded as the best of all time, Grange has proved a failure," Maxwell wrote in the February 1, 1926 edition. "Little Joe Sternaman has out-starred him in every game they've played. But as a gate attraction, Red can be said to have been a winner. We're wondering what sort of attraction he'll be next fall."

As it turned out, not much. Pyle and Grange tried to buy their way into the Bears but were refused. Instead, they created a new team, the New York Yankees, and after another refusal, this time from NFL, the nine-team American Football League was created. It lasted only one year.

By 1929, Grange was done with Pyle and back with the Bears, for whom he played for six seasons. Grange was paired with another legend-in-the-making in Bronko Nagurski. Together, they won consecutive championships for the Bears in 1932 and 1933. Nagurski was the better player of the two. The Bears also went 13–0 in 1934 but lost to the Giants in the championship game.

The barnstorming tour should be remembered as a wild, grueling success. Nearly 300,000 fans paid to see Grange, who was known as the Galloping Ghost or the Wheaton Iceman, which came from his summer job.

"He was very humble and very talented, but he was a great attraction," McCaskey said. "It was a terrific idea to sign him and then go on that coast-to-coast tour."

The largest crowd was 75,000 at the Los Angeles Coliseum, which was a record at that time. The most impactful was in New York, where 65,000 watched Grange at the Polo Grounds. It immensely benefited the Giants. The game wiped out the debts of Giants owner Tim Mara, which was beyond encouraging for him.

"Grange earned about $125,000 on the tour in a little over two months—more than enough to cover the final payments on the coonskin coat he'd bought on credit before his pro debut," Halas wrote in the *Chicago Tribune* in January 1967. "Grange was a great favorite with other Bears players. Nobody resented Red's success. He was a topnotch player—drew the crowds which paid all the salaries—and shook off a series of painful neck and leg injuries without a whimper."

When it came to the future of professional football, the tour convinced Grange that professional football could be more popular than the college version, that he was right to leave school early, too. At the time, it might have seemed impossible.

National sportswriters accompanied the Bears throughout their tour. The team visited president Calvin Coolidge, while Grange met with New York Yankees slugger Babe Ruth. And there was the money—a lot of it, especially then. The Bears reportedly made $100,000 as a team.

"I believe professional football is a big thing," Grange said, according to February 15, 1926 edition of the *Chicago Daily Tribune*. "I predict that within five years' time the pro game will be bigger than the college game.... It will be run on just as big a scale as professional baseball is now."

Grange was wrong, though. It became bigger.

44

DECEMBER 18, 1932

After three seasons in a row seeing the rival Green Bay Packers claim NFL titles, it was important the Bears were seen in 1932 when they returned to prominence.

But a snowstorm blanketed Chicago. Wrigley Field, the site for the championship game on December 18 against the Portsmouth Spartans, was covered by it. Because of the conditions, the championship game was moved inside to Chicago Stadium.

"The decision to bring back the Bears and Spartans indoors from the snowy wastes of Wrigley Field was more in the interests of the spectators than the players," Wilfred Smith wrote in the *Chicago Daily Tribune* a day before the game. "These professionals are a hardy lot and neither rain, snow nor cold has caused postponement in the regular season."

But Bears owner George Halas always had the best interests of his team and the entire league at heart, especially when both were in their infancy. Halas and league president Joe Carr preferred what Chicago Stadium could offer, even though the Salvation Army Benefit Circus had just left it—stinky.

"It was a smart move financially, with the mercury entirely out of control, and, after all, professional football is a business," Smith wrote.

On a field that was shortened to 80 yards and with goalposts now on the goal line and the building still reeking like the circus, the Bears defeated the Spartans 9–0 in front of a near capacity crowd of 11,198. It's a victory that's remembered for where it was played but for also how it was won.

It took an iconic moment from two football icons in order for the Bears to win their first title since they were named the Staleys in 1921. With 10 minutes remaining, fullback Bronko Nagurski threw a short touchdown pass to Red Grange. It was set up by an interception and return by Dick Nesbitt to the Spartans' 7-yard line.

Portsmouth coach George "Potsy" Clark protested the touchdown. At the time, there was a league rule that said that all forward passes had to start from five yards behind the line of scrimmage. He didn't think Nagurski's pass qualified. But the touchdown stood.

"It was very controversial," said Larry Mayer, who has chronicled the 1932 title game as a writer for the Bears' website since 2001. "The next year, they changed the rule that you could throw it from anywhere behind the line of scrimmage."

It was one of several league developments rooted in that game. With the smaller field, the goal posts were moved to the goal line and kept there until 1974. Hashmarks also were introduced because of the field and kept. As chairman of the rules committee, Halas saw the changes as beneficial to the future of the game.

"Even though the Bears had won their first pro title in 11 years, it was hard for me to view the season as a resounding success, inasmuch as a final audit of the books revealed a net loss of $18,000!" Halas wrote during a series of entries for the *Chicago Tribune* in 1967. "It occurred to me that something must be wrong with our style if a championship team lost money—and attendance figures also were declining all over the league. I decided we were playing dull football—too many ties—and the remedy was to open the game up to more scoring."

The Bears had six ties that season, but they didn't factor in because of league rules. Champions were previously based on winning percentage. It would change. In 1933, divisions were introduced in the NFL.

"[The 1932 game] was obviously incredibly historic," Mayer said. "And it was played right after the circus. Everyone said the smell was of elephants."

For the Bears, it marked their return to the top of the NFL standings. With coach Curly Lambeau, the Packers won the previous three titles. The Bears ended their rivals' run by defeating them 9–0 on December 11, which included a legendary 56-yard run by Nagurski. The Bears previously had a scoreless tie with the Packers in their season opener on September 25 and a 2–0 loss to them later on October 16.

"Ironically, the Packers finished with ten victories against only three losses and a tie," Halas wrote. "But ties didn't count in the standings, so the Packers wound up in second place even though they topped the Bears by the three games in the victory column!"

The championship also preceded Halas' deadline to buy out co-owner Dutch Sternaman. Halas owed $38,000, and after losing $18,000 on the 1932 season, he was $15,000 short during the Great Depression.

It took $5,000 from his own mother, a bank loan of $5,000, and Charles Bidwell (a close friend of Halas' who later became the owner of the Chicago Cardinals) buying $5,000 in stock to make it work. Halas wrote that he made the deadline for the payment by 50 minutes. The Bears were in such dire straits that coach Ralph Jones—who implemented the man-in-motion in the T formation—resigned to be the athletic director at Lake Forest College.

"The loyalty of the Bears players also was a big help when the money was the shortest," Halas wrote. "I couldn't pay off everybody at the end of '32 players so some of the players agreed to take promissory notes."

It included Nagurski and Grange. In 1933, the two icons were the Bears' top two rushers as the franchise went 10–2–1, won the first-ever West Division and then won back-to-back NFL championships with a 23–21 victory against the New York Giants. And this time, the Bears played outdoors at Wrigley Field in front of 26,000 fans.

45

THE 14 RETIRED NUMBERS

Ed O'Bradovich can still remember all the screaming that linebacker Bill George did at him and others on the defense. And O'Bradovich, a bruising defensive end, also remembers that he always listened.

"It happened almost every game," O'Bradovich said. "I'd be playing, obviously, my position, left defensive end, and they'd come out, the offensive line would get set and we're ready to go, and then all of sudden I hear, 'OB jump inside! OB jump inside! They're coming! They're coming!'"

There was a play to be made, and George, a member of the Pro Football Hall of Fame, needed O'Bradovich to be in place to make it.

"It's like that," O'Bradovich said. "He's screaming out in a second or half a second. And I'd jump inside the tackle, which I'm never supposed to do. Guess what? I'd get across the line and make the tackle. He made me a hero."

The Bears are a team full of them, and every year that number grows. Figuring out where every player fits throughout the generations and different eras of Bears football certainly has its difficulties.

In 2020, two more Bears players were inducted into the Hall of Fame as senior candidates, and they came from different eras: Jimbo Covert, the starting left tackle from the Bears' Super Bowl–winning team in 1985, and Ed Sprinkle, a member of the Bears' 1946 title-winning team whom owner/coach George Halas once called the "greatest pass rusher I've ever seen."

The Bears' 1963 championship team featured five All-Pros on defense: George, defensive end Doug Atkins, linebacker Joe Fortunato, and safeties Richie Petitbon and Rosey Taylor. Atkins, like George, is a Hall of Famer. He was an intimidating 6'8" defensive end who also happened to be an exceptional athlete. And legend has it that Atkins never worked out.

"The most feared man in the National Football League was Doug Atkins," O'Bradovich said. "He was unbelievable."

Still, a certain reverence is held for those who have their numbers retired by the Bears. They have the most Hall of Famers of any team and the most retired numbers. But considering the full duration of their 100-year history, the 14 numbers that the organization no longer has in circulation seems few.

When current players walk into the renovated and expanded Halas Hall, the Bears' home base in Lake Forest, Illinois, they're greeted by the numbers that they can't wear.

No. 3: Bronko Nagurski
No. 5: George McAfee
No. 7: George Halas
No. 28: Willie Galimore
No. 34: Walter Payton
No. 40: Gale Sayers
No. 41: Brian Piccolo
No. 42: Sid Luckman
No. 51: Dick Butkus
No. 56: Bill Hewitt
No. 61: Bill George
No. 66: Clyde "Bulldog" Turner
No. 77: Harold "Red" Grange
No. 89: Mike Ditka

All of them are not only worthy of their chapters, but their own books. Many already have had them written. Similar to Piccolo, Galimore has a tragic story, one that shouldn't be forgotten over the generations.

Nicknamed the "Wisp," Galimore, a running back, died in a car crash with teammate John "Bo" Farrington on July 27, 1964, in Rensselaer, Indiana, where the Bears held training camp at St. Joseph,

College. Galimore was a second-team All-Pro in 1957 and 1958 and a member of their title-winning team in 1963.

"This was the saddest day in Bears history," Halas told his players after their deaths. "We all share the same sad feelings. Something like this reaches the heart and makes everything else seem petty. It's going to take a great deal of will power to carry on, but I know you can do it. A great honor can be bestowed to Willie and Bo if you dedicate the season to them."

McAfee, Hewitt, and Turner might not carry the same household-name value as Nagurski or Grange, or later Butkus, Sayers, and Payton. But their place in the history of the Bears is considered just as important.

"They all rank very high," said longtime Bears writer Dan Pompei, who co-authored the team's centennial scrapbook with Don Pierson, which included ranking the best 100 players. "Don and I thought it was a mistake that Bulldog Turner was left off the NFL's all-time team that came out over the summer. No question he was a major part of the Monsters dynasty.

"Hewitt was the Bears' first truly great defensive player, but he was a truly great offensive player as well. Given his contribution to the great teams of the 1930s, you could say his impact on winning games was as significant as almost any Bear in history.

"I'm a little biased on McAfee. My dad was a season-ticket holder in the 1940s, and I grew up listening to stories about him. He wasn't just a great two-way player. He was a great three-way player, the best three-way player in Bears history."

Similarly, it's why George is unique, too—why his jersey is retired with McAfee, Hewitt, and Turner, who all played before him.

George was a revolutionary player who is regarded as the NFL's first modern middle linebacker. He was moved off the line and away from the middle guard position by innovative Bears assistant coach Clark Shaughnessy.

George then became an extension of defensive coordinator George Allen on the field during the Bears' championship season in 1963. He was voted to eight Pro Bowls and named a franchise-best first-team All-Pro eight times. The Bears' legacy of linebackers begins with him.

"Bill George was the smartest defensive player I ever coached," Allen told the *Chicago Tribune* in 1982. "He called the defensive signals for the Bears when they were at their best defensively. He studied films, kept a notebook of his own, did his homework every week and always prepared to play his best. He practically invented the middle linebacker position and the 4-3 defense."

46

BRONKO AND ALL THE BACKS

It was 1943 and the Bears needed Bronko Nagurski to be their hero once again. The issue was that Nagurski hadn't played football in six years.

His days of running over tacklers or carrying them on his back—all the stuff that made him a legend in the NFL—were gone. Or so he thought.

The Bears were in a transition year with owner/coach George Halas and players serving during World War II.

Nagurski, who once said he was born to play football, was convinced to return by Luke Johnsos, a former teammate who was now coaching the Bears with Hunk Anderson.

Only five teammates remained from when Nagurski last played for the Bears in 1937. The team had new stars in quarterback Sid Luckman and center Clyde "Bulldog" Turner, both of whom looked up to Nagurski. Johnsos told Nagurski that he would primarily play only tackle and that his running would be kept to a minimum.

On September 23, 1943, the Bears announced that Nagurski would start at left tackle. It came three days before the team's regular-season opener against the Green Bay Packers.

"Nagurski, who retired a couple seasons ago after a long and brilliant career as a full back, is attempting a comeback as a lineman and apparently has exceeded even his own expectations," *Chicago Daily Tribune* sportswriter Edward Prell wrote.

But that's who Nagurski was. He's always been more myth than man—and that man was damn good at football. Halas' ability to sign him out of the University of Minnesota in 1929 for $5,000 was a pivotal moment for the franchise. They had the league's first superstar in Red Grange and now the league's first soon-to-be legend in Nagurski.

Born in Canada and raised in International Falls, Minnesota, Nagurski grew up as a real-life Paul Bunyan, chopping down trees, plowing fields, and living through the frigid cold. Nagurski's strength became legendary as a teenager and his real name was transformed from his given Bronislau into "Bronko."

Now in 1943, another chapter to Nagurski's book of tall tales would be added. In the final week of the regular season, the Bears were 7–1–1, but on the verge of losing their championship bid from the Western Division to the Packers in a tight game against the winless Chicago Cardinals, their old rival. The Cardinals had a 10-point lead entering the fourth quarter. In desperate need of a spark throughout the game, Johnsos and Anderson turned to Nagurski. He was back at fullback.

"Then Bronko carried the ball 15 times for 84 yards as he powered [through] the middle or slanted off the right side of the Cardinal line," Prell wrote. "When a yard was needed for a first down, the Nag squirmed for every inch."

It included a one-yard touchdown in the fourth quarter—the first of three unanswered touchdowns by the Bears. Nagurski did it all while wearing a metal brace on his back. The Bears defeated their old rivals 35–24 to win the Western Division.

On December 26, 1943, at Wrigley Field, the Bears prevailed 41–21 in the championship game against the Washington Redskins. Nagurski scored on a three-yard run in the second quarter. It was the Bears' third title in four seasons during their Monsters of the Midway run. For Nagurski, it was his first since winning back-to-back championships in the 1932 and 1933 seasons.

"Well, I'm retiring again," Nagurski said after the game. "It's not a game for a 35-year old, and I can't listen to George Halas' songs my entire life."

* * *

When the Bears were at their best, they always had great running backs. Along with the linebackers, it's what the franchise will forever be known for. It started with Grange in the late 1920s and took off with Nagurski in the 1930s.

Then came George McAfee, Rick Casares, Willie Galimore, Gale Sayers, and, of course, the one and only Walter Payton. There are more, too. It's a very proud history.

"That's the thing: there's always pretty much been a good running back here in town," said WGN-TV broadcaster Jarrett Payton, the son of Walter Payton. "Gale Sayers is the guy that came before my dad that everybody knew. My dad kind of took it and set the bar super, super high.

"But I've always said, other guys that came after that, they just needed to do what they needed to do. I always wonder how it is in the mindset of a new running back coming into the organization when you look at the records and you know the position."

The conversations always start with Sayers and Payton, but Casares—who played for the Bears from 1955 to 1964—was voted to five consecutive Pro Bowls over the first five years of his career. He trails only Payton in Pro Bowl appearances.

"In those days, everybody wanted to be the running back, not the quarterback," said Hub Arkush, the Bears' former radio broadcaster and the publisher of *Pro Football Weekly*. "He embodied the whole tough and blood-and-guts image of the thing."

In the draft following the Bears' Super Bowl XX victory against Patriots, the organization selected its successor for Payton with the 27th overall pick: Neal Anderson from Florida. In 1988, Anderson went to his first of four consecutive Pro Bowls. He was a second-team All-Pro in 1990. His 6,166 rushing yards rank third.

"Neal Anderson is the most underrated player in Bears history," said Larry Mayer, the Bears' full-time writer for their website since 2001. "This was a guy that was a first-round draft pick, but he came in right after Walter Payton and people were completely spoiled by him. [Anderson's] attitude was so great that he played only on special teams as a rookie and was the best special teams player I've ever seen. He was just an amazing special teams player. Then when we finally got the chance, he did a great job. Nobody really talks about him as one of the better running backs."

During the Bears' Super Bowl run during the 2006 season, Lovie Smith's team relied on Thomas Jones and Cedric Benson. Jones' 3,493 rushing yards are the sixth-most, which is right behind Sayers, who still holds the record for touchdowns scored by a rookie with 22 in 1965.

In 2008, the Bears selected Matt Forte out of Tulane in the second round. He didn't get the accolades that other running backs received throughout the Bears' long history, but his 8,602 rushing yards are only behind Payton's never-to-be-touched 16,726.

"Forte was very productive and a good leader in that locker room," said Mark Potash, who covered Forte's career for the *Chicago Sun-Times*. "He was a more quiet type of a leader, but people respected him.

"His versatility, his consistency—from a team perspective—he was just good to have on your team. Maybe, one who wasn't your No. 1 or a top-10 pick, but if you want a running back to build a winning team, to me, he was a good guy to have in your locker room and on your team."

* * *

Of all the stories that the Bears came to love and share about Nagurski, Halas' favorite might have occurred on November 26, 1933, against the Portsmouth Spartans at Wrigley Field.

In a story shared by Halas during his journal series in the *Chicago Tribune* in 1967, Nagurski was said to be infuriated that he failed to cover receiver Ernie Caddel on a touchdown that gave the Spartans the lead in the fourth quarter.

Nagurski demanded the ball from Carl Brumbaugh on the next series and took off for a long touchdown run in the Bears' 17–14 victory.

"Six Portsmouth tacklers had shots at Nagurski on his scoring run—but Bronko ran right over them," Halas wrote. "He was running so hard when he hit the end zone that he skidded slowing down and plowed helmet-first into the concrete wall of the dugout. It took a concrete wall to stop an aroused Nagurski."

As legend has it, Nagurski, who was known for his soft-spoken demeanor, later said, "That last guy really hit me." Halas and the Wrigley Field groundskeepers would later say that Nagurski's helmet left a crack in the wall.

"I always used my strength in football," Nagurski said, according to the Pro Football Hall of Fame. "I liked to meet guys head-on when I was carrying the ball. Then I'd drop my shoulder, and catch him with that, and then brush him off with my arm. It worked—most of the time."

Grange once said that Nagurski was a blend of linebacker Dick Butkus and running back Larry Csonka. Beattie Feathers became the NFL's first 1,000-yard rusher in 1934 by running behind Nagurski. Feathers averaged 8.4 yards per carry, which is still a record.

When Nagurski walked away from football the first time after the 1937 season, he did so because he couldn't get a raise from Halas but also because he had a successful professional wrestling career. In the 1930s, Halas paid him and Grange through IOUs during some financial difficulties for the team during the Great Depression.

In 1963, Nagurski became part of the first class inducted into the Pro Football Hall of Fame Class, along with Halas and Grange. His 1963 championship ring was measured at 19½, which is still the largest of all time.

In the same *Tribune* entry in 1967, Halas also shared the story of how Nagurski's three collisions with Philadelphia Eagles linebacker John "Bull" Lipski in a game resulted in Lipski being unconscious three times. It happened on two violent Nagurski runs and a forceful block on a sweep play that also took out two of his Eagles teammates.

"Bronko overtook Lipski and the two subs about five yards from the sideline and—WHAM—Bronk threw a block that sent all three of them flying into the Eagles' bench," Halas wrote said. "Poor Lipski was knocked out for the third time—a record that should stand until another Nagurski comes along, if one ever does."

There won't be.

47

THE MEN BEHIND THE SCENES

If there is going to be a book written about the Chicago Bears, Tom Thayer, a starting guard for the 1985 Bears and a radio broadcaster for decades, wants to make sure that Clyde Emrich is in it—that there is a reason why the Bears' weight room at Halas Hall is named after him.

"What he did for the development of Chicago Bears football from rehabbing Gale Sayers to teaching Dick Butkus to the development and understanding of organized strength—no matter who you are—don't leave him out of it," Thayer said. "Anybody's biography that starts with, 'The first man in the world to...' It's pretty special."

In Thayer's opinion, Emrich deserves consideration for the Pro Football Hall of Fame as the first recognized strength coach in the history of the NFL.

When Emrich retired as a professional weightlifter in 1968, he was offered a contract by George "Mugs" Halas Jr. Since then, the handshake of Emrich, who was in the Olympics in 1952 and won a gold medal at the Pan Am games in 1959, has been the strongest on the team.

"I really owe so much to Clyde because I really bonded with Clyde," said former safety Doug Plank, whose No. 46 became the name of Buddy Ryan's defense. "He was honest and truly helping anyone that wanted help. He could see the phonies from the real guys."

It's guys like Emrich who are really the driving forces behind sports teams. He's one of the behind-the-scenes staff members whom former players highlighted for their help and unseen contribution. They're that important to them.

"There's no one that has more hands-on knowledge in the game than Clyde Emrich," Thayer said. "[It's] his own successful experiences, the inception of just generations and years of weightlifting and how it benefits players and how to use the equipment to benefit the players.

"He's a lot like Tony Medlin. Nobody was bigger than anybody. Clyde took an equally important hands on approach to every guy he ever touched. I just think that he's such an important guy in the strength history of the NFL."

As Thayer said, Medlin belongs in this conversation, too. He's another "important guy" in the history of the Bears as their head equipment manager since 1997.

"He's irreplaceable," said Lance Briggs, a linebacker for the Bears from 2003 to 2014. "His address is right there at Halas Hall. You think Chicago, you think 'T Med.' T Med's been there and seen a lot of generations, seen a lot of guys coming through. And he's going to continue to do that. It's hard for me to imagine the organization without him."

Former Bears players also pointed to former trainer Fred Caito, who worked for the team for 30 years before being dismissed in 1997, and Ken Mrock, the longtime groundskeeper who started working for the Bears after the 1985 season.

They're all part of the family-like culture that has been fostered by the Bears, especially under the McCaskey family. It's what they want. There is loyalty and it works both ways. Fans might not see it, but it will be rewarded if they continue to excel and improve within their respective responsibilities. Emrich, Medlin and Mrock are just three examples. So is longtime scout Jeff Shiver, who began working for the team in 1987. There are more, too, just not directly involved in the football side of the franchise.

During the 1960s, Halas viewed weightlifting and isometrics as a new way to improve his team as the NFL game evolved. He was always looking for a winning edge. It's why he turned to Ralph Jones and Clark Shaughnessy to improve the T formation with the man-in-motion during the 1930s, and why decades later, he was calling Emrich to his office. Emrich was invited to training camp before the 1963 season, which ended with the Bears first title since 1946. In 1968, Emrich—the first man under 200 pounds to clean and jerk 400 pounds—was hired full time by the Bears.

"He would also demonstrate how to do something correctly," Plank said. "And everything was explosive. I remember one time Clyde

Emrich... telling me never to bench press. Bench press is looking good for the girls. Everything Clyde taught was explosive. Picking weights up off the ground and throwing them over your shoulders, bringing them up to your shoulders or throwing it over your head. It was for your back and your thighs and your stomach and your shoulders. The other thing that Clyde did a lot, he did a lot of strength drills for your hands, your grip."

Emrich, of course, has been replaced by younger versions of himself. His official title is now "administration" in the Bears' media guide. Emrich, though, will still consult players if they need it. After safety Eddie Jackson went to the Pro Bowl and was named All-Pro after the 2018 season, Emrich told him to have higher goals—to start working with the mindset of being a Hall of Famer.

"Obviously, an organization has many, many different layers to it," said radio play-by-play broadcaster Jeff Joniak, who has been with the Bears since 2000. "You take Clyde, he's the best. He's a legend by name and moniker. That's what he's referred to and he remains somebody of great importance to that organization."

Medlin joined the team as an assistant to Gary Haeger in 1988, the final year that running back Walter Payton was on the roster. Over the years, Medlin formed lasting bonds with players such as Payton, Richard Dent, Otis Wilson—"Tony's one of the brothers for life," Wilson told The Athletic in 2018—and then later with Devin Hester, Lance Briggs, Charles Tillman, and Matt Forte.

"To me, being in this business," Medlin told The Athletic, "it's probably the most unique relationships that you could develop—ever—in my opinion because you see people come in as young people and then they grow."

Since 1991, Carl "Hyde" Piekarski has been Medlin's right-hand man with the Bears. He was nicknamed "Hyde" after the leather hide of a football by quarterback Jim McMahon. In 1984, McMahon had hit Piekarski, then a ball boy, in the head with an errant pass. But nicknames stick only if the person does. Piekarski, just like Medlin, is a behind-the-scenes fixture for the team, another driving force that fans don't always learn about.

"These are guys that care very much about their jobs and they care about being great," Joniak said. "They understand the mission to try and win a championship. It goes beyond that.... The rewards are the environment, not just the payday. The environment is special. It's a family business, but a really tight-family company."

48

THE VOICES OF THE BEARS

Bears radio play-by-play broadcaster Jeff Joniak took over when returner Devin Hester did in early in the fourth quarter of his first NFL game, which just happened to be on the road against the rival Green Bay Packers.

Hester fielded a punt from Jon Ryan at the 16-yard line—and the NFL, for the next 10 years, would never be the same.

"And with a burst to the 25, 30," Joniak said in his broadcast, his voice becoming more emphatic with every word. "Opening 35, 40. Right side. Midfield. No chance! Goodbye! Touchdown! Welcome to the NFL, the Windy City Flyer."

It was Hester's first return touchdown in the NFL. A special play was made by a special player, and it got a memorable, special call from Joniak. A better one was coming, however. In Week 14 against the St. Louis Rams, Hester scored two touchdowns on kickoff returns in a 42–27 victory.

"Hester starts at the 10, veering right," Joniak said, his voice intensifying with each second. "Now angling to the middle. Now at the 20, hits the gas—25, 30, 35, 40. Forget it! Nobody's going to get him. Long gone. Devin Hester, you are ridiculous!"

It stuck. Everyone heard it and everyone was talking about it. Mike Mulligan, a columnist for the *Chicago Sun-Times* at the time, stopped Joniak before he reached the team bus after the game and told him as much. It was a viral sports moment in Chicago before there was a term for such things.

"It was the second return and I literally started giggling," Joniak said. "I knew he was going to score. And it just was a jaw-dropper because I could not believe what he was doing and they still kicked to him. He was unstoppable. And that's when I just let it out. And because I say that term routinely, it just came out. I just lost my mind, but I didn't think anything of it."

Memorable plays can even more so when they have memorable calls. In this case, "ridiculous" stuck with Joniak and Hester—forever. With television networks controlling their own broadcast teams, a team's radio play-by-play broadcasters tend to become their "voice." It's why their calls become part of highlight-reel packages.

For the Bears, Joniak is the 11th voice, starting his run in 2001. He followed Gary Bender, Wayne Larrivee, Joe McConnell, Jay Scott, Jack Brickhouse, Red Grange, Bert Wilson, Jack Drees, Jimmy Evans, and Bob Elson. In terms of years, Joniak only trails Brickhouse, who is more known for his Cubs calls but called Bears games from 1953 to 1976. Larrivee was a favorite but left for the Packers.

For Joniak, the job wouldn't be the same without Tom Thayer, his broadcast partner who was a starting guard for the Bears' Super Bowl-winning team in 1985. Any praise that Joniak said he gets, Thayer deserves it, too, if not more. Thayer's longevity is more than notable. Thayer began his career as an analyst for the Bears in 1997 with Larrivee and Hub Arkush. Linebacker Dick Butkus, defensive lineman Dan Hampton and safety Gary Fencik also spent time in the broadcast booth.

Players from coach Lovie Smith's best teams have told Joniak and Thayer that they're the "soundtrack of their careers." It's particularly true for Hester, who had "Windy City Flyer" painted on the wall of his home with the Chicago skyline. "Touchdown, Bears!" is another Joniak staple.

"I take great pride in being a voice for the fans and a voice for that organization," Joniak said. "It's what I love. It's my passion and that passion has to come through on your broadcast, too, otherwise you have no chance. You're not going to resonate with people."

Joniak's "ridiculous" connection to Hester is an example. It'll live on, likely forever.

"Devin honestly brought everyone to their feet and had everybody's attention from teammates to fans to broadcasters," Joniak said. "He embraced it, too. He loved it."

* * *

When the officials stopped the game for the two-minute warning in the fourth quarter of the Bears' matchup against the Rams in the NFC Championship Game on January 12, 1986, public-address announcer Jim Riebandt saw an opportunity to add some extra emotion to the team's in-game experience.

Earlier in the fourth quarter, outside linebacker Wilber Marshall picked up a fumble and returned it 52 yards for a wild touchdown, an insurmountable lead and an eventual 24–0 victory. It was time to celebrate the inevitable.

"It's two minutes... then I paused... to New Orleans," Riebandt said. "The crowd got a bang out of that one."

Starting in 1982 and ending in 2019, Riebandt was the Bears' PA announcer at Soldier Field. In 2002, the Bears played at the University of Illinois in Champaign, when Soldier Field was being renovated. With a better address system, it's where Riebandt's most famous call took off.

"There's a timeout!"

"Where?"

"On the field."

"Oohh..."

Riebandt knows he'll be remembered for it because Bears fans mention it all the time when they meet him. But it's a line that's always been in the script for Bears games. It was a cue for Ben Arden and Bill Archer's Big Bear Band. Riebandt was simply following the instructions of the late Chet Coppock, whom Riebandt backed up in 1979 as the Bears' PA announcer.

"Chet made a point to tell me, that once you say a timeout, give the pause so the band can be ready to play as soon as you say on the field," Riebandt said.

Over 38 years, there were plenty of memorable moments for Riebandt, a full-time lawyer whose PA run with the Bears started by writing a letter to general manager Jim Finks in 1979. Riebandt became the PA announcer for DePaul University's men's basketball team under legendary coach Ray Meyer in 1977.

During the Fog Bowl on December 31, 1988—a 20–12 win for the Bears in the playoffs against the Philadelphia Eagles—Riebandt called out the down and distances and more with the help of the NFL stats crew, who relayed information to him via radios. CBS broadcaster Verne Lundquist complimented Riebandt live on air for what he was doing. He was later interviewed by newspapers because of it.

Over the years, Riebandt's responsibilities changed as more music was played at Soldier Field. Live shots with others were introduced on the large video screens inside the stadium. The NFL also became more involved in teams' game productions. But for a long period of time, Riebandt was an enduring in-game link between the Bears' current teams and their beloved ones from the 1980s.

Riebandt also was one of the voices of the Bears, calling games played by Walter Payton and Mike Singletary and Jay Cutler and Brian Urlacher.

"The bottom line is I sometimes had to think to myself, you know, I'm a lawyer; I'm not a professional broadcaster," said Riebandt, who grew up on the Northwest Side of Chicago. "And I'm sitting here and I'm the only connection between the Bears organization and their fans at all these home games. I'm the only one. It was a little surreal."

49

THE CHICAGO MEDIA

On May 28, 1968, the Bears were front-page news in Chicago. A legend was finally done. And this time, it was for good "George Halas brought the most colorful and successful coaching career in the history of football to a dramatic close yesterday. He retired as head coach of the Chicago Bears."

Those were the words written by George Strickler in the first paragraph of his front-page story of the *Chicago Tribune*. Strickler covered the "Old Man's" retirement a day earlier.

"I have made this decision with considerable reluctance but no regrets," Halas said in his announcement. Strickler described those at the news conference as stunned.

The Bears' long, storied history wouldn't be the same without the long tenures of the sportswriters who wrote the stories about them. It's unlike any other city.

During the 1920s, Halas was desperate for coverage for his team. He needed the publicity for the NFL to help spur its growth. In order to get it, Halas either wrote his own articles or provided complimentary tickets to journalists. Signing halfback Red Grange out of the University of Illinois and taking him on a cross-country tour in 1925–26 changed that. The Bears and the NFL had its first true draw and superstar in Grange.

Of course, much has changed since then. There is almost too much coverage of the NFL and its teams. The NFL doesn't need newspapers, but television contracts with ESPN, NBC, ABC and CBS. In 2003, the NFL Network debuted.

But Chicago, starting with Strickler, has a special place in the coverage of the NFL. In 1964, Strickler founded the Pro Football Writers of America. In 1969, he also became the first winner of the Dick McCann Memorial Award "for long and distinguished reporting on professional football." It's an honor presented to a reporter at the enshrinement ceremony for Pro Football Hall of Fame. The *Chicago*

Tribune has produced three others: Cooper Rollow (1985), Don Pierson (1994), and Dan Pompei (2013). They're forever linked to the Bears.

"The Bears are in my blood," said Pompei, now a writer for The Athletic who started covering the Bears in 1985 for the *Chicago Sun-Times*. "My father was a season-ticket holder from the 1940s. I remember Bears games on the TV from the time I could watch TV. When I started covering the team, the first thing I did after a game was call my dad to talk about it. I think that gave me an insight into what the team was about, their tradition, and how their fans thought. I always tried to convey that in my writing."

Pompei isn't alone in his deep ties. In all mediums, many of those who have had distinguished careers covering the Bears or talking about them are from Chicago or its surrounding suburbs. It includes Peggy Kusinski (WMAQ-TV, NBC Ch. 5), Hub Arkush (*Pro Football Weekly*), John "Moon" Mullin (*Daily Herald*, *Chicago Tribune*, NBC Sports Chicago), Bob LeGere (*Daily Herald*), Mark Potash (*Chicago Sun-Times*), Jeff Dickerson (ESPN), Mike Mulligan (*Chicago Sun-Times*, 670 The Score), Dan Bernstein (670 The Score), Laurence Holmes (670 the Score, NBC Sports Chicago), and Larry Mayer (Bear Report, ChicagoBears.com).

It's really a never-ending list that also includes notable columnists in Rick Morrissey (*Chicago Tribune*, *Chicago Sun-Times*), Bill Jauss (*Chicago Tribune*), Bill Gleason (*Chicago Sun-Times*), Barry Rozner (*Daily Herald*), and Mike Imrem (*Daily Herald*)

"Within Chicago, the Bears are the best team to cover just because everybody is interested in every single thing about the Bears," said Potash, who started working full time for the *Sun-Times* in 1990. "They're always important. People love the Cubs, they love the Sox, they love the Bulls, but they're addicted to the Bears. It's an addiction. You just feel that.

"Even as a disappointment, the Bears are a big story…. Nobody unites this town like the Bears do. That's always been the history."

The media is part of that history, too. It's their own longevity. Brad Briggs, a writer for the *Chicago Sun-Times* and then the *Chicago Tribune*, isn't a native Chicagoan, but he's covered the Bears since 2001.

In Chicago, the experience is substantial. Media members have built their own legacies through their coverage. In some cases, they're more famous than some of the Bears players that they cover year after year. When the Bears hire new coaches, they're being covered by media members who have dealt with several of their predecessors.

"It's always football season in Chicago," said LeGere, who covered Dave Wannstedt, Dick Jauron, Lovie Smith, Marc Trestman, John Fox, and Matt Nagy in his long career for the *Daily Herald*.

"Yeah, the Cubs lately are trendy and they've always been fairly popular. But people in Chicago want to talk Bears, and not necessarily football—Bears—year-round. If you go to the gym or somewhere else, as soon as somebody finds out what you do for a living, that's all they want to talk about. They will literally go down the roster: 'What about this guy? What about this guy? What are they going to do here?' We all grew up like that as Bears fans, especially some of us through horrible years and we're still diehard Bears fans. There's just so many people like that. You realize how special it is covering the Bears. You know how important other people consider the Bears. Even casual sports fans are Bears fans."

It helps to know what that feels like growing up in the Chicago area, what it feels like to watch or hear stories about Walter Payton or to dance to "The Super Bowl Shuffle" as a child. But disconnecting yourself from a certain level of fandom always is the goal.

"Everybody that's from here, you grew up being a fan of the team," said Dickerson, who started covering the team for ESPN Radio in 2004. "Anyone that covers the team that's from here that says, 'I wasn't a Bears fan.' Well, they're a liar. Why would they be covering sports, if they didn't like sports? What are you talking about? Of course, you legitimately have to divorce yourself from that."

It's understanding and appreciating that Chicago is a tough town that wants tough coverage of its favorite teams, particularly the Bears.

"To tell the truth when they're bad and to credit them when they're good. To analyze the play as best you can," said Arkush, whose magazine, *Pro Football Weekly*, was founded by his father in 1967. "I've always prided myself on trying to be the voice of the fan.... Our purpose as media is to be your conduit to your team and your game."

But covering one of the founding franchises of the NFL—a team that had Bronko Nagurski, Dick Butkus, Walter Payton, and Brian Urlacher—definitely carries weight.

"My Bears message has been is that you're the luckiest fans in the world because you have the most important franchise in the NFL and everything's always spun off of that," Arkush said.

It's having an appreciation for the game of football and the Bears place in it.

"Having been a steel worker and a truck driver, it beats a real job covering football," Mullin said. "I think the end game is just to put a good piece of meat on everybody's plate first thing in the morning and don't get in the way of the story."

"BILL SWERSKI'S SUPER FANS"

O n January 12, 1991, some certain fans of a certain football team that had carved out a special place in the pantheon of professional football greats sat down together at Ditka's restaurant and offered their predictions for the Bears' playoff game against the Giants the next day.

Pat Arnold: "Da Bears, 62 to tree [3]."

Todd O'Connor: "Bears. 79–zip."

Carl Wollarski: "I say Bears, 52 to 14."

Bill Swerski: "74 to 2! I mean, after all, our civic pride is on the line."

It was the debut of "Bill Swerski's Super Fans" on *Saturday Night Live*. First conceived by writer Robert Smigel after attending a Cubs game and sitting in the bleachers of Wrigley Field, it took years for the skit to come to fruition. But it became one of the most memorable *SNL* skits of all time.

The sketch doesn't work without actual diehard Chicago sports fans. In a humorous way, the Super Fans reflected them, especially their loyalty and love for the Bears, despite all the losing seasons since the days of Mike Ditka.

The Super Fans' roots are uniquely Chicagoan. When Smigel moved to Chicago in 1983, he met Bob Odenkirk, who is from nearby Naperville, during an improv class. The two later became part of *SNL*'s writing staff. Jim Downey, who was *SNL*'s head writer at the time, also was from south suburban Joliet. In 1991, the writers got their perfect lead for the skit when Joe Mantegna, who went to Morton East High School in the suburb of Cicero, hosted SNL in January. With the Bears in the playoffs against the Giants, it was the ideal time to debut it.

Chicago provided more, too. In 1985, *The Sportswriters* debuted on WFLD-TV. It was a roundtable discussion full of distinctive Chicago accents: Bill Gleason of the *Chicago Sun-Times* and *South Bend Tribune*, Bill Jauss of the *Chicago Tribune*, Rick Telander of *Sports Illustrated*, and Ben Bentley, a boxing promoter and the first spokesman for the Chicago Bulls.

The television show was an extension of what Gleason, Jauss, and Bentley already said on WGN radio. But now on screen for everyone to see, the foursome smoked cigars around a poker table and mess of newspapers and simply talked sports and so much more. It was a successful and truly ground-breaking program—one that served as a seminal spark for the all talk shows that came about later on ESPN, NFL Network, and other stations.

"Jauss was North Side. Bentley was West Side. He was like Humboldt Park from back in the day. And Gleason was South Side," said Telander, who was from Peoria but played football at Northwestern and later became a columnist for the *Chicago Sun-Times*. "So there were variations in Chicago dialect—and boy, they had it. I loved it."

SNL did, too. *The Sportswriters* served as more inspiration. Instead of journalists talking around a table, there would be fans that talked like them and offered their own biased thoughts on their favorite teams, while drinking beer, smoking cigars, and gorging on unhealthy amounts of red meat. It was a grand time for Chicago sports, too. In those days, Chicago had Mike Ditka and the Bears and Michael Jordan and the Bulls to root for as they won.

"They obviously did their own take on it, but they got those accents that are just hilarious," Telander said. "I know when they started, they didn't know if the rest of the country would think it was funny."

But it was—it was extremely funny. In the original skit, Mantegna played host Bill Swerski, while Mike Myers, Chris Farley, and Smigel handled the roles of Pat Arnold, Todd O'Connor, and Carl Wollarski, respectively. Comedian/actor George Wendt, who grew up in the Beverly neighborhood on the Southwest side of Chicago, became a regular in the skit as Swerski's brother, Bob. Since then, the Super Fans have been featured in advertisements, including ones for the NFL and the Bears when their 100th seasons were celebrated in 2019.

"One thing I found, a lot of people hate New York, a lot of people hate L.A., [but] everybody loves Chicago. Everybody," Telander said. "There is no reason not to. Everybody's got a relative in Chicago or passed through or immigrated there or something. I think that was a big part of it, why it was so successful."

After Ditka was fired by the Bears in 1993, Jordan became the focal point of the Super Fans' adoration. But four days after his firing, Ditka made an appearance in the cold open of *SNL* that featured Wendt—or Bob Swerski—and the rest of the Super Fans. Ditka appeared again on October 25, 1997, but this time he was the head coach of the New Orleans Saints. With their thick mustaches and sunglasses, the Super Fans always was an ode to Ditka.

"It's mostly reverential and he knows that," said Telander, who wrote the book, *The '85 Bears: We Were the Greatest*, with Ditka.

The players that Ditka coached and also played with in the 1960s loved the Super Fans, too. Former safety Gary Fencik, a member of the Bears' 1985 team who spent 12 years with the team and is from north suburban Barrington, called the skit outstanding.

"Just outstanding because we all know people who are not too far off of those characters," Fencik said. "Being a lifelong Bears fan and living in the city my entire adult life, there are Bears fans that take this very, very seriously. It's almost scary.

"But those were just great skits. I still laugh when I see those Ditka sweaters. You see people at Soldier Field and they're dressed up like Ditka. That is just so funny to me. To be that iconic, and there is just no question who they're trying to be."

They're Bears fans—real-life, super ones, too. The Bears, as an organization, wouldn't exist without them.

"Ultimately, it's a city that respects the people in it, and if you work, they always respect it," Telander said. "If you work hard as a player or a coach or just a worker, you're respected."

Football is just different in Chicago. It's generational, dating back to the very beginning of the NFL. It's Halas, Butkus, Payton, Ditka, and more—thousands of mini-Ditkas.

Or as Bill Swerski famously once said: "The city of big shoulders, and home, of course, to a certain football team, which has carved out a special place in the pantheon of professional football greats. That team, which is known the world over, as... Daaaa Bears!"

[Acknowledgments]

In the final weeks of writing this book, I spent an unhealthy amount of time at my local Starbucks, processing the history of the Bears, finding the right details and stories to share, and injecting the needed caffeine into my bloodstream in order to piece all of it together.

It was a grind—but a worthy one. I've covered the Bears as a sports reporter since 2012, but I came away with a greater appreciation for what this team means to the McCaskey/Halas family, the players who wore the Bears uniform, the city of Chicago, and the NFL.

You can literally write hundreds of books about the Bears—and it feels like there have been. That's why I set out to be different from the start. I knew it would be difficult when there are so many good books written about the Bears already, especially the 1985 team.

In order to find new stories, I kept the fans in mind and sought out the people who have been around the team the longest, either as players or media members or a combination of both.

I also focused on the post-1985 history of the team. It's why I'm extremely thankful for the time that Brian Urlacher, Lance Briggs, Devin Hester, Charles Tillman, Olin Kreutz, Robbie Gould, Jason McKie, and Patrick Mannelly gave to me for this book.

Mannelly—the longest tenured Bears player in team history—deserves special mention. The book started with him. He was the first person interviewed. I tried to weave him into as many chapters as possible because he has so many memories and stories to tell.

In the end, I'm grateful that Mannelly was willing to write the foreword for this book. The Bears history is his history. It's better explained in his own words.

As for other former players, I want to thank Tom Waddle, Gary Fencik, Ed O'Bradovich, Bob Wetoska, Dan Hampton, Tom Thayer, Doug Plank, and Jay Hilgenberg for all the stories that they were willing to share.

Sitting with Jarrett Payton, eating cheeseburgers together and hearing stories about his father, was my favorite moment in the compilation of this book. In Chicago, it's Walter Payton and Michael Jordan. Walter had a life and story that's worth his own encyclopedia of books.

Hearing Payton's son, Jarrett, whom I consider a friend, explain what his father means to Chicago, to the team, and to the NFL was an emotional and memorable experience. If there are football gods, Walter Payton surely is one.

To encapsulate everything, I turned to some of my role models in the Chicago media: Rick Telander, Dan Pompei, John "Moon" Mullin, Fred Mitchell, and Hub Arkush. I came up through this profession reading all them. This book wouldn't be complete without them.

I often turned to the *Bears' Centennial Scrapbook* that Pompei and Don Pierson—two Hall of Fame writers—wrote with team owner Virginia McCaskey. All of them helped record the history of the most important franchise in the history of the NFL.

The same is true for Jeff Joniak, the voice of the Bears. Sharing a coffee with Joniak in Lake Forest and hearing him relive some of the best moments in recent team history brought back the goosebumps felt from those very plays. He recorded the unofficial soundtrack for the Bears.

Zach Zaidman and Marc Silverman provided invaluable perspective from different points of view in the Chicago radio business, while Jim Riebandt, the team's longtime public-address announcer at Soldier Field, is full of unique stories.

Jack Silverstein is a Bears fan, writer, and Chicago sports historian that readers should know more about, too.

I also turned to my friends on the Bears beat who have covered the team longer than myself: Jeff "J.D." Dickerson, Mark Potash, Larry Mayer, and Bob LeGere. Spending time with them resulted in great background and details about the team but also ample amounts of laughter.

I wanted to express a special thank you to Patrick McCaskey, a team board member and one of George Halas' grandchildren. A published author himself, McCaskey is the team's historian. Getting his input and insights enhanced everything, from start to finish.

At Triumph Books, Jesse Jordan, my editor and a Bears fan, was beyond flexible and helpful throughout the process. My work is Jesse's work. He helped this come to fruition. Bill Ames made all of this happen, too.

Finally, my family, where do I even begin?

I always wanted the challenge of writing a book. It was a career goal—and I plan on writing more of them. But it wouldn't have been possible without the endless patience and love of my beautiful wife, Colleen. I am where I am in my sportswriting career because of her. It started with your belief in me—your tough love. My love for you is endless.

And to my three young sons, I know one day you'll read this book.

Just know that playing football with you three in our back yard will always be better and more rewarding than writing anything professionally about it—ever.

[Sources]

Books

Halas By Halas. George Halas

Chicago Bears Centennial Scrapbook. Dan Pompei and Don Pierson

Bear with me: A Family History of George Hallas and the Chicago Bears. Patrick McCaskey

Papa Bear: The Life and Legacy of George Halas. Jeff Davis.

Amazing Tales from the Chicago Bears Sideline: A Collection of the Greatest Bears Stories Ever Told. Steve McMichael, John Mullin, Phil Arvia

The 50 Greatest Plays in Chicago Bears Football History. Lew Freedman

McMahon. Jim McMahon

If These Walls Could Talk: Chicago Bears. Otis Wilson with Chet Coppock

Monster of the Midway: My 50 years with the Chicago Bears. Doug Buffone as told to Chet Coppock

The Bears: A 75-year Celebration. Richard Whittingham

Videos

ESPN *30 for 30: The '85 Bears*

NFL Films

Periodicals

Sports Illustrated

Chicago Tribune

Chicago Tribune archives

Chicago Sun-Times

Websites

ESPN.com

TheAthletic.com

Grantland.com (oral history of "The Super Bowl Shuffle")

Pro Football Reference

ChicagoBears.com

Windy City Gridiron